TRANSFORMING
SCHOOLS

TRANSFORMING
SCHOOLS

Using Project-Based Learning, Performance Assessment, and Common Core Standards

Bob Lenz

with Justin Wells and Sally Kingston

JB JOSSEY-BASS™
A Wiley Brand

Published by Jossey-Bass

A Wiley Brand

One Montgomery Street, Suite 1200, San Francisco, CA 94104-4594—www.josseybass.com

Jossey-Bass books and products are available through most bookstores. To contact Jossey-Bass directly call our Customer Care Department within the U.S. at 800-956-7739, outside the U.S. at 317-572-3986, or fax 317-572-4002.

Wiley publishes in a variety of print and electronic formats and by print-on-demand. Some material included with standard print versions of this book may not be included in e-books or in print-on-demand. If this book refers to media such as a CD or DVD that is not included in the version you purchased, you may download this material at **http://booksupport.wiley.com**. For more information about Wiley products, visit **www.wiley.com**.

Library of Congress Cataloging-in-Publication Data is on file and available from the Library of Congress

ISBN 978-1-118-73974-7 (pbk.), 978-1-118-73970-9 (epdf), 978-1-118-73966-2 (epub)

Printed in the United States of America

FIRST EDITION

PB Printing 10 9 8 7 6 5 4 3 2

Contents

Breadth versus depth—it's an old struggle. Stop struggling. Go with depth. It's the only way to engage students in the present and to prepare them for their futures.

Everything maps backward from a redefinition of what it means to graduate from high school. Know, do, reflect: our unified theory.

A school that is dedicated to deeper learning is a school that has established a coherent, schoolwide, standards-aligned performance assessment system. We explain what this means, why it's vital, and how to work toward this challenging but transformative goal.

Learning is deepest when it culminates in an act of creation. As we walk through an example project, we show how PBL is the most effective and efficient means to our ends: preparing students for rigorous performance assessments, meeting state standards, and, most important, making learning matter to students.

DVD Contents

Videos

Videos can be found on the accompanying DVD as well as at http://www.wiley.com/go/transformingschools.

DOCUMENTS

1. Envision Schools Course Syllabus Template

2. Envision Schools College Success Portfolio Performance Task Requirements: Scientific Inquiry

3. Envision Schools College Success Portfolio Performance Task: English Language Arts Textual Analysis

4. What Is the Most Effective Method for Cleaning Oil, Dispersants or Absorbents?

5. Envision Schools College Success Portfolio Performance Assessment: Creative Expression

6. Performance Assessment Planning Template

7. SCALE Performance Assessment Quality Rubric

8. Envision Project Planning Template

9. Envision Sample Daily Schedule

10. 9th Grade Envision Schools Advisory Curriculum

11. The Six A's of Designing Projects

12. Project Sharing Protocol

13. City Arts and Tech High School Holistic Grading Rubric

14. Envision Core Values

15. Decision Making at Envision Schools

16. Ground Rules for Meetings

17. Meeting Agenda Template

18. NSRF Tuning Protocol Guidelines

To the students, teachers, and leaders of Envision Schools—past, present, and future.

Acknowledgments

Without Daniel McLaughlin, Envision cofounder, as well as the original Envision Schools staff and board, there would be no book to read because there would be no Envision. Thank you to Daniel and all Envision founders for believing that schools can transform lives.

We acknowledge and thank all of the Envision teachers, leaders, and students who cocreated this transformational school model through their practice. Having a vision for a transformational school is only half of the equation; the blood, sweat, and tears of our colleagues and students made it a reality.

At the core of Envision Education is a credible and defensible deeper learning student assessment system, which owes its existence to our partnership with the Stanford Center for Assessment, Learning, and Equity (SCALE). We will always be indebted to Linda Darling Hammond and Ray Pecheone for their belief in and support of our vision. Stanford's Ruth Chung Wei has been an invaluable partner in creating many of the tools that drive our assessment system.

The genesis of Envision, and therefore this book, is Sir Francis Drake High School in San Anselmo, CA. Bob acknowledges his colleagues and mentors at Drake High, whose work has inspired educators around the country and the world to rethink school and learning.

Thank you to Kate Bradford, our editor, whose positive attitude inspired us to never give up on this project. We thank Tony Wagner for acknowledging our work and pushing our thinking.

Finally, we recognize our families and partners for their sacrifices and their inspiration—not only through the writing of this book but also across our careers at Envision. We couldn't have done this without you. We love you!

About the Authors

Bob Lenz is the Founder & Chief of Innovation for Envision Education. He is a nationally recognized leader in high school redesign, deeper learning, project-based learning, 21st century skills education, and performance assessment.

Since Envision opened its first school in 2002, Bob has led the organization's expansion to operating three high-performing schools in the Bay Area and training other educators in the Envision model through Envision Learning Partners. Today, more than 90% of Envision Schools graduates go to college, compared to just 40% of all California high school graduates; the college persistence rate for Envision students is 85%, compared to 60% nationwide.

Seeking to impact education on a broad level, Bob directed Envision's efforts to create Envision Learning Partners. ELP works with education leaders across the country to create vibrant schools that successfully prepare all students for college, career, and life. As Chief of Innovation, Bob works to bring the Envision model to schools across the country, and to guide the national conversation on school reform and student success.

Bob was the first in his family to receive a college degree, obtaining a BA from St. Mary's College and an MA in education from San Francisco State University.

Justin Wells is a founding faculty member of Envision's first school, where he helped develop Envision's graduation portfolio and defense system. For nine years, he taught English and led teacher teams in the design and implementation of semester-long, multi-disciplinary projects that drew recognition, media coverage, and research attention from ABC News, the Buck Institute for Education, KQED, Stanford University, the Oracle Education Foundation, and the Partnership for 21st Century Skills. Along the way, Justin served as the associate research director for performance assessment at the Stanford Center for Assessment, Learning, and Equity (SCALE), where he designed prototype performance tasks for the Smarter Balanced Assessment Consortium (SBAC). Currently, he works as a consultant and coach for Envision Learning Partners, helping schools and school districts develop performance assessment systems guided by the principles of deeper learning and project-based learning.

Sally Kingston, PhD, is senior education analyst for Applied Engineering Management Corporation. She has over 25 years of experience as leader and teacher across the P-16 pathway, including serving as executive director of Envision Learning Partners. Sally writes about education for the Partnership for 21st Century Skills. She is co-author of *Leading Schools: Distinguishing the Essential from the Important* and *The Leadership We Need: Using Research to Strengthen the Use of Standards for Administrator Preparation and Licensure Programs*. She holds an MA in Education and a PhD in Educational Leadership and Organizations from the University of California Santa Barbara, where she was named Distinguished Alumnus in 2008.

Foreword

This important book describes some very different approaches to teaching and learning for high school students, which are proving to be much more successful than the conventional methods widely used in schools today. Bob Lenz and his colleagues understand that a good education means much more than preparing students to take a test. They focus relentlessly on teaching and assessing the skills that matter most for college, work, and learning in the 21st century. They motivate students by giving them authentic and challenging work; they assess students' portfolios of work to determine college readiness, and require every student to present and defend their work. Perhaps most important, even though their approach is both challenging and demanding, they have been especially effective working with the students most at risk.

In their introduction, the authors describe some of the reasons why a very different approach to education is essential today. But in my experience, many educators, parents, and community leaders do not fully understand the economic consequences for our students and for our country if we do not reimagine America's schools.

The global economic meltdown that began in 2008 has hastened the elimination of many kinds of jobs. In their important book *The Second Machine Age: Work, Progress, and Prosperity in a Time of Brilliant Technologies,* MIT economists Erik Brynjolfsson and Andrew McAfee discuss the accelerating pace of robotization of jobs. Half a dozen years ago, no one thought that machines could handle a task as complex as driving in heavy traffic. The Google driverless car has proved otherwise, and computers now compile and write complex financial reports and compete successfully against humans in chess and *Jeopardy!*

Although the popular media have reported the declining rates of unemployment as good news, the reality is that growing numbers of people—especially young people—have given up looking for work altogether. As I write this in the spring of 2014, the percentage of Americans who either have jobs or are looking for work is 63 percent and is at the lowest point since women began entering the labor force in significant numbers in the late 1970s. Young people in their twenties have been hardest hit of all, with one in five neither in school nor employed.

Nor does the unemployment rate say anything about the quality of jobs available. The vast majority of jobs that have been created in recent years are minimum-wage service and sales jobs. The result of all of these trends, economists tell us, is that the gap between the rich and the rest of us is greater than at any time in this country's history since 1929.

Historically, college graduates have always had an easier time finding jobs and earned considerably more than high school graduates over the course of their work life. It is no surprise, then, that an increasing number of young people are enrolling in college in response to this jobs crisis. Indeed, the mantra of many of our policymakers and educators is that all students should graduate from high school "college ready." As a result, the college attendance rate in this country is the highest it has ever been.

However, there is a growing body of evidence that attending college might not be the good investment it once was. College tuitions have increased 72 percent since 2000, while income earned by twenty-four- to thirty-five-year-olds has declined nearly 15 percent and median family income has declined 10 percent. To close this gap, students and their families are borrowing more money than ever. College debt recently exceeded credit card debt in this country—over $1 trillion. Students now graduate with an average combined family debt of more than $30,000.

That is, if they graduate at all. Colleges have done nothing to stem the horrible attrition rate of students. Of the students who enroll in colleges, only about half complete any sort of degree. The completion rate at our community colleges—where many of our most disadvantaged students enroll—is less than 30 percent.

Then there is the problem of the job prospects for our recent college graduates. The combined unemployment and underemployment rate of recent college graduates is 53 percent—and is *up* slightly from a year ago. Far too many of our college graduates are finding that the only kinds of jobs they can get do not require a BA degree and certainly do not pay a college-graduate wage. We talk a lot about government debt in this country, but the debt I worry about most is the debt of our college graduates. It is the only form of personal debt that cannot be eliminated by filing for bankruptcy.

This dismal employment picture for recent college graduates exists at a time when employers say they cannot fill available positions for highly skilled workers. This is because there is a profound mismatch between what students learn in college and what employers say they need. It is not merely a matter of students picking the wrong college major. Employers say they do not care what job applicants' college majors are. They care about skills. According to a recent survey of employers conducted on behalf of the Association of American Colleges and Universities, "Nearly all those surveyed (93 percent) agree, 'a candidate's demonstrated capacity to think critically, communicate clearly, and solve complex problems is more important than their undergraduate major.'"[1] The Seven Survival Skills that I wrote about in *The Global Achievement Gap* are more important than ever to employers.

As necessary as these skills are, they are no longer sufficient. Employers want something more from new hires now. Over and over again, business leaders have told me that they want employees who can "just go figure it out"—who can be creative problem solvers or innovators. In my most recent book, *Creating Innovators: The Making of Young People Who Will Change the World,* I explore what parents and teachers can do to develop these capacities. I describe the teaching methods that most successfully develop the skills needed in an increasingly innovation-driven economy—precisely the same methods, in fact, that Bob and his colleagues are using.

One of my most striking findings in interviews with young creative problem solvers in their twenties is that many became innovators in spite of their excellent schools, not because of them. Students who went to Harvard, MIT, Stanford, and Carnegie Mellon all told me that it was the rare outlier teacher who had truly made a difference in their development.

Too many of our college graduates are not learning any of the skills that matter most. In a recent study that involved twenty-three hundred undergraduates at twenty-four institutions, Richard Arum and Josipa Roksa analyzed data from the Collegiate Learning Assessment, a state-of-the-art test of writing, problem solving, and critical thinking skills. They found that, after two years of college, 45 percent of the students tested were no more able to think critically or communicate effectively than when they started college. Their book, *Academically Adrift,* makes a compelling case for the need to fundamentally rethink the nature of a college education and accountability for results.

Employers are beginning to wise up to the fact that students' college transcripts, GPAs, and test scores are a poor predictor of employee value. Google famously used to hire only students from name-brand colleges with the highest GPAs and test scores. However, according to recent interviews with Laszlo Bock, senior vice president of people operations at Google, these data are "worthless" as predictors of employee effectiveness at Google. The company now looks for evidence of a sense of mission and personal autonomy and is increasingly hiring people who do not have a college degree.

Even the interview questions they pose have changed. In the past, Google interviewers asked prospective employees brain-teaser questions like how many Ping-Pong balls can you get into a 747 or how many cows are there in Canada. Now they want them to talk about a complex analytic problem they have tried to solve recently.[2]

Our schools are not failing, as many claim; rather, they are obsolete. We continue to focus far too much time on teaching and testing content knowledge that can be retrieved from the Internet as needed. Knowledge has become a free commodity, like air, so the world no longer cares how much our students know. What the world cares about — what matters most — is what our students can do with what they know.

The Envision schools are successfully preparing all students for college, as the results of the recent SCOPE studies show.[3] And they are doing so much more than that. Through their project-based approach to learning, they are equipping students with the skills needed to be "innovation ready," as well as preparing them for the complex challenges of continuous learning and citizenship in the 21st century. Finally, the Envision schools are contributing in significant ways to the essential "educational research and development" needed to reimagine our schools for the twenty-first century.

Tony Wagner

Tony Wagner currently serves as Expert In Residence at the Harvard University Innovation Lab and is the author of five books. Previously, he was the founder and codirector of the Change Leadership Group at the Harvard Graduate School of Education for more than a decade.

NOTES

1. Hart Research Associates. (2013). *It takes more than a major: Employer priorities for college learning and student success.* Retrieved from http://www.aacu.org/leap /documents/2013_EmployerSurvey.pdf

2. See Bryant, A. (2013, June 19). In head-hunting, big data may not be such a big deal. *New York Times.* Retrieved from http://www.nytimes.com/2013/06/20 /business/in-head-hunting-big-data-may-not-be-such-a-big-deal.html?page wanted=all&_r=0. Also see Lohr, S. (2013, April 20), Big data, trying to build better workers. *New York Times.* Retrieved from http://www.nytimes.com/2013/04/21 /technology/big-data-trying-to-build-better-workers.html?pagewanted=all

3. Cook-Harvey, C. M. (2014). *Student-centered learning: Impact Academy of Arts and Technology*. Stanford, CA: Stanford Center for Opportunity Policy in Education (SCOPE); Lewis-Charp, H., & Law, T. (2014). *Student-centered learning: City Arts and Technology High School*. Stanford, CA: Stanford Center for Opportunity Policy in Education (SCOPE).

TRANSFORMING
SCHOOLS

Why Learning Must Go Deeper

My first year in college was amazing. Everything that you guys taught us here, I use. Every, single, thing.

— Envision Schools graduate (2011)

You've either heard the claim or reached the conclusion on your own: the world is changing, and our schools are not keeping up.

If you still need some convincing, there are entire books that lay out the argument persuasively. There may be some disagreement around how we got to this point and which facet of the complex problem is most pressing, but those who worry about our schools point to the same facts. America's public education system once led the world; now it wheezes in the middle of the pack. A system meant to break down walls of class and race is now implicated in building them up. Because of globalization and advances in technology, the kinds of jobs that created and defined the American middle class are vanishing before our eyes. A troubling number of kids don't like school; a tragic number are dropping out. And despite generations of rhetoric around reform, the typical student's day-to-day classroom experience has hardly changed in a hundred years.

> ## Great Books on the Need for Educational Change
>
> Ted Sizer (1985), *Horace's Compromise*
>
> Deborah Meier (1995), *The Power of Their Ideas*
>
> Linda Darling-Hammond (1997), *The Right to Learn*
>
> David Conley (2005), *College Knowledge*
>
> Tony Wagner (2008), *The Global Achievement Gap*

It's this last fact that most concerns this book, not because it is more important but because it is the one that educators can act on most concretely. It is also a fact easily overlooked. In recent years, education has enflamed intense debate. You would think it was the direction of change, rather than the absence of change, that could provoke such anger. But examine the labels on all our hot buttons: testing, tenure, teacher evaluation, charter schools, vouchers, trigger laws, unions, rubber rooms, No Child Left Behind. . . . While these controversies crash into adult sensibilities, they barely ripple into the typical day of the typical student at the typical school in America. Harvard education professor Jal Mehta (2013) sums up the last hundred years: "On the whole, we still have the same teachers, in the same roles, with the same level of knowledge, in the same schools, with the same materials, and much the same level of parental support."

This book is for those who agree that school should be different and are wondering *how* to go about making it better. It is a book about school design. It's not the only thing that must change to fix the problems of American education, but it's an essential one and the one our experience speaks to.

ABOUT ENVISION EDUCATION AND THE AUTHORS

Over ten years ago, after earning acclaim for his leadership of an innovative academy within a comprehensive high school, Bob founded the first Envision school, dedicated to the ideas of performance assessment and project-based learning. He recruited a team of teachers before he had a school building secured. Justin was the second teacher hired.

The summer before we opened our doors, there was a building but still no furniture. For two months, we sat on the floor of an empty room and designed our school.

That initial design grew into three schools, a small charter management organization, an educational consulting division, and now the book in your hands.

Along the way, Envision Schools garnered national recognition for its innovations in performance assessment, its graduation portfolio system, its rigorous and integrated approach to project-based learning, its workplace learning internships, and its personalized learning environment that have been so successful in getting students into college who were statistically not likely to go. We serve students who come from low-income families (almost 70 percent qualify for free and reduced lunch) and whose parents did not go to college (almost 80 percent of our students will be the first in their families to graduate from college). (Figure I.1 details the demographics of Envision Schools.)

Because college success is the goal we have for our students, college success is how we measure our performance. Case studies on our schools, published by Stanford University researchers (Cook-Harvey, 2014; Lewis-Charp & Law, 2014), found that Envision Schools graduates are entering and persisting in college at rates far ahead of their demographically comparable peers. One hundred percent of African American and Latino 2012 graduates completed the courses required for University of California/California State University eligibility at Impact Academy, an Envision school. Statewide, the rates are 34 percent and 39 percent, respectively. Whereas only 8 percent of all low-income students nationwide earn a bachelor's degree by their mid-twenties (Mortenson, 2010), at our City Arts and Tech High School (CAT), 72 percent of 2008 graduates and 85 percent of 2009 graduates are persisting into their fourth and fifth years of college or have

Figure I.1 Envision Schools' Demographics, 2013–2014

Latino	57%
African American	23%
White	7%
Asian and Pacific Islander	3%
Other	10%
English Language Learners	11%
Free/reduced lunch	69%
First in their families to graduate from college	79%

Figure I.2 College Persistence Rates

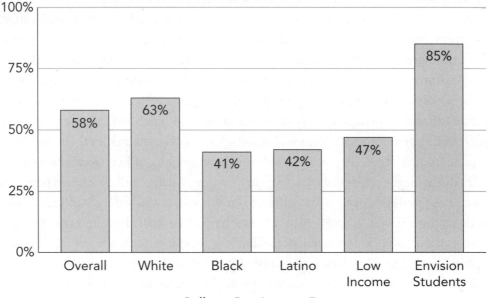

College Persistence Rates

Note: Nationwide numbers indicate the percentage of students who attained a bachelor's degree within six years of matriculating at a four-year college (2004–2009). Adapted from *Persistence and Attainment of 2003–4 Beginning Postsecondary Students: After 6 Years,* by A. W. Radford, L. Berkner, S. C. Wheeless, and B. Shepherd, 2010, Washington, DC: National Center for Education Statistics. Retrieved from http://nces.ed.gov/pubs2011/2011151.pdf. The Envision Schools number indicates the percentage of all Envision alums who are enrolled in college and working toward a bachelor's degree or have already earned one. Based on data from the National Student Clearinghouse.

already graduated. Figure I.2 provides more detail on how Envision's college persistence rates compare to relevant national averages.

From this success was born Envision Learning Partners (ELP), a division of Envision Education that partners with schools and districts nationwide that are inspired by our school design and the results it has generated. (Sally served as the executive director of ELP from 2013 to 2014.) Currently ELP is working directly with teachers and schools in seven states (New York, Delaware, Washington, Massachusetts, Michigan, California, and Hawaii), impacting more than ten thousand students; in addition, we are supporting the efforts of several large school systems, including Los Angeles Unified, the Educational Achievement Authority in Detroit, Sacramento City Unified, Oakland Unified, and awardees of the US Department of Education's Race to the Top - District competition.

THE COMMON CORE IS NOT A HURDLE; IT'S AN OPPORTUNITY

Envision accomplished all of this during a time of enormous pressure not to. The organization was founded in 2001, at the same tine as the No Child Left Behind (NCLB) legislation was passed. That law, while broadening awareness of the achievement gap, simultaneously narrowed the purpose of our nation's schools, boiling the whole endeavor down to the incremental movement of some numbers attempting to say something about student literacy and numeracy. Like many others (we've never been alone in our thinking), Envision defined success for its students as something bigger, more aspirational, and with a longer time horizon. For us, it has always been about preparing students for college and life success, and we never believed that standardized testing alone would get us there. We did what NCLB told us to do, but stayed true to our philosophy of building schools predicated on deeper learning (more on that in a moment).

Fast-forward to today, where we seem to have entered the era of Accountability 2.0. Performance assessment is "trending," and fast. A concept that for decades — and especially the last decade — has been fervently tended to by a small and forward-thinking group of educators is now on the tipping point of becoming mainstream practice in schools across the nation.

That's because of the new Common Core State Standards (CCSS). Improbably, over just a few years, the Common Core was adopted by forty-three states and territories and became a de facto set of national standards for math, reading, and writing across the curriculum.

Many factors were at work in the Common Core's swift adoption by so many states, but significant among them is the increasingly shared verdict that NCLB, for all its good intentions, demanded accountability without offering any educational vision. All value was placed on the act of counting, with scant attention paid to what it was that was being counted. A few states held themselves to a high standard, invariably one that was established before NCLB was passed. Most states, however, opted to test themselves on what could be bubbled in. We now have a decade of evidence to support the aphorism that "what gets tested is what gets taught." And when bubble tests define what gets taught, we end up with narrow and shallow curriculum.

Federal pressure certainly played a big role in its spread, but the Common Core would never have caught on if it wasn't riding a groundswell of recognition that in order to succeed in the 21st century, our kids need to not only learn content and basic test-taking skills but also achieve deeper learning outcomes.

The change that the Common Core demands from us is considerable, but it's not radical. Two simple ideas sum up the Core:

1. College and career readiness is the primary goal of school.
2. Higher-order thinking skills, communication skills, and conceptual understandings are just as important as fact-based content knowledge, if not more so.

Is the Common Core an important agent of change? Yes. But is it the *driver* of change? No. The Common Core is following, not setting, the direction of education. Hundreds of schools, including ours, were Common Core aligned before the standards ever existed. Properly viewed as an opportunity rather than as a compliance hurdle, the Common Core makes it easier for educators to do what they've been wanting to do all along.

The next generation of assessment is coming. By the 2014–15 school year, standardized tests, as administered by the two major assessment consortia, Smarter Balanced and the Partnership for Assessment of Readiness for College and Careers (PARCC), will look different from what we've gotten used to. These new performance assessments are being designed to measure skills in higher-order thinking, research, argumentation, modeling, data analysis, reading across the curriculum, even speaking and listening. (We know this firsthand: during a stint as an educational researcher at Stanford, Justin was part of a team that prototyped performance tasks for the Smarter Balanced test.)

Many educators welcome the coming challenge, but they also need help. After ten years of working within the cramped confines of NCLB, teachers and school leaders are crying out for tools, examples, and coaching that will help them guide their students into the next generation of assessment and, ultimately, the 21st century.

This book is an answer to that call.

DEEPER LEARNING

Put simply, here is the message of the book:

- Define a unified, schoolwide, mission-level outcome for your students.
- Map backwards from that goal.
- Rely on performance assessment and project-based learning to get you there.

Obviously, as anyone even remotely connected to a school can attest, there are lots of moving parts to this, and the complexity is in the details (thus seven more chapters).

But the reason we can distill our message into just three steps is that they operate as a coherent system.

Deeper learning is the term we (and others) use to name this coherent system of school design. It is at once a statement of goals (or desired outcomes), a commitment to certain methods (or pedagogies), and a declaration of beliefs (or principles).

THE COMPETENCIES OF DEEPER LEARNING

The Hewlett Foundation is among several forward-looking organizations that have taken up the term *deeper learning* to advance the cause of education. Envision Education has been a leading member of Hewlett's Deeper Learning Network.

Hewlett's list of desired student outcomes is representative of what is emerging all over the country when groups of thoughtful educators sit down and inventory what students should know and be able to do in the 21st century:

- Master core academic content

- Think critically and solve complex problems

- Work collaboratively

- Communicate effectively

- Learn how to learn

- Develop academic mindsets

We define the goals of our schools in chapters 1 and 2 and detail the methods in the chapters that follow. Underlying all of this is a set of beliefs—an educational philosophy—that suffuses the entire book. We list those beliefs here so that you're better able to notice how they inform our school design.

Deeper learning …

- Insists on depth over breadth
- Creates something that did not exist before
- Attends to the present, not just the future
- Is learning you can tell a story about
- Is best realized through an integrated approach within a "holonomous" organization

Think of these as our design principles.

Deeper Learning Insists on Depth over Breadth

Teachers have long struggled with the tension between breadth and depth.

It's a hard choice, hard enough that one is tempted to avoid it or dismiss it as a false choice or contend that it is a dilemma that can be dissolved through tinkering. Maybe we don't have to choose between covering a lot of content and focusing on a particular concept or skill. Maybe we can find a way to do both at the same time.

We shouldn't kid ourselves. The tension is inescapable, and the choice is unavoidable: **go with depth.**

Depth is what this world demands from us. The explosion of human knowledge is not a 21st century phenomenon; it happened in the last century. Now, in this era of Big Data, *explosive* can hardly describe the rate of growth of human knowledge. "Every two days," says former Google CEO Eric Schmidt, "we now create as much information as we did from the dawn of civilization up until 2003" (Siegler, 2010).

But those days aren't getting longer. And our minds aren't growing faster than evolution allows. And although we have prolonged adolescence over the last couple hundred years and added a college degree to what it means to be an educated citizen, it is doubtful that we can, or should, extend adolescence any further.

So the answer to exploding knowledge is not more schooling but a *different kind* of schooling. This is what the concept of deeper learning is all about and why it came to be. To pretend that we can "cover" everything that students need to know is to tilt at windmills. We must rid ourselves of any residual notions that education is the transmission of needed knowledge. Rather, we are teaching skills, and one skill most generally: how to ride a tsunami of knowledge whose future content we can't even begin to imagine.

What this means, ultimately, is that content, though still vitally important, is always a means to the end of some underlying, conceptual understanding. Decades of research bear this out: when deep, conceptual understanding is attained, learning is enduring, flexible, and real.

Some educators have paid attention to this message; unfortunately, most policymakers in our country seem unaware of this research and its implications. It is commonly observed in our field that "Singapore is where good ideas born in America go to grow up." It is tempting to roll your eyes when you hear about Singapore's test scores, while you imagine a classroom where kids sit politely and homogeneously in neat little rows, their creativity starved by a diet of drill-and-kill. But the reality there is different, and Singapore's own educational mantra, announced by Prime Minister Lee Hsien Loong in 2004, sums it up best: "Teach less, learn more."

> "Teach Less, Learn More" (TLLM) is a call for all educators to teach better— to engage our students and prepare them for life— rather than to teach more for tests and examinations.
> — Singapore Ministry of Education press release, September 22, 2005, retrieved from http://www.moe.gov.sg/media/press/2005/pr20050922b.htm

Deeper Learning Creates Something

One of the highest forms of learning is creation. The act of creation allows for the deepest expression of understanding.

Educational theorists have been telling us this in different ways for many years. The pioneering developmental psychologist Jean Piaget concluded that "education means making creators" (Bringuier, 1980, p. 132). Lorin Anderson, a former student of Benjamin Bloom, led an effort to revise Bloom's famous learning taxonomy so that the verb *create* went to the top of the hierarchy (Anderson et al., 2001; see Figure I.3). According to Grant Wiggins and Jay McTighe (1998), the fullest assessment of students' understanding is through the exhibition of created products or performances (p. 127).

As designers of schools and curriculum, we distill all this wisdom into the following rule of thumb: for learning to be meaningful and long lasting, it should culminate in the creation of something that never existed before.

Creativity is strongly associated with the arts, but here we define the word expansively. The "something" created can be an argument, a scientific conclusion, a story, an interview, a research report, a short film, a photograph, a relationship, a script, a slide deck, a lesson plan, a video game, a puzzle, a proposed solution, an advertisement, a recommendation,

Figure I.3 Bloom's Revised Taxonomy

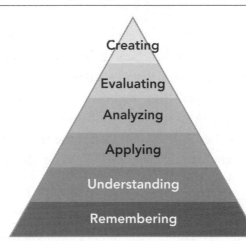

Source: Adapted from *A Taxonomy for Learning, Teaching and Assessing: A Revision of Bloom's Taxonomy of Educational Objectives* (Complete ed.), by L. W. Anderson (Ed.), D. R. Krathwohl (Ed.), P. W. Airasian, K. A. Cruikshank, R. E. Mayer, P. R. Pintrich, J. Raths, & M. C. Wittrock, 2001, New York, NY: Longman.

an editorial, a website, a blog, a proposal, a logo, a sign, a map, a dramatic performance, a historical interpretation, a business plan, a piece of music, a cost-benefit analysis, a symposium, a caption, an exhibit, a slogan, a translation, a letter, a computer program, a blueprint, a data chart, a brochure, an app, a review … You get the idea, and probably have many of your own to add to the list.

As elastic as it is, this conception of creativity does not stretch to include much of what kids do at school: multiple-choice tests, worksheets, fill-in-the-blanks, formulaic essays, banks of math problems, memorized lists of words, follow-the-recipe science labs, and the recall of historical names and dates. And it almost goes without saying that what standardized testing has done to the two skills that have commanded its attention—numeracy and reading comprehension—has been to strip them of their creative potential.

Of course, many hours of important, noncreative work must often happen before creative acts are possible, but creation should always be the conscious end goal of what students do at school. Creativity is what this new global, digital economy values and almost the only thing it rewards. Creativity is what Americans are traditionally known for. (Imagine an education system that deliberately plays to our national strength!) And, most significant, creativity is what excites and engages us, forging an emotional connection to our learning that is as critical to the process as the content of learning itself. What we learn cannot be untwined from how we learn it.

Look upon an object that you've made by hand. Compared to the received objects that surround it, notice how much more alive it is to you—its detail, its beauties and its imperfections, the pride it evokes, the memories it triggers. That's how it should feel to reflect on your education.

Deeper Learning Attends to the Present, Not Just the Future

Learning is inherently forward looking. It is, after all, the work of fulfilling potential. Much of what schools do for children is done with an eye to the payoff down the line.

Equally, problems in education are painted with tomorrow's implications, often in economic terms. You don't hear about the high school dropout rate, for example, without hearing that the lack of a diploma will cost the dropout hundreds of thousands of dollars over a lifetime.

But this focus on the future, though natural and appropriate, makes us vulnerable to forgetting the value of the present. Children are precious to us for who they are now, not for who they will become. Time spent learning is not any less valuable than the time spent doing what you learned. Practice isn't less critical than the performance it makes possible. As John Dewey famously declared over a century ago, "Education, therefore, is a process of living and not a preparation for future living" (1897, p. 7).

What this means is that the design of a school must pay as much attention to our students' present as it does to their future.

This may seem to run counter to our design process, which does start by looking into the future, imagining our students as college graduates, ready and prepared for what the world may hold in store for them. But in the details, we keep in mind that the work plays out in the present, during actual days of real lives.

Eventually, all of our backwards mapping maps back to today. What kind of a day is it? Is it a day fully and richly lived?

Deeper Learning Tells a Story

What do you remember most vividly from high school? We've made a point to ask that question of adults over the years, and here are typical responses:

- Prom [or some other social event equivalent]
- That cliffhanger of a [fill in the sport] game
- Performing in the [arts event]

- (Occasionally) the fond recollection of a favorite teacher (testifying to the lasting influence that good and caring teachers can have in our lives)

What we find striking is not what's said but what goes unsaid: there's hardly ever a mention of a specific academic learning experience—a paper that led to an intellectual discovery, a science project that pointed the road to a college major, a debate that opened the door to a new sense of self.

Striking but perhaps not surprising. We remember what is memorable. Sporting events, performances, and prom parties have features in common that make them memorable: anticipation, rising action, possible conflict, climax, and resolution. These are the raw materials of storytelling.

Humans are storytellers. Storytelling is the primary way that we make sense of our experience. It is the way that we hang on to our experience. It is the way that we communicate our experience. If learning doesn't intentionally harness this truth, then it's not plumbing as deeply as it should.

In this book, we use a more general term—*reflection*—to name this critical component of learning. Built into every step of the student's journey, from the lesson to the milestone, reflection is an opportunity for the student to tell a story of what she has learned. More often than not, telling that story is the moment when the learning takes hold. As Bob likes to say, reflection leads to retention.

A school design that elevates reflection to its rightful place in the learning process must accept an attending challenge: if we want students to tell stories of their learning, school must provide experiences worth telling stories about. Here is where football games and spring musicals and prom parties can teach us something: experiences are often memorable because they've been designed to be memorable. Every academic experience can—and should—have all the makings for a good story.

Deeper Learning Is Best Realized through a "Holonomous" Organization

Our school design is deeply informed by the concept of *holonomy*, a term based on the work of Arthur Koestler (1972) to name the relationship between a whole and its parts. (The Greek *holos* means "whole," and the suffix *on* means "part.") Complex systems tend to be made up of parts that are simultaneously independent and interdependent. Every individual part, Koestler observes, has the dual tendency to "preserve and assert its autonomy" while serving "the demands of the (existing or evolving) whole" (p. 112).

This is true for educational communities, say Arthur Costa and Robert Garmston (1994):

> Effective teachers, for example, are autonomous individuals: self-asserting, self-motivating, and self-modifying. However, they are also parts of larger wholes: a department, a school, a district. They are influenced by the norms, attitudes, values, and behaviors of the collective. The school, in turn, is an autonomous unit interacting within the influence of the district and the community. (p. 123)

A holonomous learning organization pays attention to the whole and the parts simultaneously. It works to balance autonomy and interdependence by supporting individuals to become independent and self-actualizing while maintaining a community that serves to regulate the norms, values, and concerns of the individual. And by harmonizing parts to the whole, it transforms potential tension into amplified energy.

Holonomy also warns us that one part of a system cannot reach its potential if it is not working in harmony with other parts of the whole. If, for example, it is the mission of a school to teach students how to collaborate productively, then teachers and leaders must themselves be working to collaborate productively. Every part is a window into the whole; the success of the whole can only be assessed through consistency of the parts.

A fundamental premise of this book is that educational organizations cannot deepen learning without striving to be holonomous, or "consistent throughout [the] entire system — self, classroom, school, district, and eventually the community" (Costa & Kallick, 1995, p. 6). We have adapted this philosophy into our own Envision Schools transformation model (see Figure I.4), and it structures not only the design of our schools but also the organization of this book.

Think of a holonomous organization (and the chapters of this book) as a series of nested layers:

- At the heart of it all, of course, are our **students**; a graduate profile describes what they need to know and be able to do to graduate college and career ready (chapter 1).

Figure I.4 The Envision Schools Transformation Model

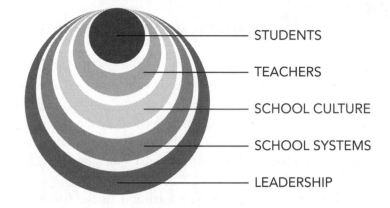

STUDENTS

TEACHERS

SCHOOL CULTURE

SCHOOL SYSTEMS

LEADERSHIP

- Surrounding the students are the all-important **teachers**; chapters 2 and 3 discuss what they need to know and be able to do to help students actualize the vision of the graduate profile.

- A holonomous organization must always be intentional about its **culture**, the permeating force that surrounds the people (chapter 4).

- **School systems**, or structures, should align with the goals and values of the organization (chapter 5).

- **School leaders** have the important job of looking across all these layers and stewarding the organization toward consistency (chapter 6).

CAN THIS KIND OF SCHOOL WORK FOR ALL KINDS OF KIDS?

Yes.

The high school design presented in this book is what's best for all students, regardless of race, socioeconomic status, language, neighborhood, school size, school location, or parental support.

We've tested the model under the broad array of conditions that American society has to offer. Our first school served mostly white middle-class kids in the suburbs. After that we opened two schools in San Francisco, serving students of color, many Hispanic. We have a school in downtown Oakland, one of the most wonderful and vibrant cities in America, but one that, as many know, presents all the challenges associated with urban education. We have a school in Hayward, nominally a suburb but one that reflects the new reality of American suburbia, now home to over half of our country's metropolitan poor (Tavernise, 2011).

And prior to opening these schools, Bob, Justin, and Sally taught in and led schools representing an even wider cross section: comprehensive public, parochial Catholic, public elementary, and elite independent.

We have yet to encounter a single student who was either not ready or somehow too advanced for the kind of performance- and project-based education that we advocate.

But we do encounter skeptics when we describe what we do. Interestingly, the skepticism comes from opposite sides. Project-based learning is a luxury, people will say, for the well-resourced and well-prepared upper-middle class, but kids on the wrong side of the achievement gap can't afford to waste time on projects when there is so much work to do in shoring up their basic skills.

And now that we are serving students at risk, we hear it from the other end: project-based learning may be necessary for engaging low-achieving students, but high-achieving students are already motivated to do more rigorous work.

Both criticisms are two sides of the same misconception: that project-based learning is some kind of soft-skill sideshow to the real and hard work at hand. What's true is the opposite: project-based learning is the only realistic path to the deeper learning outcomes that this new century demands of us. That is why this book's message is for those who work with all students, all of them coming of age in a new age.

TRANSFORM, NOT REFORM

One of the reasons that we like to use the word *transform* is that it connotes our desire to discuss matters that move beyond—transcend—the struggle that pits "reformers" against "the establishment," a debate that is often more political than pedagogical and has become downright tribal in its ferocity.

Most of the ideas we espouse in this book can be realized in both big and small schools, in both private and public schools, with or without charters, with or without testing, with or without unions and tenure and vouchers and, yes, even the vagaries of state and federal policy. We're not saying that such factors don't make it harder or easier to transform your school. (They do.) We are saying that you don't have to wait for the political battles to end in order to accomplish deeper learning outcomes for your students.

In many ways, we are traditionalists, and we admit that most of the ideas here are as ancient as philosophy. To learn by doing. To learn by asking questions. To learn with people. This isn't innovation, nor is it—to use a buzzword of the day—"disruptive." The concepts are not radical; they're fundamental. The deeper the learning, the more human it feels.

Video 1. Envision Philosophy, Practices, and Design

This overview of the Envision philosophy explores how Envision rises to the challenges of engaging students, accelerating their basic skills, and getting them ready for college. Grounded in equity and social justice, Envision schools help students become self-advocates  for their own learning processes, skills that will be with them in college, career, and life.

REFERENCES

Anderson, L. W. (Ed.), Krathwohl, D. R. (Ed.), Airasian, P. W., Cruikshank, K. A., Mayer, R. E., Pintrich, P. R., Raths, J., & Wittrock, M. C. (2001). *A taxonomy for learning, teaching and assessing: A revision of Bloom's taxonomy of educational objectives* (Complete ed.). New York, NY: Longman.

Bloom, B. S., Engelhart, M. D., Furst, E. J., Hill, W. H., & Krathwohl, D. R. (1956). *Taxonomy of educational objectives: The classification of educational goals. Handbook I: Cognitive domain.* New York, NY: David McKay.

Bringuier, J.-C. (1980). *Conversations with Jean Piaget* (B. M. Gulati, Trans.). Chicago, IL: University of Chicago Press. (Original work published 1977)

Cook-Harvey, C. M. (2014). *Student-centered learning: Impact Academy of Arts and Technology.* Stanford, CA: Stanford Center for Opportunity Policy in Education (SCOPE).

Conley, D. T. (2005). *College knowledge: What it really takes for students to succeed and what we can do to get them ready.* San Francisco, CA: Jossey-Bass.

Costa, A. L., & Garmston, R. J. (2002). *Cognitive coaching: A foundation for Renaissance schools* (2nd ed.). Norwood, MA: Christopher-Gordon.

Costa, A. L., & Kallick, B. (1995). Systems thinking: Interactive assessment in holonomous organizations. In A. L. Costa & B. Kallick (Eds.), *Assessment in the learning organization: Shifting the paradigm* (pp. 3–7). Alexandria, VA: Association for Supervision and Curriculum Development.

Darling-Hammond, L. (1997). *The right to learn: A blueprint for creating schools that work*. San Francisco, CA: Jossey-Bass.

Dewey, J. (1897). *My pedagogic creed*. New York, NY: E. L. Kellogg.

Koestler, A. (1972). *The roots of coincidence*. London: Pan Books.

Lewis-Charp, H., & Law, T. (2014). *Student-centered learning: City Arts and Technology High School*. Stanford, CA: Stanford Center for Opportunity Policy in Education (SCOPE).

Mehta, J. (2013, April 12). Teachers: Will we ever learn? *New York Times*. Retrieved from http://www.nytimes.com/2013/04/13/opinion/teachers-will-we-ever-learn.html

Meier, D. (1995). *The power of their ideas: Lessons for America from a small school in Harlem*. Boston, MA: Beacon Press.

Mortenson, T. G. (2010, November). Family income and educational attainment 1970 to 2009. *Postsecondary Education*. Retrieved from http://www.postsecondary.org/last12/221_1110pg1_16.pdf

Radford, A. W., Berkner, L., Wheeless, S. C., & Shepherd, B. (2010, December). *Persistence and attainment of 2003–4 beginning postsecondary students: After 6 years* (NCES 2011-151). Washington, DC: National Center for Education Statistics. Retrieved from http://nces.ed.gov/pubs2011/2011151.pdf

Siegler, M. G. (2010, Aug. 4). Eric Schmidt: Every 2 days we create as much information as we did up to 2003. *TechCrunch*. Retrieved from http://techcrunch.com/2010/08/04/schmidt-data

Sizer, T. (1985). *Horace's compromise*. Boston, MA: Houghton Mifflin.

Tavernise, S. (2011, Oct. 24). Outside Cleveland, snapshots of poverty's surge in the suburbs. *New York Times*. Retrieved from http://www.nytimes.com/2011/10/25/us/suburban-poverty-surge-challenges-communities.html

Wagner, T. (2008). *The global achievement gap: Why even our best schools don't teach the new survival skills our children need—and what we can do about it*. New York, NY: Basic Books.

Wiggins, G., & McTighe, J. (1998). *Understanding by design*. Alexandria, VA: Association for Supervision and Curriculum Development.

Chapter 1

Transforming the Graduate

> I get it. This is about learning.
>
> —Carlos Ramos, Envision student, reflecting on a realization
> that came to him halfway through a portfolio defense

It's twenty-seven days until Kaleb Lawson's graduation ceremony, and he has just been told that he is not ready to graduate.

Standing alone at the head of the room, Kaleb can't believe what he has just heard. His face is losing color, and he is struggling to maintain composure. The lights are too bright. The fan of the digital projector whirs too loudly.

The audience, loosely packed in rows of chairs that face Kaleb and the screen behind him, numbers around twenty, an assortment of fellow students, interested parents, and supportive teachers. Fronting the audience is a long table, behind which sit four adults who have been asking questions and taking notes. Obvious to anyone who has ever seen an episode of *American Idol*, this is a panel of judges.

One of the panelists, a digital media teacher named Mr. Harris, breaks an uncomfortable pause: "Your reflections on your leadership skills don't show the depth that we are looking for. Plus, we don't see evidence that you have practiced this presentation enough. You relied way too heavily on your notes. You didn't make enough eye contact with your audience."

Staring at the floor, Kaleb nods slowly to acknowledge what he has heard. He is taking this hard. Preparation for this presentation was not a matter of days, weeks, or even months. This was years in the making. For the last forty-five minutes, he gave a presentation that told his entire high school story. He showed examples of his best academic work, reflected on his successes and failures, tried to make a case that he was ready to graduate.

"You're not ready, Kaleb," Mr. Harris continues. "You can do better than this. Work with your advisor to revise your reflections. Polish your delivery. In ten days, you need to make a second attempt."

WHY SCHOOLS NEED TO REDEFINE GRADUATION

We'll follow up on Kaleb's story later in the chapter. (Unsurprising spoiler alert: he passes on his second attempt.) But first, let us explain what we just witnessed.

In order to graduate, every Envision Schools student must go through what Kaleb did. We are not referring to the failing part, but the standing before a panel and making a sustained, evidence-based claim that one is ready to move on from high school. It is the culminating moment of what we call a Deeper Learning Student Assessment System, and it is what defines an Envision Schools education.

The concept is nothing revolutionary, an idea as old as the trial of the hero's journey and as traditional to education as the relationship between apprentice and master. It is the PhD defense, the bar exam, the IPO presentation, and the playoff game. Many learning journeys culminate with a challenge that draws on everything that you have learned to meet it, proving to all that you are ready to move on.

But how do we know when a high school student is ready to move on?

In most high schools in America, the de facto answer to that question seems both arbitrary and abstract. Four years of seat time, 120-something "credits." Perhaps a certain number on a standardized test. We count the inputs with one abstraction (course credits) and diffusely assess them with another abstraction (letter grades). After decades of this approach, our high schools have lost touch with any concrete sense of what their students know and are able to do at the end of four years. And with vague purpose have come uninspiring outcomes.

It's not OK. Every organization should know its purpose and should design itself accordingly. For institutions of learning, that purpose must articulate the future for its students. What do we want for our students? What are we preparing them for? What do we want them to know and be able to do by the time they move on? What kind of people do we want them be?

Transforming a school must start with thoughtful answers to these big-picture, purpose-driven, goal-oriented questions. Although there are different ways to answer these questions legitimately, there are kinds of answers that we should not accept.

For one, the answers must come in the form of words, not numbers or symbols. Test scores, numerical school ratings, and statistics on grades are abstractions of reality, not descriptions of reality.

And a school's overarching goal must be framed around its students, not reflect circularly back on the school. A student's success is its own end; its purpose is not to make the school successful, which is effectively what happens when a school defines its goals in terms of its ranking based on test scores.

The mission of Envision Education—our particular answer to the question of purpose—is to prepare all students, especially those whose parents did not go to college, to succeed in college, career, and life.

Our mission may sound straightforward, but there is an ambitious nuance in the way we have framed our mission. Getting *into* a college is not how we define success for our students; graduating *from* college is where we have set the bar.

Having clearly defined the goal, we could now design our school. Once we had a vision for our students' future, we could establish what it would require to graduate, with all the skills and content knowledge and habits of mind that it would take to succeed in college.

Although the answer to that was not and is not easy, it is easy to see that the traditional graduation requirements are not adequate. An arbitrary number of credits earned over four years, perhaps a standardized test thrown in, will not cut it. Indeed, they don't.

"MAPPING BACKWARDS" FROM GRADUATION

In 1998, Grant Wiggins and Jay McTighe published a seminal book called *Understanding by Design*, a culmination of two decades of evolving thinking on how to assess student learning. As with many watershed moments in a field, their thesis resounded not because it was radical, but because it crystallized what our common sense already knew.

Teachers are designers, they argue, and belong to the field of design professionals that includes architects, engineers, and graphic artists. Students are the primary clients, and "the effectiveness of curriculum, assessment, and instructional designs is ultimately determined by their achievement of desired learnings" (p. 7).

Curriculum, then, is a means to an end. Therefore, the most effective way to design curriculum is "backward": you start with the end—identifying the learning goal—and then map out the steps that will get you there.

Again, this is good common sense, but what made *Understanding by Design* such a landmark was not simply its call to map backwards but its challenge to make assessment the entry point of design:

> Rather than creating assessments near the conclusion of a unit of study . . . backward design reminds us to begin with the question, What would we accept as evidence that students have attained the desired understandings and proficiencies—*before* proceeding to plan teaching and learning experiences? (p. 8)

Though built on the thinking of those who came before, Wiggins and McTighe's eloquent spin on curricular design caught us at the right time, a turn-of-the-century moment when the American collective consciousness started to question its approach to education. Fifteen years later, "mapping backwards" is now a stock phrase in the world of education, and performance assessment has gone from a commonsense idea to common wisdom to a mandate of the Common Core.

We summarize *Understanding by Design* not simply because we believe in it but because we seek to broaden its scope. Schools themselves, not just the courses offered within them, are a means to an end. Like teachers, school leaders are designers. Everything that Wiggins and McTighe say about the design of a course can and should be applied to the design of a school.

This is the thinking that informed the design of Envision Schools. If we were to begin with the end, we had to start by envisioning the graduate. And if we were to gather evidence that the graduate was indeed ready to move on, we needed to design a meaningful and holistic assessment of the graduate. To apply backwards design to a school as a whole, there had to be something substantive and rigorous from which to map backwards—not simply a ceremony handing out diplomas.

The solution that emerged is our Deeper Learning Student Assessment System.

Once it was in place, we discovered that such a cumulative assessment system is the single most effective way to move from having a school mission to living a school mission. It has become our unifying theory—the element of school transformation that catalyzes all the others.

DEFINING SUCCESS: KNOW, DO, AND REFLECT

Before designing a way to measure our graduates, we had to determine what to measure. As we've said, the goal for our students is college success. We are not content with getting students into college; we want them to navigate the university with confidence in their knowledge and skills and with perseverance in the face of inevitable adversity. Put more plainly, we want them to graduate instead of drop out.

Research by such thinkers as David Conley (2005) helped us take inventory of what's needed for success in college. When Conley surveyed professors on this question, they responded with a refrain: intellectual skills and habits of mind; "these were considered by many faculty to be more important than specific content knowledge" (p. 173).

The professors emphasized some of the general skills we would expect: critical thinking, analytical thinking, problem solving, reading and writing skills. But they were equally adamant about the importance of certain attitudes:

> an inquisitive nature and interest in taking advantage of what a research university has to offer; willingness to accept critical feedback and to adjust based on such feedback; openness to possible failures from time to time; and ability and desire to cope with frustrating and ambiguous learning tasks. (p. 173)

The implications of Conley's study were clear as day: the high school must do more than teach content to its students; it must teach intellectual skills and instill habits of mind.

The next step was exciting but daunting: How do we wrestle this complex picture of what it takes to be a successful student in college into a measurable and manageable set of outcomes for our high school students? Our mission statement was too general. The state standards were incomplete. What we needed to create was our own *graduate profile*.

Key term: **graduate profile**—a community-wide vision statement describing what a learner should know and be able to do before he or she graduates from the school

In creating our graduate profile, we didn't have the luxury of working from a clean slate. We are still living in traditional structures. Colleges still have course-credit requirements and are still looking at transcripts and test scores. Our state still has content standards; our district has curricular requirements. Content knowledge hasn't lost its importance; it's just sharing space.

In the end, we structured and balanced our graduate profile around three simple verbs: **know**, **do**, and **reflect**. The prepared graduate *knows* the content and the discrete skills of her academic subjects. She can *do* what typical college courses demand (research, analyze, inquire, and create) using her intellectual, interpersonal, and executive skills to make things happen. And she has the ability to *reflect*, a habit of self-awareness and revision that sets her on the path of continued growth.

> We created a template that helps our teachers develop their course syllabi so as to reflect our graduate profile. See the Envision Schools Course Syllabus Template in the appendix.

THE ENVISION SCHOOLS GRADUATE PROFILE

Here are the specifics of our Envision Schools graduate profile, with annotated commentary:

Envision Schools graduates are ready for success in college and future careers because they know, do, and reflect (Figure 1.1).

Figure 1.1 Envision Education's Know-Do-Reflect Triangle

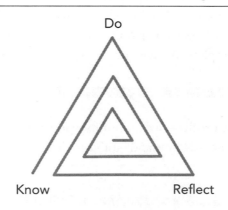

Envision graduates **KNOW**. They master academic subjects, which makes it possible to

- Meet the University of California's A-G Requirements
- Pass the California High School Exit Exam
- Demonstrate proficiency on California state standards tests
- Perform successfully on college entrance exams

> KNOW covers more traditional graduation requirements. But notice that we align our course requirements to meet the prerequisites of our state's university system. Most public high schools don't. We couldn't well say that we are preparing kids for college if we didn't do this.

Envision graduates **DO**. They

- Use core competencies required to perform the role of a college student: **inquiry**, **analysis**, **research**, and **creative expression** in core content areas
- Use the four C's: **communicate** powerfully, think **critically**, **collaborate** productively, and **complete** projects effectively
- Participate in at least one Workplace Learning Experience in which they do real work and complete a project that not only benefits their workplace but also demonstrates their ability to use leadership skills as well as inquire, analyze, research, or express themselves creatively in the workplace (We will talk more about the Workplace Learning Experience in chapter 5.)

> DOING is where our graduate profile rises above traditional graduation requirements. It gets at the important distinctions between knowledge and skills, between passive and active learning, and between learning content and applying it. DO is where we address what the college professors have been calling for. A Psychology 101 professor doesn't expect background knowledge in psychology, but she expects incoming students to know how to conduct inquiry and write a research paper.

Envision graduates **REFLECT**. They

- Recognize and acknowledge growth, accomplishments, and successes as well as areas for future growth and development

- Revise work to proficiency based on feedback from teachers and peers

When students REFLECT on their growth and on the quality of their work, they develop habits of mind that are as essential to college and career success as their knowledge and skills. Self-awareness, persistence, confidence, and equanimity are not personality traits one is born with but habits of mind that can be developed with practice.

Video 2. Envision Defense Montage

In this "highlight reel" from several portfolio defenses, Envision students talk about education and why it matters, demonstrating the power of knowing, doing, and reflecting.

THE NUTS AND BOLTS OF ENVISION'S DEEPER LEARNING STUDENT ASSESSMENT SYSTEM

As Wiggins and McTighe (1998) remind us, once you have described your educational goal, you must design a way to measure whether you've reached it. Measuring the **knowing** was relatively straightforward; traditional means—course grades and standardized tests—were adequate, not to mention still expected by the colleges. Measuring the **doing** and **reflecting** is where things get complex. But here again, we didn't have to reinvent the wheel. Portfolios have long been the means by which people demonstrate what they can do. And the PhD defense has long served as a ritual of formal reflection. These two analogues would form the basis of our assessment system.

Critical elements of the Deeper Learning Student Assessment System include

- *Evidence of academic work.* Students assemble a portfolio of their best work across the core academic disciplines, including science, math, language arts, social studies, and world languages. In addition, students are required to produce a college-ready research paper and a multimedia product, and to complete a Workplace Learning Experience, or internship. The assignments that are eligible for a portfolio, referred to as "tasks," are embedded in the regular curriculum rather than presented as an adjunct to students' studies.

- *Rubrics.* Each task is evaluated against carefully vetted standards that are clear, challenging, and attainable. The evaluation rubrics used to measure the quality of tasks were developed with educational experts at Stanford University. The rubrics are shared with the students at the start of the freshman year, giving them a clear understanding of exactly what is expected of them and how they will be evaluated.

- *Reflection.* As each task is completed, students write a reflection that describes both the end product and the process they used to create it. They reflect on what they've learned, what they would have done differently, and how they will apply this learning to future projects. In addition, students must describe how they applied at least two deeper learning competencies to complete the task. Examples might look something like these:
  - "During our science project, my group got stuck on a part of the process; I collaborated productively by taking leadership of the group to help us agree on a solution and a way to move forward."
  - "I managed my project effectively by creating an action list organized by due dates, and then I checked the list and adjusted it regularly to keep myself on track."

Figure 1.2 maps the structure of Envision's Deeper Learning Student Assessment System.

Five Proficient Artifacts

Forming the backbone of the portfolio are five pieces of deep and rigorous academic work, all meeting or exceeding a standard of proficiency (more on how we define proficiency in the next chapter). Students must populate their portfolios with one each of the following:

- A **research paper**
- An **inquiry**
- An **analysis**
- An artifact of **creative expression**
- An artifact from the **Workplace Learning Experience**

Figure 1.2 The Structure of Envision's Deeper Learning Student Assessment System

Significantly, this list is not a list of the traditional subject disciplines: science, English, math, and social studies. In our first iteration of the portfolio, it was. But our thinking has evolved over time. Conley's work challenged us to think more deeply about what it means to prepare students for college success. Discipline content is of course important, but what is more important, and has been neglected, are key academic competencies demanded of all college students across disciplines. We continue to imagine our students as freshman in college, scanning the course syllabus on their first day in Psychology 101 and feeling relieved when they see the types of assignments they have already mastered in high school.

Our portfolio targets four core competencies that we see as vital for college readiness. (The fifth item on our list, the Workplace Learning Experience, draws from one of the previous four.) Each one of these is assessed as its own rigorous performance task.

By **research**, we mean that students will present an argument about a historical, social science, scientific, or other issue. To demonstrate their mastery of research, they must select a writing sample that embodies the following expectations, which are aligned to the Common Core Reading and Writing Standards for Literacy:

- Responds to a research question
- Develops an argument
- Supports the argument with evidence
- Analyzes the evidence
- Knows and uses accurate content knowledge
- Structures the argument in a coherent way
- Uses discipline-specific writing conventions to communicate ideas

By **inquiry**, we mean that students will formulate a question that can be explored by scientific or historical investigation. To demonstrate mastery of inquiry, they must select a writing sample or lab that embodies the following expectations:

- Formulates an investigable question
- Designs and performs the investigation
- Collects data/evidence, and analyzes and interprets it
- Draws conclusions and assesses the validity of the conclusions
- Knows and uses accurate content knowledge
- Structures information in a coherent way
- Uses discipline-specific writing conventions to communicate ideas

By **analysis**, we mean that students will demonstrate the ability to read and think critically and communicate their ideas powerfully, with work that embodies the following expectations, which are aligned to the Common Core State Standards for English Language Arts:

- Develops an argument
- Supports the argument with evidence
- Analyzes the evidence
- Organizes and structures ideas for effective communication
- Uses language to skillfully communicate ideas

By **creative expression**, we mean that students will think critically and creatively and communicate their ideas powerfully, persuasively, and artistically. We expect students to demonstrate an understanding of artistic thinking and artistic practice. Students shall use the arts as a tool to investigate and discuss topics and concerns that are relevant to artistic traditions and their lives. To demonstrate mastery of creative expression, they must select a piece of work that embodies the following expectations:

- Shows command of the technique of the artistic discipline
- Constructs and makes a work of art with personal meaning and intent
- Explains the connection of the work of art to artistic and cultural traditions
- Envisions, explores, and persists with an aesthetic idea
- Questions, discusses, and judges own work

By laying down these core competencies as the foundation of the portfolio, we proclaim their priority. But let us be clear: the traditional subject areas are not sidelined by this design. We don't have research teachers and inquiry teachers and analysis teachers; we have history teachers and science teachers and English teachers. Instead, the content-area requirements overlay the core competencies. Intentionally, our design reflects our pedagogical philosophy: competencies are the foundation on which content knowledge is built. Figure 1.3 shows how it works.

The circles denote the subject areas through which the corresponding core competency (in the rectangles on the left) must be performed. This gives students the opportunity to exercise some choice in how they show what they know. But those choices must be strategic, because each artifact must come from a different subject area. For example, if a science artifact is used for research, then a social studies artifact must be used for inquiry. In this way, the portfolio signals, to students and teachers, what kind of work needs to be produced in their content classes.

Figure 1.3 Envision Schools' Four Core Competencies

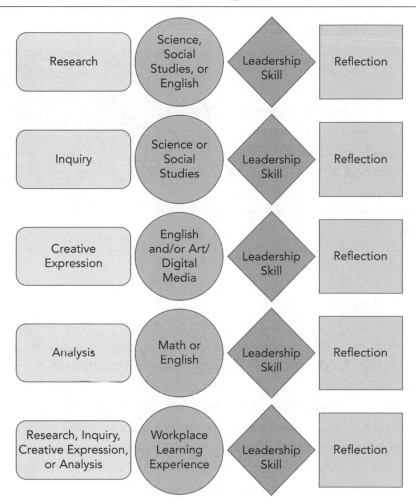

Five Artifact Reflections That Include the Four C's

Students must write a reflection on each of the five artifacts, in which they tell the story of how the artifact was created, what it taught them about the core competency it represents, and how it demonstrates their growth as a learner. In addition, the reflection must connect its artifact to one of the four C's: *communicate* powerfully, think *critically*, *collaborate* productively, or *complete* projects effectively. The reflection explains how this artifact is evidence of growth in that skill.

Video 3. The Four C's

How do the four C's—*communicating* powerfully, thinking *critically*, *collaborating* productively, and *completing* projects effectively—help students get to and succeed in college? Listen to teachers and students discuss the difference these skills make in taking ownership of their own education.

The Cover Letter

The purpose of the cover letter is to provide students with an opportunity to build their defense. Done well, the cover letter also creates a sense of closure and accomplishment—a chance to share what they know and can do with people who are important to them. At the core, a cover letter introduces the portfolio and sets the defense stage where students share what they know, can do, and reflect on.

The short reflections completed after each artifact serve as scaffolding for the cover letter. Because the cover letter synthesizes a student's mastery of the core competencies and the deeper learning outcomes, the cover letter itself is a major reflection—three to five typed pages. A cover letter is like a college admissions personal statement, only richer because the students draw their examples from deep student work and experiences in their school.

The Digital Element

Once students have reached proficiency on five tasks and the cover letter, they upload their certified artifacts (including reflections for each artifact) into the digital archive. Certified artifacts are then available to all Envision staff members so that we can share student work with each other as well as measure how we are doing.

Finally, students prepare a digital presentation driven by their cover letter to organize and highlight the three artifacts that are part of their portfolio defense.

Proficient Defense of Three Artifacts

This is the final step of the portfolio process, and what Kaleb was doing when we started this chapter. In a culminating rite of passage, each student identifies and publicly defends three of the certified work artifacts from his portfolio. Citing this work as evidence, the student defends his mastery of the Envision four C's and details how the presented work both meets the school's criteria for graduation and supports his personal and professional goals. The event takes roughly one hour, with over a third of it devoted to a rigorous Q&A session with the panel.

THE POWER OF PORTFOLIO DEFENSE

Envision schools are not the only ones doing this. We are part of a growing group of schools all over the country that are tying graduation to a powerful academic rite of passage, generally known as a defense of learning. The idea is catching on in high schools and middle schools because of our field's maturing understanding and rising estimation of performance assessment (more on that in chapter 2).

What students defend, and to whom they make their defense, varies in creative, practical, and school-specific ways. At Kamaile Academy, a school on the leeward coast of Oahu that serves disadvantaged native Hawaiian youth, students must not only argue their mastery of academic skills but also explain their plans for embodying the value of *kuleana*, or responsibility to the world, one of the cultural values of the school. Local community elders join teachers on Kamaile's defense panels.

At Health Professions High School in Sacramento, California, students defend a year-long, cross-disciplinary senior project. It starts with an extended explanatory research paper on a chosen medical issue, evolves into a stance expressed in an argumentative essay, and is then taken to the streets in a public advocacy campaign, working in collaboration with a local medical professional. Anyone who watches a student defend one of these projects knows, without having to read the school's graduate profile, what kind of student Health Professions has aspired to mold: "a student prepared for college and career, a responsible citizen, an independent critical thinker, a lifelong learner, and an excellent communicator."

That's the mark of a well-designed defense of learning—watch one, and you know exactly what the school is about: whom it serves, what it values, and the quality of work its students produce. It's the ultimate in "show, don't tell." Schools have long codified their goals in the form of mission statements, standards, declarations of values, and the like. The premise of performance assessment—that to evaluate skills we must observe them in action—challenges schools to take the aspirational words in their handbooks and on their posters and embody them in real-life student performances.

Regardless of the variations on well-designed defenses, the transforming effect that they have on learning communities is similar. For one, defenses help schools focus on the fundamental. There is a logic to defense design—that need to distill—that converges on a set of performance tasks that express what is elemental to the core subject areas and to college and career readiness in general: research, textual analysis, experimental design, mathematical reasoning, historical argument, artistic judgment, collaboration, communication, and critical thinking. Most defense systems are built around some subset of this list. Not incidentally, they also align with and encompass the essence of the Common Core.

Just as defense helps teachers focus their teaching, it also helps students make sense of their education, seeing it not as a collection of credits but as a multiyear project toward a unified end. We never encounter students as eloquent about their learning as students who go to a school that requires them to defend. These students have a deep understanding of what they must learn. They are asked not just to do the work but to reflect on what it means. If they don't pass, they try again.

Designing and implementing portfolio defenses is a huge job for all involved: the students, teachers, and school leaders. But we haven't met anyone who regrets it once she is able to look back. And we can't name another mechanism that offers a school more leverage for transforming itself into a place of deeper learning.

SO THAT'S THE GOAL; HOW DO WE GET THERE?

We've laid out an ambitious goal for our students and their teachers.

So now what? What happens when a school implements a deeper learning assessment system? What needs to change to ensure its success? The answer is "Everything," and the chapters that follow tell the rest of the story.

But here is the sneak preview: deeper learning means rooting a school's curriculum in performance assessment (chapter 2), best served by project-based learning (chapter 3). It means nurturing a school culture of trust (chapter 4), without which many teenagers won't take the risks or develop the self-confidence to succeed in what is effectively a four-year project. It means structuring a school into human-scaled learning communities that allow teachers to mentor students over multiple years (chapter 5). And it means a different kind of school leadership (chapter 6).

All of these changes are good ideas in their own right. But for us, they became necessary changes when we committed to our Deeper Learning Student Assessment System. That system became the focal point of our schools' design, from which everything else maps backwards.

Video 4. Tiana: Profile of a Deeper Learning Student

Deeper learning makes a real difference: for Tiana, her deeper learning education at City Arts and Tech High School meant becoming the first person in her family to go not only to college but also beyond tenth grade. Within a few months at CAT, she realized she had what it took to imagine that future for herself. She and other students reflect on the opportunities and the mentors that got them where they are today.

THE REST OF KALEB'S STORY

Years later, when we interviewed Kaleb and asked him to recollect that day when he did not pass his first defense attempt, he admits that he cried when he got outside the building. In addition to being disappointed in himself, he felt embarrassment for failing in front of a crowd, and, perhaps most stingingly, shame over letting down people who believed in him. At the top of that list was Tony Harris; the panelist who delivered the bad news was also his advisor and one of his most trusted mentors.

Justin was also on the panel and remembers that Kaleb's failed first attempt had been a surprise. By senior year, Kaleb had emerged as one of the sharpest minds and most thoughtful communicators in the class, and as his English teacher for the past two years, Justin knew Kaleb's work firsthand. In American Literature, Kaleb wrote an essay on the author James Baldwin that would prove to be a seminal moment in Kaleb's intellectual awakening and a linchpin artifact of his graduation portfolio.

But on reflection, we had to admit that our surprise was also testament to how far Kaleb had come in the three years he had attended our school. Neglected by an absentee father and raised by a working-class mother, Kaleb came from the toughest neighborhood we served. His biracial background — half black, half white — made him question his identity. He had spent years bouncing around dysfunctional schools. When he came to us as a sophomore, Kaleb was angry and academically ill-prepared. His sophomore year was punctuated by academic setbacks, outbursts of rage, even the occasional fight; Tony Harris had to coach Kaleb through every one of these episodes.

In short, this was a kid who was no stranger to inconsistency and setback, nor to the process of overcoming it. After the tears dried, he went back to work. Over the week that followed, Kaleb rewrote his reflections on his "four C" skills, grounding them with more evidence of his growth over time. He developed an overarching and unifying metaphor, polished his delivery, reorganized his speaking notes to be more user-friendly, and tidied up his PowerPoint slides. He rehearsed in front of the mirror, start to finish, multiple times. These were all things Kaleb knew how to do and admitted he should have done the first time.

Keep in mind that Kaleb already had a college acceptance letter in his back pocket. So during a time when most college-bound seniors have long since succumbed to the lethargy of senioritis, Kaleb, faced with the threat that a diploma would not be handed to him on graduation day, was wrestling his way through a transformational learning experience.

The oral defense often feels higher stakes to the students than it really is. For Kaleb, the heavy lifting had already been done. He had already written the papers and performed the experiments and created the art that needed to fill the portfolio. His teachers had already guided him through the revisions that lifted his work to standard and had, as content specialists, signed off on that work as college ready. By most measures, Kaleb had already proven he was ready for college.

So why did he have to go through all this? Was this unnecessary abuse, a trial that amounted to little more than theater?

No. The oral defense is essential to the overall assessment. It must be passed, and the students who have had to show up in the summer for a third or fourth attempt, delivering their defenses to empty classrooms, can attest that it is not theater.

But Kaleb and his peers do overestimate the relative weight of the oral defense, for two good reasons: first, public speaking is inherently nerve wracking, and second, it is natural to invest symbolic significance in the final step of any journey, even though every step was vital to reaching the destination.

This is by design. We *want* students to attach major significance to this culminating experience. It is designed to give their graduation meaning and depth, to give them something concrete to point to, celebrate, and be proud of. In fact, we see the defense as the achievement of the pedagogical sweet spot, a created space that requires and inspires the learner's best effort while still cushioning failure's fall with second (and third and fourth) chances. In other words, although Kaleb was sweating it now, his teachers knew he was going to do fine in the end and that they would be there to support him along the way.

And he did do fine. Ten days later, Justin sat on the panel for Kaleb's second attempt at his oral defense and remembers how much more smoothly and persuasively Kaleb made his case. "Unlike the first time, I felt well prepared," Kaleb recalls, "and because I could feel that it was going well, I got increasingly confident. I started strong and got better from there. Before it was even over, I knew I had passed. It felt so good!"

After he passed, Kaleb went on to be the first in his family to attend a four-year university (Bob's alma mater, St. Mary's College) and, more crucially, would graduate from that university with a degree in sociology. He now works as a compliance officer to prevent discrimination and abusiveness in the banking industry.

"The grad portfolio taught me lessons that I have carried into the work world," Kaleb told us when we recently asked him about it.

> For example, the job I have right now came out of a temp position. It wasn't handed to me, and I could tell that it wasn't going to be. First, I had to figure out what I wanted. Then I had to size up the situation, document my work, prove my diligence. In the end, I had to *make a case* [emphasis Kaleb's] that I was someone this firm should bring on full time. And I had a sense of how to go out about it because I had *practiced this before* [emphasis ours].
>
> As I continue to work in a large organization, I am realizing this is true about everything. If you want something—change a policy or get a promotion or whatever—you have to make the case. And it's not just doing the work; you have to show the work. . . .
>
> I remember that all of us seniors were frustrated by the grad portfolio requirements at the time. I mean, we had already done all these big assignments, and we didn't understand why we had to go through this extra step of reflecting on them.

Kaleb was part of the first Envision class ever to put together a graduation portfolio and defense; as pioneers, they were particularly resistant to the process because it was easy to imagine school without it. (Over the years, as younger students have watched seniors prepare for and deliver their defenses, the process has become embedded in our school culture and is no longer resisted as it was during that pioneer year.)

> We were used to the normal way of doing school. You churn out an assignment or take a test, usually after cramming for it, you hope you get an A on it, and you move on.
>
> But the graduation portfolio forced us to go beyond just doing the work. We had to learn how to be confident about our own work. If you can do that in a safe high school environment, that's the place to start. It was so positive . . . so smart what you guys made us go through back then.

Even the trauma of failing that first attempt?
Kaleb recalls,

> I was crushed. I went outside, and I was crying. But it wasn't long before I could appreciate why Mr. Harris failed me the first time. I felt that he respected me, rather than letting me sell myself short. What I realized, even then, was that Mr. Harris believed in me more than I did. And in order to pass the defense, that needed to change.

No, this is not theater; it is backwards design. This is what we must do if we are to send students off into the world and expect them to succeed. Because what we see up there during an oral defense, the culminating moment of a four-year project, is not Kaleb convincing his teachers that he is ready to graduate; it is Kaleb making—and winning—the case to himself.

Video 5. Student Profile, Portfolio Defense

An Envision student and teacher talk about preparing for the "final moment" of the portfolio defense; Yvonne reflects on her growth as a student and a learner.

Yvonne
12th Grade Student
Metropolitian Arts & Tech High School,
San Francisco, CA

REFERENCES

Conley, D. T. (2005). *College knowledge: What it really takes for students to succeed and what we can do to get them ready.* San Francisco, CA: Jossey-Bass.

Wiggins, G., & McTighe, J. (1998). *Understanding by design.* Alexandria, VA: Association for Supervision and Curriculum Development.

Chapter 2

Designing a Standards-Aligned Performance Assessment System

> People learn more when they do something.
>
> — Dedranae Tucker, Envision student

Consider the driver's test. Your fellow citizens won't share the road with you until you pass it, proving you can drive skillfully and responsibly. There may be variations to the licensure process, but they all culminate in your getting behind the wheel of a car, an assessor buckled into the seat next to you, and showing you can drive *by driving*.

Compare that to the driver's permit exam, which in most states is a standardized written or electronic test that assesses one's knowledge of the rules of the road. It is a significant step in the process; indeed, passing the permit exam is what allows you to get on the road and practice driving—under the supervision of a licensed driver.

No one questions the distinct purposes of these two assessments. One tests what you know about driving; the other tests how you drive. They are both important, but not equally so. Common sense tells us that a basic knowledge of traffic laws does not provide sufficient evidence to answer the ultimate question at hand: Is the license seeker qualified to drive a car on his or her own? That's why the process culminates with a performance assessment.

Our K–12 education system has much to learn from such common sense. We give our students lots of permit exams and hardly any driver's tests. We measure (or attempt to measure) what they know, hoping it serves as a proxy for what they can do. The upshot is that many young adults leave high school unprepared to drive the metaphoric roads of college or career.

This is not a news flash to most of our readers. We'd rather take up the question that follows: Knowing that performance assessment is a better way to measure and prepare our students, how do we elevate it to its proper role in education, shifting the emphasis of assessment from knowing to doing?

Answers are out there, but they typically direct attention to teachers (here is how their courses should change) or to the larger school system (here is how standardized testing should change).

But the most effective agent for transforming assessment is overlooked. It is neither the teacher nor the state. It is the school.

PERFORMANCE ASSESSMENT DEFINED—AND REFINED

Performance assessment is a fancy term for a simple concept: **evaluating what you can do by observing you doing it.**

The musical director auditions singers by hearing them sing. The coach tries out players by watching them play, both through drills (which isolate certain skills) and in scrimmages. The performance doesn't necessarily have to be observed in the doing. A record or product of a performance satisfies in many cases: a photographer's portfolio, a cook's prepared dish.

Performance assessment doesn't have a direct opposite, but it does have counterpoints. A multiple-choice test is the most commonly cited example of what performance assessment is not (Darling-Hammond & Adamson, 2010). For an assessment to merit the qualifier *performance*, the test taker must construct an answer for himself, rather than selecting an answer from predetermined options. By definition, a performance assessment evaluates **a product or performance, requiring some kind of constructive or creative act.**

Another counterpoint is assessment by proxy. When it's not possible to measure someone's abilities directly, we try to measure them indirectly. An example is the traditional job interview. Employers generally can't observe on-the-job performance before they put you on the job. Instead, they sit you down on the other side of the desk and ask you interview questions.

Because your palms are sweating, you certainly feel as though your performance is being assessed. What is really happening is that your ability to do the job is being inferred from proximal data: the confidence and intelligence of your answers, the professionalism of your dress, the details of your reported experience. Most job interviews cannot directly assess your ability to do the job; rather, they measure how well you can interview. (Exceptions abound, of course, including the "demo lesson" often demanded of applicants for a teaching position.)

Before something can qualify as performance assessment, its challenge must be aligned to its purpose. It is not enough to see someone writing or experimenting or singing or interviewing—in other words, engaged in some creative or constructive activity—and then slap the word *performance* onto its assessment. First, you must name what you want to measure. Only then can you judge whether the observed product or performance gives you the evidence you seek.

This is why defining performance assessment as everything non–multiple choice is simplistic. We can, for example, fool ourselves into thinking that if students are merely writing something—whether a short answer or a developed essay—then we have definitively moved them into the land of performance assessment.

But writing can be as formulaic as any bubble test, especially when it doesn't challenge students to tap a higher-order thinking skill. There's a good reason why English teachers, for example, challenge each other and their students to move beyond the book report as a response to literature. Summarizing plot is not a higher-order thinking skill. If your goal is to assess students' ability to analyze or evaluate text, then the traditional book report, even though it is an open-ended writing assignment, does not qualify as a performance assessment. By definition, **a performance assessment must enact the skill you are intending to measure.**

To qualify as a **performance assessment,** what is evaluated must be

1. A product or performance
2. An application of a *targeted* skill (or skills)

You know you have a genuine performance assessment if preparing for the test, taking the test, and then applying the skill in real life all look the same. Consider the skill of parallel parking. How is it tested on the driver's test? By parallel parking. How do you practice for that part of the test? By parallel parking. And what do you do with the acquired skill after you pass the test? You parallel park.

AN OLD PEDAGOGY FOR A NEWLY DEMANDING WORLD

Long before the term *performance assessment* ever existed, Professor Henry Higgins took Eliza Doolittle to the horse races (Lerner & Loewe, 1956). Proof that Eliza's learning had gone deep was not to be found in the cozy confines of Higgins's library, where she recited "the rain in Spain" until her accent was perfectly aristocratic. The bet was that Higgins could make her pass as an aristocrat; naturally, she needed to prove her skills among them. So off they went to the "Ascot opening day."

It was a challenging test in a new and authentic context. Of course, in one of the more memorable scenes of musical theater, Eliza, until that moment indistinguishable from the blue bloods surrounding her, exhorts her horse to "move your bloomin' arse!!!" (p. 78). Eliza wasn't quite ready to pass this famous example of a performance assessment.

Jargon deserves our skepticism. So often it turns out to be wrapping paper. You tear it off and are miffed to find an old concept, regifted.

Performance assessment, as a term, can make us feel that way, especially when it is uttered in a tone that pretends to be some revolutionary new invention. But good teachers have, through their own judgment and sense, been designing good performance assessments for as long as humans have been teaching each other things. Many of us can think back to a teacher whose course culminated with some demanding assignment, one that required us to *do* the subject rather than just learn it, one that not only challenged us but *helped us make sense of what the course was ultimately about*. Student-designed experiments, research projects, presentations of learning—such oft-cited examples of performance assessment were around long before the term gained currency. Visual and performing arts teachers have always dwelt in the land of performance assessment, never left, and have good reason to wonder what all the hubbub is about.

Still, performance assessment, though not describing a new thing, is an increasingly useful term, for two reasons. One, a lot of non–performance assessment has grown up around it, competing for sunlight. The denser the thicket, the more attentive we must be to the difference between what to prune and what to let grow.

Two, though performance assessment has always been good pedagogy, it is fast becoming the only pedagogy that can possibly address the demands of this changing world. Tony Wagner, an education professor at Harvard, has been a consistently eloquent voice on the matter:

> Today, because knowledge is available on every Internet-connected device, what you know matters far less than what you can do with what you know. The capacity to innovate—the ability to solve problems creatively or bring new possibilities to life—and skills like critical thinking, communication and collaboration are far more important than academic knowledge. As one executive told me, "We can teach new hires the content, and we will have to because it continues to change, but we can't teach them how to think—to ask the right questions—and to take initiative." (Friedman, 2013)

That job falls to our schools. And that list—thinking critically, communicating, collaborating—keeps popping up every time someone thinks about preparing students for their future, whether for college, career, or citizenship. It is a set of skills, not a body of facts. It's a list of verbs, not nouns. If we agree on their importance, then we must design educational experiences that allow students to practice and teachers to coach those skills *in action.*

A multiple-choice question is not inherently bad. It can be an appropriate and certainly efficient way of assessing certain kinds of content knowledge. But when cast in the light of the task at hand, it just looks woefully inadequate, even irrelevant. We realize that performance assessment—however jargony it may sound—is our only possible means for measuring what our students need measured.

Actually, there is much to appreciate about the term performance assessment, because the words it comprises point in the direction that school design needs to go. The word *performance* connotes action, creativity, and the presence of an audience. The word *assessment* suggests something ongoing—a process—in a way that the word *test* does not. These are important themes for the design of a schoolwide performance assessment system.

THE ENVISION PERFORMANCE ASSESSMENT SYSTEM

The linchpin of Envision's Deeper Learning Student Assessment System is the portfolio defense, described in chapter 1. We see high school as a four-year project, everything building toward that one final performance.

But as we explained in the previous chapter, that one final performance in fact brings together four performances:

- A research paper
- An analysis
- An inquiry
- A creative expression

This list emerged from a decade of rigorous dialogue, not only among our teachers but also with educational experts at Stanford, who themselves have carefully studied the articulation between high school and college in the United States. This is our organization's distillation of college and career readiness (and it therefore subsumes the Common Core State Standards as well). We have planted four flags in the ground: if our students can master each of these tasks, they can succeed in college.

Each of the performance tasks is guided by its own scoring rubric, used by students and teachers to determine whether a given performance has missed, met, or exceeded the standard of proficiency.

Much of the professional development at Envision Schools centers on how to implement these performance tasks and use their associated rubrics. A weeklong session orients new teachers to the system. August pre-school planning requires all teaching teams to map out the number of opportunities students will have to perform these tasks. And over the course of the year, during both weekly collaborative meetings as well as dedicated days of professional development, teachers use the rubrics to score and discuss student work together, a never-finished process of interpretation and calibration. It then becomes the job of principals and lead teachers to ensure that the tasks are taught frequently enough and deeply enough so that, by the end of four years, students have had a chance to attain mastery of each of these skills.

By the junior and senior years, students are actively working with their subject area teachers to craft their best possible research papers, analyses, inquiries, and representations of creativity. Senior year, they choose the best of each, then revise it to proficiency if it is not already, or polish it to an advanced level if it is already deemed proficient. When ready, the artifact is submitted, reflected on, and finally defended.

Key Features of the System

Over the years, the design of our system has evolved, and as long as we remain committed to being a learning organization, it will continue to evolve. Still, certain features have developed into design principles that are holding fast.

The List of Performance Assessments Is Short

It has to be.

A commitment to performance assessment—whether from a teacher, a school, or a school system—is a commitment to focus. The number of performances considered central must be kept small, ideally no more than the fingers on one hand.

There are two reasons for this. The first is practical. Learning is a process of repetition, and repetition can only occur if there is time for it. Having twenty priorities is the same as having none. Performance assessment is ultimately about goal setting, and we all know that one of the biggest barriers to reaching goals is having too many of them.

The second reason is pedagogical. One of the fundamental purposes of education is to help us make sense of a complex world. We can't reduce that complexity, but we can learn how to navigate it. We do this by discerning patterns, building systems, and molding theories.

A well-designed performance assessment is exactly that: a theory of action that focuses the learner and the teacher, unifying a complex web of skills and content into a comprehensible whole.

The Performance Assessments Distill the Standards

Standards setting is inherently an act of analysis. A set of standards is always an answer to the question, "What is quality?" Naturally, we seek the answer by taking the subject in question and breaking it down into its parts.

What makes for a great tennis player? Few of us would be satisfied with the answer, "A player who wins a lot of games," even though it's true. The purpose of the question is to parse the performance: the mechanics of the backhand and forehand; the speed of the serve; the player's fitness, grit, and grace under pressure. Whether it's a performance or a machine, we take something apart when we want to see how it works. And after we're done, we end up with a lot of parts spread across the floor.

So it's unfair to complain, as many often do, that academic standards come to us as long, overwhelming to-do lists. Even standards that attempt to condense and prioritize, as the Common Core standards do, fill pages and pages with their discrete items, broken down by skill areas, broken down by grade level, and so on. If it were an engine and you wanted to see how it works, then a quality education would have many parts to spread across the floor.

So we describe quality with analysis; in contrast, we *assess* quality with synthesis—or at least we should. Assessment is most convincing when we can see how all those parts come together. Many athletes look great on paper, analytically, but greatness is ultimately achieved on the court, in the game. You can survey all those engine parts spread across the floor—all of them accounted for and gleaming—but you don't know if you have a quality engine until you put it together and turn it on.

Yet we make this mistake in our schools all the time. We approach standards as though they were a checklist, testing kids on discrete skills and tidbits of knowledge without ever asking them to synthesize and apply. Education becomes a practice session toward a game that is never scheduled. It's an engine tinkered with in the garage that never hits the street.

We shouldn't blame the standards for this. It's not the job of standards to tell us how to put the engine back together. In fact, most standards consciously avoid doing so; often they preface themselves as the *what* instead of the *how*. The how is the job of educators. (And truth be told, we wouldn't have it any other way.)

This is the purpose of a performance assessment system: to take all the various goals vying for attention, from all realms—state standards, district initiatives, college entrance requirements, school mission, academic traditions, and 21st century skills—and synthesize those into a few key performances, whose achievement convincingly makes the claim, "This is quality."

When Envision undertook the work of distilling all of its educational goals, we ended up with four fundamental skills to master: writing a research report, making an inquiry, conducting an analysis, and actualizing a creative vision. Within the first week of her first year at school, a ninth grader knows that these are the four things that she must learn how to do well. And for the next four years, all of her courses, assignments, lessons, and projects—the component parts of school—feed into her mastery of those skills. In the end, there is a unified assessment, the defense of her portfolio, that challenges the student to *put it all back together*.

None of the Performance Assessments Is Tied to a Particular Subject Discipline

At first glance, the subject disciplines—English, math, history, and science—appear absent from our list of performance assessments. In fact, they are baked in, because these are the courses in which students learn to accomplish these tasks. Particular tasks naturally emerge from particular subject disciplines. But—and here is the advantage of a list that is not discipline specific—it is a one-to-many, rather than a one-to-one relationship. The responsibility for teaching how to perform each of these tasks is, in every case, shared. This design embodies the zeitgeist of the Common Core era, which proclaims that the teaching of literacy must be shared across subject areas.

Moreover, by untethering a research paper from, say, history, we can prepare students for the reality that certain modes of discourse will show up in subject disciplines that are not taught in high school, that are encountered for the first time in college, and that many of our students will go on to major in: sociology, political science, geology, and so on.

Still, it is important to note—especially for the proud defenders of academic tradition—that although our design may sometimes blur the distinctions between traditional subject disciplines, it does not erase them. In fact, we've observed the opposite: the more the subject disciplines collaborate together, the more we are learning of the important differences in subject specific thinking. Historical research, for example, is intrinsically different from literary analysis, though both require close and careful reading. Such differences are not merely respected; they are nurtured and celebrated, and they often serve as fodder for impressive reflections during portfolio defenses.

The Rubrics Are Commonly Shared

A rubric is not merely an assessment tool; more fundamentally, it is a communication tool. Using words instead of numbers or symbols, a rubric serves to explain what it means to do a good job.

For that communication to be most effective, a rubric should be used both before the performance ("What is expected of me?") as well as after ("How did I do?"). The same rubric should also be used across multiple performances, offering many chances to meet one clearly articulated set of expectations. Mastering a skill comes not only through practice but also through a deepening understanding of the expectations. For this to happen, the learner needs more than one opportunity to demonstrate progress in relation to the same expectations.

The more opportunities, the better. The benefits of a rubric's repeated use within one course only compound when the rubric is used across multiple courses and multiple years. At Envision, we have designed rubrics that work across "grade bands"—ninth/tenth and eleventh/twelfth—allowing students to work with a given rubric for two years.

If a school community is converging on a set of performance assessments, then it should also converge on an associated set of common rubrics. Envision's rubrics are shared across our whole network of schools. You can find samples of Envision's rubrics in the appendix.

Designing Performance Assessments

A complete performance assessment has three parts:

1. **The outcome(s)**

    Designing a performance assessment begins with announcing what you hope that the learner achieves, specifying the targeted skills or standards to be measured. Often, the outcomes are framed as "learning targets" or "objectives."

2. **Demonstration of the outcome(s)**

    This is the "task," the "assignment," or the "prompt" — what the learner is asked to do, resulting in a product or performance that provides direct evidence of the targeted skills or standards.

3. **Measurement of the outcome(s)**

    The criteria for success must be established before the learner creates the product or delivers the performance. Typically, this is documented in the form of a rubric.

> Teachers at Envision are able to focus their design efforts on the task (part 2), because the outcomes (part 1) and the rubrics (part 3) have already been established and are shared schoolwide.

With this three-part structure in mind, let us look at two examples of Envision performance assessments.

A Scientific Inquiry: Disaster in the Gulf

Here is an example of a performance assessment, designed by Envision teachers Stanley Richards and Ben Rosen, that is nested within a larger interdisciplinary project that explores the question, "Who is responsible for the 2010 BP oil spill in the Gulf of Mexico?" Students researched the policy and laws pertaining to the spill in their Government class. In their English class, they researched and wrote first-person accounts of how the spill affected people in the gulf, the oil company, and the government, and delivered these accounts at a mock congressional hearing. In art class, students created works that interpreted the effects of the spill on nature. For science, the students conducted an experimental inquiry into the best methods for cleaning up the oil spill. Here is an overview of the three parts:

Part 1: The Outcomes   To demonstrate their mastery of the inquiry competency in science, students must complete a performance assessment that embodies the following outcomes:

- Initiating the Inquiry

  What is the evidence that the student can formulate questions that can be explored by scientific investigations as well as articulate a testable hypothesis?

  - Asks empirically testable, scientific questions
  - Constructs drawings, diagrams, or models to represent what's being investigated
  - Explains the limitations and precision of a model as a representation of the system or process
  - Formulates a testable hypothesis that is directly related to the question asked

- Planning and Carrying Out Investigations

  What is the evidence that the student can design and perform investigations to explore a natural phenomenon?

  - Designs controlled experiments (with multiple trials) to test the suggested hypothesis
  - Identifies and explains the independent and dependent variables in the hypothesis
  - Clearly communicates the details of the procedures so that they can be replicated by another group of students
  - Creates a detailed and clear data collection method for all trials
  - Conducts multiple trials

- Representing, Analyzing, and Interpreting Data

  What is the evidence that the student can organize, analyze, and interpret the data?

  - Organizes the data in tables and/or graphs
  - Expresses relationships and quantities (units) using mathematical conventions

- Explains mathematical computation results in relationship to the expected outcome

- Analyzes and interprets the data and finds patterns

- Draws inferences from the data

- Suggests strengths or weaknesses in inferences from which further investigation could result

- Constructing Evidence-Based Arguments and Communicating Conclusions

    What is the evidence that the student can articulate evidence-based explanations and effectively communicate conclusions?

    - Constructs a scientific argument, explaining how data and acceptable scientific theory support the claim

    - Identifies a counterclaim (possible weaknesses in scientific argument or in one's own argument)

    - Provides multiple representations to communicate conclusions (words, tables, diagrams, graphs, and/or mathematical expressions)

    - Draws conclusions with specific discussion of limitations

    - Uses language and tone appropriate to the purpose and audience

    - Follows conventions of scientific writing, including accurate use of scientific/technical terms, quantitative data, and visual representations

Part 2: The Task   The Disaster in the Gulf inquiry task challenges students to analyze techniques for removing spilled oil from the water and wetlands. Students research various cleanup solutions, generate a hypothesis, and then create and implement a scientific investigation to determine whether their hypothesis is correct. The task was designed so that students could practice toward and produce evidence of the desired outcomes listed in part 1.

In the appendix, a sample of student work illustrates one student's journey through the performance assessment, from his research to his hypothesis to his experiment using oil, detergent, and cotton balls.

Part 3: The Rubric   In the appendix, you will find the scientific inquiry rubric used to evaluate the student work for this performance assessment. It breaks down the outcomes listed in part 1 and communicates how to measure those skills across four performance levels: emerging, developing, proficient, and advanced. The same rubric is used across multiple assignments over multiple years. Teachers use it to map what they must teach, and students use it to understand what is expected of them and to plot the development of their skills.

Two documents in the appendix provide fuller detail on the Disaster in the Gulf performance assessment:

- Scientific Inquiry Performance Task and Rubric
- Disaster in the Gulf Student Work and Reflection

A Textual Analysis: Dante's Inferno

This performance assessment is also nested within a larger project, called the *Inferno Mosaic Retelling Project*, designed to engage eleventh- and twelfth-grade students in a rigorous reading and analysis of Dante's 14th century epic poem, the *Inferno*. (The mosaic retelling also works with ninth and tenth graders using Homer's *Odyssey*.)

The project revolves around two portfolio-eligible performance assessments: an artistic expression and a textual analysis. (Rubrics for both are included in the appendix.) After the class reads the poem, each student chooses some of Dante's lines to interpret artistically in the medium of her choice. The students present their art publicly as part of an ensemble retelling of the poem. In the final step, each student writes a literary analysis essay based on the lines that she has interpreted artistically.

We'll talk more about project design principles in the next chapter. Here we focus on one of the performance assessments—the textual analysis:

Part 1: The Outcomes   To demonstrate their ability to read and think critically and to communicate effectively, students must complete a performance assessment that embodies the following expectations, which are aligned with the Common Core State Standards for English Language Arts:

- **Argument**

    What is the evidence that the student can develop an argument?

    - Responds to the texts with a controlling idea or argument that demonstrates engaged reading and critical thinking
    - Acknowledges and responds to key questions, concerns, or alternative claims relevant to the controlling idea/claim

- Makes insightful connections, raises implications, and/or draws meaningful conclusions as a result of the reading and analysis

- **Evidence and Analysis**

  What is the evidence that the student can support the argument and analyze evidence?

  - Examines one or more significant works of fiction and/or nonfiction
  - Examines and analyzes the ideas and points of view presented in the texts and the author's language used to convey those ideas (for example, figurative language, literary elements, rhetorical devices)
  - Provides relevant textual evidence to support ideas and claims

- **Organization**

  What is the evidence that the student can organize, analyze, and interpret the data?

  - Presents the controlling idea/argument in a way that is clear and guides the paper's organization
  - Demonstrates a coherence and an internal structure that supports the argument
  - Consistently uses transitions that relate and connect one idea to another
  - Develops ideas and claims in appropriate depth

- **Conventions**

  What is the evidence that the student can use language skillfully to communicate ideas?

  - Uses grammar, language, and techniques that are appropriate to the student's purpose and audience
  - Observes appropriate language conventions
  - Engages the reader with a strong voice and rhetorical technique (for example, anecdotes, "grabber" introductions, repetition, sentence variety, parallelism)
  - Cites textual evidence accurately and consistently

Part 2: The Task   In a textual analysis essay, students take the lines from Dante's *Inferno* that they have already interpreted artistically and now interpret them analytically, presenting and supporting a student-generated thesis.

Before developing the paper, each student must propose a thesis to the class for feedback and approval. A structural outline is also required before work can begin on the first draft. These steps help the student address the expected standards of the performance assessment (listed in part 1).

Many students struggle with interpreting another's words—especially a great author's—with words of their own. This is exactly why the art task, perhaps counterintuitively, comes before the writing task. By drawing the students into a different medium of expression, the art task effectively forces the students into an act of interpretation. For the textual analysis paper, students return to the land of words to explain what their art helped them notice.

One student, for example, noticed something surprising after creating a sculpture of the monster-guardian Geryon, made from parts he found in a junkyard. Once it was sculpted, the monster appeared horrifying to the student, yet in his initial reading of the poem's lines, the monster sounded "cool," not scary at all. Upon further analysis, the student noticed that the narrator describes Geryon, who guards a lower circle of Hell, in a tone very calm and matter-of-fact, unlike the narrator's high-pitched, fearful, connotation-rich descriptions of earlier monsters guarding higher circles of Hell. This observation led the student to a sophisticated thesis linking style to theme: the deeper his journey into Hell, the more calmly, even coldly, Dante the Pilgrim accepts what he sees there, which is exactly what Virgil, and God, expect from him.

Part 3: The Rubric   Student essays are evaluated, both formatively and summatively, using the English Language Arts Textual Analysis rubric (included in the appendix).

Video 6. The *Inferno* Mosaic Retelling Project

Watch how Justin's assignment to interpret Dante's *Inferno* through art helped his students gain a deeper understanding of the epic poem and its themes, enabling them to write more perceptive textual analysis papers.

> ### Resources for Designing Performance Assessments
>
> - *Envision Performance Assessment Planning Template (in the appendix)*
>   Envision developed this tool to help our teachers and our client-partners design performance assessments. The template guides your thinking through all three parts of a complete performance assessment: (1) What are your desired outcomes? (2) How will students demonstrate those outcomes? and (3) How will you measure them?
> - *SCALE Performance Assessment Quality Rubric (in the appendix)*
>   Longtime assessment experts at the Stanford Center for Assessment, Learning, and Equity (SCALE), in consultation with practitioners in the deeper learning community, developed this rubric for evaluating performance assessments. The tool helpfully isolates the various features of a quality performance assessment, including alignment to standards, clarity of task prompt, and level of student engagement. Excellent professional development can be built around this tool; for example, a group of teachers can gather to share designed assessments and use the rubric to give each other constructive feedback.
> - *Designing for Deeper Learning: How to Develop Performance Assessments for the Common Core (a free online course: novoed.com/learning-design-common-core)*
>   Our colleagues at SCALE, who helped Envision design its performance assessment system, introduced a MOOC (massive open online course) on performance assessment design in fall 2014. Envision's Campaign Ad Project serves as a featured example in the Stanford course.

THE CHALLENGES ARE THE STRENGTHS

Performance assessment is hard. It is complex and time consuming at every stage, and it requires constant maintenance. Doing it well, beyond the scope of a single classroom, comes with all the challenges of collaboration. As soon as you start to scale it across a department or school or school system, you run into problems of validity and reliability (technical terms from the world of standardized testing).

But the power of performance assessment lies guarded within these very challenges. Only by facing them does the work reach its potential. Here we catalogue the perceived problems and show how each one is a latent strength.

The Challenge: Performance Assessment Is "Costly"

The Upside: The Size of Our Investment Is Equal to the Size of Our Return

Compared to its alternatives, performance assessment is almost always more expensive, time consuming, and resource intensive.

Again, compare the driver's permit exam to the driver's test. One requires a piece of paper or a computer and can be scored by a machine. Draw up the test once, and it can be disseminated to thousands. The other requires one trained human being to sit in a car for up to an hour with every single person seeking a driver's license. In comparison to the permit exam, the driver's test is incredibly costly.

But we do it because we, as a society, have decided that it's worth it. When it comes to putting skilled and safe drivers on the road, performance assessment is what it takes to ensure the outcome that we seek.

Clearly, this book argues that performance assessment in K–12 education is also "worth it." Value is not simply a function of cost; it is equally a product of investment. The more time you invest in something, the more value it holds for you. The more valuable it is to you, the more you care to invest in it. This is a virtuous cycle.

We've seen this time and again in our schools. When teachers see good performance assessment design as one of their primary responsibilities, and when they are given appropriate support to fulfill that responsibility, they treat these performance assessments with great care. A carefully designed, skillfully implemented, and reliably scored performance assessment system requires a significant investment from teachers and school leaders, but that investment creates its own commitment. Students benefit immensely from this.

The Challenge: Performance Assessment Design Is Complex

The Upside: The Result Is Powerfully Simple

Testing companies can churn out multiple-choice questions like widgets from an assembly line.

A good performance assessment, in contrast, can only be produced with hand-craftsmanship. It requires careful thinking through every stage of design, from the targeting of skills, to strategizing how to produce evidence of those skills, to determining how to measure that evidence. Because performance assessments tend to synthesize a range of standards and subskills, the designer must puzzle a number of pieces together. It's hard work.

But when done well, what emerges from that complex wrangling can be powerful in its simplicity. What the learner sees is a coherent, singular goal, a way to apply all the parts of his learning toward a whole: after my months in this course, here is the experiment I can now design, the argument I can now defend, the art I can now create, the math I can now apply to a real-world problem. More powerfully than any other mechanism, a well-designed, unifying, and culminating performance assessment communicates to the learner the *meaning* of what he has learned.

The Challenge: Performance Assessment Tries to Measure Skills That Are Hard to Measure

The Upside: Collaboration and Revision Are Required

The world of standardized testing is nervous about performance assessment because of a concept known as *validity*. A test is valid if it accurately measures what it intends to measure.

Because performance assessments try to measure skills that tend to be complex and hard to quantify (for example, research, analysis, inquiry, and creativity), psychometricians (big word for the people who study the validity of testing) see such assessments as fraught with the potential for error.

But here the difference between hard and impossible is important. Performance assessment is hard—not impossible—to design for validity. And the difficulty can be overcome by increasing two inputs: time and manpower. The greater the number of people involved in a performance assessment's creation and the more time given to its revision, the closer to perfect it can be.

How convenient that a culture of collaboration and revision happens to be the most effective agent for improving teaching and learning. What we've noticed in our schools is that performance assessment design provides a deeply authentic reason for our teachers to come together. As Arthur Costa and Bena Kallick (1995) have written, "Teams build assessment—and assessment builds teams" (p. 141).

The Challenge: Performance Assessment Is Hard to Score Reliably

The Upside: It's the Best Professional Development Ever Invented

An argumentative essay, a historical research project, an extended science inquiry—these are assignments that can't be scored by a machine or with an answer key. They require human judgment.

When humans are making judgments about complex work, then one has to be concerned about an issue that is known in the field as *reliability*. Is the score on this performance based on predetermined, commonly understood, and static criteria, or is it a reflection of an individual and inconstant judgment? If a piece of student work earns a wide range of scores from a group of judges, then psychometricians won't trust any of those scores as "reliable."

When performance assessments are administered on a large scale—for example, AP tests—enormous effort is invested in establishing "inter-rater reliability." Many different people are judging the tests, but those people have been trained to look for similar things and reach similar judgments.

It may seem that reliability lies beyond the concern of a particular teacher giving a particular assignment at a school. As long as a student understands ahead of time what is expected of him, and the evaluation of his work follows through on those expectations, then why should it matter whether another teacher down the hall would score the work a little differently?

In a traditionally organized school, the answer to the last question is that it doesn't matter much. In a course credit system, the teacher owes little to the school beyond a letter grade for each student. What that letter means is largely up to the teacher.

But if a school moves toward a performance assessment system, and the orientation shifts from counting credits to mastering skills, then suddenly there is a real need for teachers to reach a shared understanding of "What is mastery?"

Over the last twenty years, the tool that has gained widespread acceptance for meeting this challenge is the rubric, whose defining characteristic is its insistence on words, rather than abstract symbols, to describe the quality of the work.

Educators are well familiar with the rubric's typical format—a table, levels of quality across one axis, various aspects of the performance across another, with cells containing phrases that describe features of the student work. Truth be told, most rubrics disappoint in some way. We're never quite satisfied with the wording (English teachers in particular). If created in collaboration, then they are created through compromise. And at this point, we've all seen enough of them that certain features border on cliché.

So it's not the form of the tool—that blizzard of bullets and boxes—that gives rubrics their power. Rather, it is the practices—the thinking and the actions—that surround rubrics that have made them a transformative force in education. First of all, creating a rubric requires us to do the all-important but often underemphasized mapping backwards from a goal. We must define proficiency, establish the standard. Most rubric writing starts there, filling in the boxes that give words to the expectation we have for all of our students. One of the biggest barriers to learning is lack of clarity around the learning target. Rubrics force us to describe the target, and the benefits that ripple from this act cannot be overestimated.

Second, even if the rubric has been handed down to you, as is often the case with rubrics that are common across a school, the work of calibration never ends. The student work keeps rolling in, so the conversation of what the rubric means is never finished. Just as every Supreme Court case is an attempt to interpret the words of the Constitution, so too is every scoring of a student paper or performance an interpretation of the meaning of the rubric. Teachers need to keep coming together, looking at student work together, and reaching agreement on varying levels of quality, also known as calibrating. Sometimes this leads to revision of the rubric; more often it leads to a refined understanding of students' abilities.

We hear it time and again, after a session during which teachers gathered around a table, using a rubric to score student work together: "That's the best professional development I've ever had."

Of course, a rubric makes such collaboration possible but not inevitable. The hard drives of most teachers are scattered with the bones of old rubrics, unused and forgotten. A department cooks one up during some August professional development, rolls it out with some energy that September. But by November, it's a check-in agenda item during the department meeting. By March, most of the department are grading their papers without it.

Performance assessment is a powerful engine, but it doesn't drive itself. It needs tracks to a destination. School leaders must make it a priority and build structures that allow teachers to collaborate regularly on their use of schoolwide rubrics. Sustainability comes with building performance assessment into the design of the school.

THE TAILWIND OF THE COMMON CORE

Even though performance assessment has always been the right thing to do, teachers and schools must often fight headwinds to get it done. In the last decade of the high-stakes bubble test, those headwinds have never blown stronger.

Many, including Envision Schools, have had to keep a strong commitment to performance assessment when all that "counts" are the bubble-test scores. You want to believe that it's going to work out, that if students are trained in higher-order thinking, then multiple-choice questions are just an interesting puzzle to solve on the fly. Sometimes it works out this way. ELA is an area where Envision's commitment to performance assessment has paid off in terms of test scores. It's a riskier road in the so-called content disciplines (science and history). And in math, it's a fraught endeavor. Train kids to think and do math as it is practiced in the real world, and they will suffer in the bubble tests, which seem incapable of rewarding anything but rote, algorithmic learning.

Refreshingly, the Common Core puts the wind at our back for the first time in a long time. They aren't perfect, but these standards go a long way toward closing the gap between what we have to do and what we should be doing. It has elevated the importance of literacy, shifted the focus to higher-order thinking skills, and reinforced the idea of learning how to learn.

Many of the state standards to which schools have been held in the past have emphasized what students should know over what they should be able to do. The Common Core flips the center of gravity to the other side, from knowing to doing. In ELA, the standards stress the ability to write arguments based on evidence, conduct research, read across the curriculum, engage in academic discussion, make formal presentations, and use technology effectively. In mathematics, standards stress conceptual understanding, applying mathematical thinking to real-world issues and challenges. At the high school level, there is an emphasis on mathematical modeling.

The "content" is still there. The math standards lay out a learning progression from K to 12, starting with whole numbers and addition and subtraction, and moving into geometry, algebra, probability, and statistics. In ELA, there is grammar and Shakespeare. But in reading the standards, you can't help but be struck by the radical shift of priority: content is the means; skills are the end. That's because the ultimate goal of the standards is very clear: college and career readiness. There is an acknowledgment that college is a journey into new content. Skills, not memorized packets of static knowledge, are what a student will need there.

The Common Core State Standards take pains to avoid dictating methods or even recommending approaches to assessment, as they should. But read between the lines. Notice all the attention to higher-order thinking skills. Performance assessment offers the only possible approach to assessing what the Common Core is asking us to do. Even the large-scale standardized tests, normally able to bubble-test everything, can't get around it. Smarter Balanced and PARCC both needed to develop new performance assessment components for their Common Core tests; there was no other way to align them to the standards.

Whatever the limitations of the Common Core, a set of standards that necessitates performance assessment is better than standards that don't. In a nutshell, that is why the

Common Core is an advance for education: without any kind of performance assessment, school is a glorified driver's permit exam.

It remains critical, however, that we keep the Common Core in perspective. We must not mistake the winds of policy for the pedagogical port of call.

The Common Core *is* policy, not pedagogy, and the winds will shift again. At the writing of this book, it is already clear that the journey through the Common Core will be a blustery one. The tests will be controversial. Some states will back out. Components will be revised. The tests will get rewritten. And one day, the Common Core will be replaced by something else. This is why schools must establish a graduate profile for their students that transcends any set of discrete standards, including the Common Core.

Take the long view. Treat the Common Core as an opportunity to speed your journey. Maximize its potential to help transform your school. But beware the siren song: in this policy climate, it's easy to start thinking of the Common Core as the destination. When the winds shift—and they will—you risk losing the true course.

In the meantime, we should enjoy this wind at our back, for however long it lasts. The Common Core does validate two ideas that all students deserve: college and career readiness as a goal, and performance assessment as an essential strategy. This is a huge opportunity to make our schools both more rigorous and more engaging for our students.

Video 7. The Envision Assessment Process

Envision Education, in partnership with Stanford University, developed performance assessments linked both to standards and to deeper learning skills, so that all Envision teachers use the same rigorous assessment tools. Watch teachers discussing and evaluating student work in collaboration.

REFERENCES

Costa, A. L., & Kallick, B. (1995). Teams build assessment—and assessment builds teams. In A. L. Costa & B. Kallick (Eds.), *Assessment in the learning organization: Shifting the paradigm* (pp. 141–152). Alexandria, VA: Association for Supervision and Curriculum Development.

Darling-Hammond, L., & Adamson, F. (2010). *Beyond basic skills: The role of performance assessment in achieving 21st century standards of learning*. Stanford, CA: Stanford University, Stanford Center for Opportunity Policy in Education (SCOPE).

Friedman, T. (2013, March 30). Need a job? Invent it. New York Times. Retrieved from http://www.nytimes.com/2013/03/31/opinion/sunday/friedman-need-a-job-invent-it .html

Lerner, A. J., & Loewe, F. (1956). *My fair lady*. New York, NY: New American Library.

Chapter 3

Project-Based Learning – It's the How (and the Why)

In the posteducational world, there are never assignments, only projects.
— Rob Koch, Envision graduate, reflecting on what it's been
like after high school

All the eleventh and twelfth graders at the school are packed into the largest available classroom. It's one of the first days of the first semester, and the room crackles with the natural teenage energy that comes with the beginning of the school year. Students are still catching up, giving hugs, calling out greetings, jockeying for seats with friends. But there is also the energy of anticipation, both excited and anxious, which serves as a kind of hush on the buzz, much like the excited but restrained chatter that fills an auditorium before a big show.

Having been at the school for two or three years, the students know that this is an important event. In fact, for them it is difficult to imagine what their lives will be like for the next few months, until this meeting occurs. So there is inherent interest in what is about to take place.

Yet all that is about to be announced is an academic assignment.

"Television," says one of the teachers, stepping to the front of the room to begin the meeting, "has fundamentally changed American politics. As people who are about to be voters, you need to understand the role that television plays to help you become an informed voter. And the best way to do that is for you to become television commercial makers yourselves. That's what this project is all about."

The lights go down, and the first in a queue of famous presidential campaign ads appears on the projector screen: "Ike for President, Ike for President … " The students chuckle over the corny melody and antiquated animation of Eisenhower's 1952 "spot" commercial, the first television campaign ad ever to appear in America. But they are hooked; all eyes are on the screen. We're only minutes into what will be a multimonth project, and already a major goal has been accomplished: the students will never look at a television campaign ad the same way again.

Video 8. The Campaign Ad Project

This video traces the Campaign Ad Project from kickoff to exhibition. Watch students collaborate on producing professional-quality political commercials based on focus-group research with targeted swing voters. Teacher Justin Wells reflects on designing and implementing project-based learning. The Campaign Ad Project serves as a case study through the rest of this chapter.

WHY PROJECT-BASED LEARNING

In previous chapters, we laid out a blueprint for all the things a school should map backwards from:

- A vision for its graduates, expressed in the form of a graduate profile, that is aspirational, forthright, and responsive to the demands of the world that is waiting for them

- A culminating portfolio and defense that challenges students to live up to the school's graduate profile

- A handful of performance assessments that synthesize the school's curricular goals, incorporating not only the applicable state or district standards but also the 21st century skills to which the school has committed

Now it is time to figure out how to get there.

Schools lay claim to many values: academic rigor, college readiness, learning how to learn, 21st century skills, critical thinking, social justice, tolerance, citizenship—the list goes on. But when educators buckle down to the actualizing of all these goals, it does not take long before the goals compete. And when some of the demands are external, then the competition heats up (with predictable results).

The fact is, a school's goals do compete with each other if there isn't a strategy for integrating them. That's where project-based learning steps in.

When the goals of a school and the time available for attaining them are honestly accounted for, then project-based learning becomes the best way—perhaps the only way—to reach all those outcomes at the same time.

WHAT WE MEAN BY "PBL"

The opening scene of this chapter describes the launch of the Campaign Ad Project, first developed at the Communication Academy at Sir Francis Drake High School and later refined at various Envision schools. That scene exhibits a number of features that are characteristic of a good project: assembling students, generating excitement, tapping into engaging media, and exploring a topic that is both rigorous and relevant.

But there is only one detail in the entire scene that truly defines it as a project. That's when the teacher announces that the students will "become television commercial makers [them]selves." The true launch of a project is when students hear not what they are going to learn but what they are going to create.

Project is the word that distinguishes project-based learning from other kinds. Here is a simple definition: **a project is an act of creation over time**. It gets at the two basic concepts that attach themselves to the word: production and complexity.

In *Getting Things Done*, David Allen (2001) has another simple but straight-to-the-point definition of a project: any undertaking that involves more than one step. What he is underscoring is that a project has some kind of articulated relationship with time. The desired goal cannot be realized in a single simple move. One must look some distance into the future. One must break the endeavor down into some number of steps.

Of course, that definition is a bit broad for our purposes, because we can think of many multistep processes that do not seem very "projecty." Almost everything involves more than one step, and we don't use the word project for them all. Brushing your teeth is not a project.

There is another dimension to the word that narrows its use: we typically use the word project to talk about producing or creating something. Brushing your teeth is an act of maintenance, not an act of creation.

We highlight these two concepts to remind us why doing projects brings such richness and value to education. When students do projects, they are grappling with complexity and engaging in the active production of something. By replicating how things get done in life after school, projects enroll skills that we want our students to practice.

Of course, doing a project is not the same thing as project-based learning, so let's now consider the full phrase. *Project-based learning* (PBL) is a teaching approach, a mindset, and a framework for teaching skills and content. Both our working definition and our criteria are derived from our own work, as well as the work of Adria Steinberg (1997), the Buck Institute for Education (Larmer & Mergendoller, 2012), and Expeditionary Learning.

High-quality PBL—"Envision style"—includes the following:

- **An inquiry** into a student-friendly, provocative essential question that drives the learning. This is part of PBL's philosophy that learning is most engaged when triggered by a learner's "I need to know" rather than by a teacher's "because you should know."

- **A demonstration of key knowledge and skills** in which students show evidence through a product or performance that they have mastered predetermined standards or desired learning outcomes.

- **Academic rigor and alignment with standards,** allowing students to master content knowledge and skills and to demonstrate or apply that knowledge.

- **A timeline that is short or long,** ranging from a few days to several weeks, so that students learn how to benchmark and manage projects of different sizes.

- **An engaging launch** to hook students into taking on the project.

- **Applied learning** so that students think and do something new with their knowledge or skills.

- **An authentic audience**, which ensures that the students take the project seriously, challenges them to present their learning professionally, and inspires their stretching for quality.

- **High-quality products and/or performances** that not only provide evidence of rigorous learning but also knock people's socks off.

WHAT PBL ISN'T

The kickoff to the Campaign Ad Project was deliberately designed to grab attention. We were aiming for the "engaging launch" that is one of PBL's best practices. We generated that excitement by interrupting the flow of the normal school day, moving students from their classrooms into an assembly, and presenting some engaging video.

That level of excitement is not sustained through every hour of every day of a project. After the assembly, students went back to the normal flow of their classes, and if you were to drop by one of them in the days or weeks that followed, you might see a lesson that didn't, on the surface, seem so project-based: perhaps a teacher making a presentation on how a law gets made, or an English lesson on active versus passive voice, or students working through an iMovie tutorial in their digital media class. Not every moment in a project feels like project-based learning.

Exaggerating the case for PBL can result in something worse than skepticism, and that is misconception. We don't want our enthusiasm to be mistaken for evangelism, so let us make a few qualifications here. To do PBL dogmatically is to do it poorly.

PBL Is Not an End in Itself

It always makes us nervous when we hear of any school, including one of ours, referred to as a "project-based learning school." It suggests that the goal of the school is to enact learning in one prescribed way. This is dangerous: the doing becomes more important than what is getting done. When PBL is not a carefully constructed means to a rigorously defined end, then projects tend to look fluffy: a sequence of activities that *fill* time rather than a challenging, creative endeavor that *needs* time.

PBL is not the goal. It's a particularly expedient path to the goal, an efficient and rigorous way to prepare students for what lies ahead.

PBL Is Not New

Some thoughtful educators listen to the sometimes messianic rhetoric of PBL and ask, "What's all the fuss about? I've been doing things like that for years."

Which is true. PBL is not reinventing the wheel. Formal learning through projects is at least as old as medieval apprenticeship. The model already exists in most schools, usually in the performing arts department, where large-scale, creative collaboration, working toward authentic performances to real audiences, is the modus operandi.

So let's acknowledge that good teachers all over the world have engaged their students in rigorous and enriching projects for a long time. Many reasoned their way to the PBL approach totally on their own, and they do not need the "project-based" label to validate what they do. Do not mistake our PBL enthusiasm for any pretensions to invention or even early adoption. We are simply looking to something that really works in education and saying, "In light of our goals, we need to do much more of this."

PBL Is Not "All or Nothing"

Some educators worry that taking up PBL necessarily means letting go of everything else they do. They hear tales of the grandiose projects that take place at certain schools and understandably conclude that those schools must do nothing else but PBL.

It's true that to do PBL well is to do it with commitment. And as our working definition would suggest, time is one of PBL's principal ingredients. Better to respect the commitment that PBL requires than to underestimate it. Some educators jump into PBL with the naïve belief that a project can be layered over an existing curriculum without any sacrifice at all—a practice we call "project-based learning in parallel." That approach almost always results in disappointment for all involved.

The reality is that PBL, even at schools that dedicate themselves to its practice, always coexists with other, "more traditional" forms of learning. As an English teacher at Envision Schools, Justin implemented at least a couple of ambitious projects every year, but he also gave grammar quizzes, wrote comprehensive semester exams, assigned literary analysis papers, delivered some lectures, taught vocabulary, and took stock of student progress with some multiple-choice tests. Indeed, many of these traditional-looking practices took place *within* the context of a project. Again, PBL is a tool, not a goal, and when properly implemented, it's a tool among other tools.

For the benefits of PBL to take hold, it can't be an occasional affair; it must be iterative. But that does not mean that it is, or even should be, all-consuming. Good projects can be short or long. They can be schoolwide extravaganzas or intimate classroom affairs. Later in this chapter, we offer some advice on how to integrate PBL into your classroom on a scale that is modest and manageable but still preserves its principles and its efficacy.

A TOOL FOR THE CHALLENGES THAT FACE US

In our schools, students and teachers are focused on three major goals:

- Meeting the academic standards (in our case, the Common Core)

- Developing the skills of the four C's: critical thinking, communication, collaboration, and completing projects

- Preparing for the graduation portfolio and defense

Let's look at how PBL addresses the challenge posed by each goal.

Common Core = Performance Assessment = PBL

Close your eyes, flip through a copy of the Common Core State Standards, stop randomly at a given page, and put your finger down.

Now open your eyes. We're willing to bet that your finger has landed on a standard that can't be bubble-tested. Perhaps one of these:

- Work with peers to promote civil, democratic discussions and decision-making, set clear goals and deadlines, and establish individual roles as needed. (SL11–12.1b)

- Use technology, including the Internet, to produce and publish writing as well as to interact and collaborate with others. (W6.6)

- Participate in shared research and writing projects. (W7.1)

- Conduct short research projects to answer a question (including a self-generated question), drawing on several sources and generating additional related, focused questions that allow for multiple avenues of exploration. (W8.7)

- Solve multi-step real-life and mathematical problems posed with positive and negative rational numbers in any form (whole numbers, fractions, and decimals), using tools strategically. (7.EE.3)

- Apply geometric methods to solve design problems (e.g., designing an object or structure to satisfy physical constraints or minimize cost; working with typographic grid systems based on ratios). (G-MG-3)

- Use data from a randomized experiment to compare two treatments; use simulations to decide if differences between parameters are significant. (S-IC-3)

- Make sense of problems and persevere in solving them. (Mathematical Practice #1)

Everything on this list can be addressed through good PBL. And much of it can *only* be addressed through PBL. This is exactly why David Ross, from the Buck Institute for Education, likes to say that "Common Core is the *what*; project-based learning is the *how*" (Boss & Lamar, 2013, p. 13).

Bob likes to add that PBL is also the *why*. To declare learning goals does not compel students to care about reaching them. To design performance assessments to measure those goals does not make students care about performing for them. But PBL, by definition, is devoted to engaging students and getting them to care. When we embed learning goals and performance assessments inside high-quality PBL, we are taking responsibility for helping students see *why* they are learning what they are learning.

Deeper Learning Outcomes by Design, Not by Osmosis

Academic standards are only part of the puzzle, however. All recent thinking about college and career readiness concludes that certain "noncognitive" skills — known variously as habits of mind, 21st century skills, the four C's, and so on — are as important as the academic skills and knowledge they undergird, if not more important. It is hard to put it better than has Christopher Lehman (Ferlazzo, 2013), an educator at Columbia's Teachers College:

> True "college and career readiness" is more than a particular knowledge base, more than how many hours of nonfiction one has read, more than how much evidence one has used to develop ideas. Being ready for college and career also has something to do with self-belief, care for others, taking risks, falling down and getting back up.

People all over the country have been playing with the list of what these "meta-skills" are. What is remarkable is not that they vary but how convergent they are. These are the skills that show up everywhere:

- Critical thinking
- Collaboration
- Communication skills
- Discipline/management/persistence

No matter what they are called, these are skills that must be taught, not wished for. Teaching them means devoting to them the best practices of pedagogy: introducing these skills in an engaging way, creating constructivist challenges around them, referring to them constantly, being explicit about them, coaching them, assessing them (with rubrics!), reflecting on them, and, most of all, practicing them over and over again.

Anything less is wishful thinking. It's like a parent assuming his child will develop good manners on his own. Collaboration, persistence, problem solving through trial and error, project management skills—these habits and skills do not develop by osmosis.

Perhaps it is possible to parse out each of these skills and teach it in a way that is not project based. But to integrate them authentically, to demonstrate their importance convincingly, to practice them frequently, and to assess them rigorously—there is no way other than PBL. If you are serious about deeper learning, then PBL is not merely a good option; it is a mandate.

Giving Graduate Defenses Something to Defend

At his graduation portfolio defense, Envision student Greg Intermaggio presented an analysis he had written for the Campaign Ad Project. Setting the context for the paper, he told the story of his experience in the project. He recounted the collaborative struggles and how his group overcame them. He explained why this particular project was a turning point in his project management skills. And he waxed philosophical on what he took away from the project: "I learned that you can lie and people will believe you." (Among the skills that Greg demonstrated in his portfolio defense was his ability to get people's attention.)

Portfolio defenses are typically filled with such stories of meeting challenges, overcoming them, and walking away with some pearl of wisdom or newfound self-awareness. Almost all of the stories are about particular projects. At first, we took it as a happy side effect: in addition to all the other good things that it did, PBL gave our students rich raw material for their portfolio defenses.

But the longer we've been at it, the more we've come to see our portfolio defenses as perhaps the most important—certainly the most motivating—reason to do PBL. Turns out that "creation over time" equals not just a project but also a good story, and Envision portfolio defenses are propelled by these narrative arcs: project as struggle, then turning point, then ah-ha takeaway.

In staking our educational philosophy on the triumvirate of know-do-reflect, we have taken on some deep responsibilities. Among them: reflection deserves as much attention as skills and content. If we are to live up to that principle, then making time for reflection is not sufficient; we must also attend to the quality of what students are reflecting on. A well-designed project is worthy of reflection. Indeed, when projects are a part of a student's academic experience, they are what students most remember. Projects become the primary means by which students make sense of their experience. Projects catalyze students' ability to tell stories about school, stories that are about learning instead of just about friends and sports and extracurriculars.

We instituted PBL in our schools for logical reasons. It was clearly the most efficient means to achieve multiple outcomes. But what sealed our commitment to PBL — what shifted our belief from the head to the heart — was watching student after student stand up before his graduation portfolio panel and tell these powerful stories about his learning, stories brought to life by well-designed projects. We knew we needed a culture of reflection in our schools, and more than any other factor, PBL is what gave it to us.

The most important thing that a school can do for students, especially those students who might be considered "at risk," is to nurture a self-aware and resilient academic identity. When that goal comes into focus, then PBL transcends best practice; it becomes a transformational practice.

Figure 3.1 summarizes our assessment of PBL as a strategy toward our goals. Considered independently, each of the goals cries out for PBL. Considered together, they give us no other choice.

Figure 3.1   Why PBL Is the Means to Our Ends

The Goal	PBL as the Means
Meeting Common Core Standards	Highly Recommended
Developing the Four C's	Mandatory
Meaningful Graduation Portfolios and Defenses	Transformational

HOW PBL WORKS AT ENVISION SCHOOLS

There are different ways — certainly no one right way — to integrate PBL into a school's curriculum, and over our decade-plus of existence, Envision has experimented with many of them.

On average, each of our schools implements two large-scale, multidisciplinary projects per year at each grade level. Some schools will take on three or four projects in a given year. Other times a school implements just one. We try to worry less about their number than their quality.

By "large-scale," we mean that the project stretches over weeks rather than days. Those weeks don't have to add up to months (though they certainly can). Assigning a project to a semester or quarter does not mean it must fill the entirety of the term; our projects don't. The Campaign Ad Project runs from the first week of school to the November election; the semester goes on into January.

"Multidisciplinary" simply means that teachers from different subject areas are collaborating. It can mean a complex integration of four or five disciplines, but such a project is rare. Typically, two or three subject teachers, including the ever-present digital media teacher, come together on a given project. The Campaign Ad Project, for example, is a collaboration involving government, English, and digital media.

The Campaign Ad Project is also typical in that one of the involved subjects—in this case, government—is the natural lead. Multidisciplinary does not mean "a-disciplinary." We've seen this: some teachers come to this work assuming that multidisciplinary collaboration means the sacrifice of their subject's identity. Perhaps that's why multidisciplinary learning, to some skeptics, translates to "watered down."

We've seen that too: if a project tries to do too much, it does nothing well. And we grant that blending subjects should not be done for its own sake, satisfying adult ideology more than addressing students' needs.

In practice, well-designed projects tend to emerge from the curricular goals of a particular academic discipline. Other subjects get involved because of their unique ability to support students in meeting the project's challenges. Clearly, the Campaign Ad Project is a government project, but its exploration of persuasive communication calls on English, and its culminating product (a campaign commercial) requires the skills that are taught in digital media. When well designed, a project's multidisciplinarity is organic, not forced.

Because projects tend to have a subject lead, teaching teams strategize to rotate the lead over time. The Campaign Ad Project is a natural for the fall, capitalizing on campaign season. A project emphasizing science or math follows nicely in the spring.

No matter how many or how few teachers are collaborating on a given project, a school faces the challenge of making the collaboration structurally possible. There are two primary problems to solve: (1) the sharing of students and (2) the sharing of time.

Envision addresses the first problem by organizing students into cohorts of roughly one hundred. Each cohort is "owned" by a team of four to six teachers representing the core academic disciplines. Every teacher on the team has the same set of students on his or her roster. Over a two-day block schedule, all one hundred students have seen the same set of teachers.

Equally important, those teachers collaborating on a project need time to plan, confer, and assess. Setting aside time in August, before the school year begins, for high-altitude project planning is only part of the solution. Also necessary are project meetings, at least weekly, that are insulated from the buffeting of the typical school day. Meeting after an early-release Wednesday is one solution that has worked well for our teachers.

We'll go into more detail on the structure of our schools in chapter 5.

PBL TIPS, ENVISION STYLE

This book focuses on arguing why PBL is a vital ingredient of school transformation and on explaining how to situate it properly in the context of such a transformation. It is beyond the scope of this book to be a full-blown primer on PBL. Those books already exist; we refer to them often ourselves. The Buck Institute for Education (www.bie.org) made a philosophical commitment to PBL more than a decade ago; its many books, Internet resources, and PBL workshops are excellent and a great place to start. (Disclosure: Bob is a former board member; Justin is a current one.) We also recommend the book *Real Learning, Real Work,* by Adria Steinberg (1997), whose six A's of project design have deeply informed our approach to PBL.

That said, let us finish describing the Campaign Ad Project and, in doing so, offer some specific PBL tips that we've learned in our years of designing and implementing projects. In boxes, we briefly profile a few other Envision projects, so you can see a wider range of examples.

Start with Your Curricular Goals

The Campaign Ad Project did not start with a group of teachers sitting around a table and wondering, "What would be a cool project to do this fall?" It did start with a group of teachers sitting around a table (a key detail not to be taken for granted), but the questions discussed were these:

- What are our "big idea" curricular goals this year?
- Which Common Core standards need particular attention?
- By the time the year is up, which portfolio-eligible performance tasks should be tackled by our courses?

Good multidisciplinary projects emerge from intersecting goals. In this case, both the government teacher and the English teacher identified the need for students to develop careful reading skills for nonfiction text. The digital media teacher wanted his students to apply video editing skills in the service of social issues, obviously at a crossroads with the government course. In addition, the English teacher highlighted some of his key course concepts: point of view, rhetoric (connotation), and argumentative writing. Projects also take advantage of good opportunities. It was an election year, and the Government teacher naturally wanted to explore the complexities of elections and what it takes to be an informed voter.

One of the teachers had done a version of the Campaign Ad Project before and suggested that it might be a good fit. We concluded that the project, after some tweaking, would integrate our various curricular goals nicely. (Lots of good PBL is an adaptation of what's been done before.)

At a certain point in our discussion, there were two performance assessments on the table: an essay and a video. The essay would provide evidence of nonfiction analysis and argument skills. The video would provide evidence of creativity, technology skills, project management, and collaboration. Note that we didn't yet have an essential question or a complete vision of an exhibition. But having identified two rigorous performance assessments that synthesized our curricular goals and that required student acts of creation, we knew we had a meaningful project.

PBL flourishes when seeded by performance assessment.

Project Planning: Give It Everything You've Got

We are not going to sugarcoat it: once a project takes off, it is sometimes all you can do to hang on.

Therefore, the more "front-loading" you can do on a project, the better. By that, we mean getting all the project components — the schedule, the write-ups of the various benchmarks, the various rubrics, the associated website if there is one, and so on — drafted and organized *before* the project formally launches for the students. (We've included the Envision Project Planning Template in the appendix and encourage you to use it.)

This advice comes from the school of hard knocks. We know firsthand what it's like to launch a project before you have fleshed out as many details as you'd like. Teachers do what they sometimes "gotta" do. Occasionally, through sheer grit, those designed-on-the-fly projects still manage to reach their potential. More often they fall short in some way.

PROJECT PROFILE: THE CAMPAIGN AD PROJECT

What does it take to change a voter's mind?

[Designed for grades 11–12]

On Monday, November 3, the night before the coming election, your team will present a campaign television commercial on a specific California proposition to the registered voters of the school community. The purpose of your ad is to persuade your audience how to vote in the California election on the following day.

The major products that you will create for this project are

- Research brief on the issue of your selected proposition.

- Focus group research, based on interviews you conduct with the target voters of your campaign.

- Campaign commercial (30 seconds or less) on one of the ballot initiatives in the upcoming election. Video is eligible for the graduation portfolio.

- Argumentative essay that offers a sustained and evidence-based case for the position you advocate in your campaign ad, with a developed counterargument to the opposing position. Paper is eligible for the graduation portfolio.

For complete details on this project, see http://teacher.justinwells.net/CampaignAd/.

SOME OF THE COMMON CORE STANDARDS TARGETED BY THE CAMPAIGN AD PROJECT

For grades 11–12

W1: Write arguments to support claims with clear reasons and relevant evidence.

RI6: Determine an author's point of view or purpose in a text in which the rhetoric is particularly effective, analyzing how style and content contribute to the power, persuasiveness, or beauty of the text.

RI7: Integrate and evaluate multiple sources of information presented in different media or formats (e.g., visually, quantitatively) as well as in words in order to address a question or solve a problem.

RI4: Determine the meaning of words and phrases as they are used in a text, including figurative, connotative, and technical meanings; analyze how an author uses and refines the meaning of a key term or terms over the course of a text

W7: Conduct short research projects to answer a question (including a self-generated question), drawing on several sources and generating additional related, focused questions that allow for multiple avenues of exploration.

W8: Gather relevant information from multiple print and digital sources, using search terms effectively; assess the credibility and accuracy of each source; and quote or paraphrase the data and conclusions of others while avoiding plagiarism and following a standard format for citation.

For some teachers, long-range planning comes naturally, but for many of us, it is a daunting prospect. It can even feel artificial, as if you are lesson planning long before you need to. Lesson planning far in advance is a useful way to think about project planning; it gives you a sense of how much time is required to plan a project before it begins.

But once you've experienced what it's like to feel on top of a project, it's hard to go back. Planning well and being prepared make time for two important aspects of project management: (1) monitoring student progress and (2) revising your plan accordingly.

To get to that place means giving project planning the time and space it deserves. Coming together in August, before the school year begins, for meetings devoted to project planning is a solution that is hard to beat. A similar retreat at some school-year midpoint can be used for both reflection and spring project planning.

The Campaign Ad Project demanded diligent preplanning because of its timing. To make the exhibition feel as authentic as possible, we scheduled the screening of students' campaign ads to occur on the Monday night before November's election day. That gave us only ten weeks between the first day of school and the night of exhibition. We realized that if we didn't kick off the project during the first week of school, the students wouldn't have time to learn everything they needed to learn and create the kinds of quality products we wanted them to create.

So we made sure to design a detailed and coherent project *before* the first day of school. We scheduled the benchmarks, fleshed out the key performance assessments, built up the scaffolding, tracked down supporting materials, and reserved the spaces we needed for rehearsals and exhibition. Everything was corralled into a website devoted to the project (posted at http://teacher.justinwells.net/CampaignAd).

We knew our plan would need to be revised along the way; many of our decisions were best guesses. But we had learned from experience: the more detailed your plan, the more nimbly you can change it.

Craft a Good Driving Question (But Don't Overestimate It)

"What does it take to change a voter's mind?"

That's the driving question of the Campaign Ad Project, and it exemplifies the two vital roles that driving questions (often called essential questions) play in the design of a project.

First, they serve to **focus** the project, not only for the student but also for the teacher. The Buck Institute (Larmer & Mergendoller, 2012) says that "a project without a Driving Question is like an essay without a thesis" (p. 2). That focus also tends to undergird the purpose. Buck again:

> Without a Driving Question, students may not understand why they are undertaking the project. They know that the series of assigned activities has some connection

with the time period, a place, or concept. But if you asked, "What is the point of all these activities?" They might only be able to offer, "Because we're making a poster." (pp. 2–3)

Second, driving questions **set the tone**—specifically, a tone of inquiry. They remind us that all knowledge—including anything that a student reads in a textbook—exists because there was a question posed and an answer sought. Moreover, well-crafted driving questions can be simultaneously directive and open ended, striking the right balance between structure and choice.

All that said, we caution you against assigning driving questions a be-all-end-all importance, as some educators do. Driving questions are an essential component of PBL, but their role is often overemphasized. Many see them as the necessary starting place—no planning can happen before the question has crystallized—and then get mired in philosophizing or wordsmithing, ending up with questions that are grandiose, leading, or unanswerable (at least for a group of adolescents over the course of a few weeks).

"What is freedom?" "Can we end racism?" "How is life interconnected?"

It's not that these aren't important questions to ask and for students to discuss. But if, at the end of a project, students can't answer a driving question with much more substance than they could before the project began, then we wonder whether that question is pleasing the teacher more than serving the student.

In our experience, once a project is up and running, what motivates students far more than the driving question is their vision for an exciting final product. Driving questions can be the starting point for design, but they don't have to be, just as a thesis statement doesn't have to be the first sentence that an essayist puts down on paper. An equally valid and often more practical way into the design of a project is to ask, "What is the final *product* of the students' work, and how will they share that work with others?"

When the driving question follows, it is easier to craft it into something that the students can honestly answer *as a result of creating that product*. Sometimes, the product itself can serve as the answer to the question.

In the Campaign Ad Project, we did not start with a driving question. We started with a vision of the end point: students presenting political ads on the ballot propositions. The act of creating these ads is what allowed them to have a substantive answer to the still open-ended question, "What does it take to change a voter's mind?"

Video 9. Creating a Driving Question for the Watershed Project

During a planning meeting, a group of teachers (including Bob and Justin) work together to craft a driving question for a ninth-grade project.

Thom Markham, Sr. Program Dir.
Buck Institute for Education

"What Will Thrill the Audience?" Design for the Final Product

This whole book is about student-centered learning, but sometimes the best way to a goal is to come at it obliquely. A great way to design high-quality projects is to think not about the students but about the audience.

At Envision, we strive for student work that impresses self-evidently, regardless of the creator's age. We hate the phrase, "That was so great for a high school student," and we strive to avoid it at all costs. Thanks to the miracles of consumer software such as iMovie, as well as our belief in what students can achieve, we were confident that our students could produce thirty-second campaign ads that matched the quality — in both content and style — of what is actually seen on television.

We discovered one obstacle to that, though: the student voice, literally. Almost all campaign ads have a narrative voice, and the students' ads would follow that form. But teenagers sound like teenagers; there's no getting around it. Everything about their ads could be of professional quality — well-cut digital footage, background music, on-screen text — but if a teenage voice underlies the whole thing, then the audience will unavoid-ably think, "Wow, so great for a teenager."

So we banned their teenage voices. It became an added challenge to the project. The students had to recruit an adult to read their ad's script.

This one simple project requirement raised the four C's to another level. The students had to *collaborate* on how to meet this challenge. They had to *communicate* with the recruited adult. To *complete* this task effectively, they needed to manage scheduling and technology so as to respect their voice talent's time.

But before any of that, the students had to think *critically* about what kind of a voice to recruit. The project already required them to organize focus groups and identify their target swing voter. Once that voter was identified, every design choice needed to be explicitly justified by how it was targeting that demographic. So here now was one more: What kind of voice will best deliver our message, feel most trustworthy to our swing voter? Will it be a young adult male voice with some urban inflection for a confiding tone to twenty-something male voters? Or an older female voice, with a warm and motherly tone, promoting the importance of healthy food for kids? In their ad proposals, students now needed to make this choice and defend it. It was an exciting question to consider, and it deepened their thinking.

We stumbled on this good idea not because we were thinking about the needs of the students; rather, it grew from our thinking about the audience and how to blow them away.

Define Your Benchmarks

If there is one concept that unites deeper learning, performance assessment, school design, and PBL—the themes of various chapters of this book—it is the strategy of mapping backwards. At Envision Schools, we map projects backwards by dividing them up into steps, known as benchmarks.

Benchmarks keep the students on track and the teachers in touch. Major performance assessments that are embedded in the project determine many of your benchmarks. Others are simple checkpoints where some smaller piece of the project gets reviewed or presented.

How many benchmarks? As many as are needed to scaffold your particular group of students. Freshman may need more benchmarks, seniors fewer. Or it may depend on the difficulty of the project itself. Benchmarks are one of the key mechanisms for providing structure in PBL.

Demand Proposals at Every Opportunity

Don't let the students do anything before making a proposal, ideally to the whole class.

In the Campaign Ad Project, almost every one of the benchmarks took the form of the students making a proposal to the class. That was followed by a long round of feedback, from the teacher of course but also, and mainly, from fellow students. When this happens as a matter of course, the students get so good at giving each other constructive feedback that the teacher doesn't have to pipe up much at all, often only to add or reinforce a few points at the end of the feedback session.

THE BENCHMARKS OF THE CAMPAIGN AD PROJECT

On the project website, each one of these benchmarks is hyperlinked to its own page of details. See http://teacher.justinwells.net/CampaignAd/.

- Ballot review: due 9/19

- Team platform: due 9/26

- Focus-group research: due 9/29

- Commercial treatment proposal: due 10/3

- Commercial storyboard and script: due 10/8

- First draft of campaign commercial: due 10/22

- Program notes: due 10/22

- Final draft of campaign commercial: due 10/29

- Public exhibition of campaign ads: 11/3 (right before Election Day)

- White paper (final argumentative essay): due 12/12

Yes, this is time consuming; sometimes it will take a few days to get through an entire round of proposals. But the practice functions as a true investment—there is a big payoff at the end. Problems with the students' direction or understanding can be noticed and addressed early. Teachers can effectively do their formative assessment work *during* class time rather than after school hours. And, most important, we've seen no better way for students to internalize standards of quality than to spend hours talking about quality, publicly. There is the added benefit that most of the time is spent considering work other than one's own, which makes it easier for many students to see things more objectively.

Don't Act as "Grader"; Be a Traffic Cop

At first, it may seem overwhelming to see all those benchmarks and imagine all the grading that must go into it.

Here's an easy solution: don't do it.

Instead, see yourself as a traffic cop. Reduce the complexity of your job to red light, green light. Make it clear what students need to do to get a green light for the next step. Flash red or green when a piece of benchmark work comes your way. Much of the time, this can happen in class.

Of course, certain benchmarks still generate papers to read, and there will be plenty of times when those papers will need to come home in order to keep things on schedule. But it is striking how much faster assessment can go when you are working on a "ready–not ready" binary scale rather than dithering over the gradations of the typical grade-based assessment scale. It also frees you to focus on what the students need to do to get the green light on their next attempt. Summarize in a few bullet points; reinforce your points verbally whenever possible.

This doesn't work for everything, of course. Certain student work merits the more detailed judgment of performance that we associate with a rubric, most obviously the big student products that come at the end of the project.

But if you see your job as coaching students toward earning as high a grade on those final, summative assessments as possible, then carefully examine your approach to formative assessment. If painstakingly filling out a complete rubric for a benchmark piece of work is what the student needs for later success, great. But if the student can equally improve the work through a faster form of feedback, that's the way to go.

Think Revision; Good Assessment Will Follow

Here is a trick for putting you in the mindset of good assessment design:

1. Assume the student will fail on his or her first try.

2. Then imagine what the student will need for success on the second try.

That's really all a rubric is: a tool that helps a student go from step 1 (failure) to step 2 (success).

Failure is a strong word, meant to get your attention. On one hand, it feels like a stretch to say that a paper with a broken paragraph or an oral presentation without eye contact should be called a failure. On the other hand, much of life is a two-tiered rubric. You make the team or you don't. You are admitted into the college or you aren't. You get the job or you don't. She accepts your invitation, or she turns you down.

That's why many of the best rubrics out there are the simplest, especially when it comes to formative assessment. Just two scoring criteria: you did it, or you haven't done it … *yet*. The only real reason for more gradations than that is to communicate to a student who has run out of chances.

Opportunities for revision make some teachers nervous. They fear that students won't give their first shot their best shot if they are guaranteed second and third chances.

We won't pretend that that doesn't happen from time to time. But it is vastly over-shadowed by a more powerful phenomenon. Teachers who assume failure as a matter of course — but who also believe in redemption through revision and bake that belief into the plan of the project — tend to hold students to higher standards. If there is time for revision, and a structure for it, then teachers and students don't have to settle for "almost there," that deflating, numbing state of mediocrity that pervades our schools. Instead, they are more likely to hand it back with specific directives on how to make it better. When the teacher knows that a student has another chance, she tends to be tougher on the student. This is a good thing.

~~Friday~~ PBL Night Lights

On the Monday night before November's Tuesday election, the entire school community pours into the campus auditorium.

It's 7 p.m., late enough for as many parents as possible to attend after their long work-day. Because the exhibition has been actively promoted since the first day of school, the seats for this highly anticipated event are jam-packed. The adult audience is what transforms the Campaign Ad Project into something greater than an engaging academic exercise. The parents are old enough to vote; the students are not. For the parents, this event is an opportunity to learn more about what's on the ballot the next day. For the students, it's an opportunity to influence how their parents vote; it's their first time to actively participate in our democracy.

The lights go down. The auditorium quiets. A young man and young woman step up to the podium, welcome the audience, and explain what is in store for the night.

We refer to these exhibitions as our Friday Night Lights (even though they hardly ever happen on a Friday). The reference is to the popular movie-turned-television-show set in the world of Texas high school football, where Friday night games are a powerful cul-tural ritual bringing entire communities together. Our schools work to create that same energy and community bonding through the exhibitions of learning that cap projects such as the Campaign Ad Project. Authentic audience is a fundamental principle of PBL because of an audience's power to focus and motivate. Not all exhibitions can or should be big schoolwide events like the one described here. But it's powerful when they are.

PROJECT PROFILE: THE MOVING VOICES PROJECT

Just about everyone in America comes from somewhere else. Where do you come from?

[Designed for grades 9–12]

American history is the story of people on the move, and those people are us. This project reminds us that the history of this country is not merely what happened to presidents; it's what happened to our parents, grandparents, and great-great-great grandparents. And that story is not found in textbooks; it's found in attic boxes, old black-and-white photos, and that crazy story your grandma tells you about her grandma.

The major products that you will create for this project are

- Moving Voices narrative—a historical fictional account from the point of view of one of your relatives, based on interviews and research into family archives. Eligible for the graduation portfolio (creative expression).

- Independent research paper—on a slice of American history that illuminates the context of your family narrative. Eligible for the graduation portfolio (research).

- Dramatic monologue—a dramatic interpretation of your narrative for exhibition night. Eligible for the graduation portfolio (creative expression).

- Project website—the final publishing place for everything that you have discovered and created.

For complete details on this project, see http://teacher.justinwells.net/MovingVoices/.

Two more students come to the podium and give a short, factual explanation of Proposition 1A, a controversial proposal to build a high-speed rail line in California. Four of their peers then stand up from the rows of seats that front the stage; these are the producers of a thirty-second campaign ad in support of Prop 1A, which begins to play on the big screen that hangs above them.

> Watch student-produced ads from the Campaign Ad Project at http://teacher
> .justinwells.net/CampaignAd/campaign-ads-2008.
>   The evening exhibition was also covered by a local news network; the segment
> is posted at vimeo.com/53975415.

There are many ads to screen, so the event must run like clockwork. With so many different students having to stand and sit and move to the podium at the right moments, all that rehearsal is paying off. One of the most powerful lessons that can be taught through project-based exhibitions is what it means to present professionally.

After the ads on high-speed rail, the audience learns about and sees ads on the other state propositions that round out the ballot, including ones on the treatment of farm animals, parental notification for a minor's abortion, renewable energy generation, gay marriage, and redistricting. The presentation of ads runs for a little over an hour and ends with impressed and appreciative applause.

In the lobby after the screening, it's not just cookies, coffee, and congratulatory hugs. At student-manned booths that circle the lobby, parents learn more about the issues, and students get the chance to press their case.

School community events are a good thing, no matter what they are centered around, whether a football game or a musical or a holiday party. Still, it is striking how infrequently school events in this country are centered on learning (with science fairs the notable exception). Among the many good things that PBL brings to a school are opportunities for the school community to come together to celebrate its purpose—learning. The best way to teach values is to live them.

Reflect on What's Been Learned

Exhibitions are climactic, and the day after a successful exhibition deserves some time and space for whoops of congratulation and sighs of relief. However, it is dangerously easy to get sloppy in the wrap-up of the project and not attend to loose ends. We've made this mistake more than once, and we always regret it.

Always do structured reflection during the week after an important exhibition. Ideally, there are schoolwide rubrics and reflection forms that map to your graduate profile. Students need time to weigh their strengths and weaknesses, consider how they grew on this last project and how they failed, and set goals for the next project cycle. And all of this reflection should be couched in the language of schoolwide deeper learning skills or outcomes (for Envision, the four C's: **collaborating** productively, **completing** projects effectively, **communicating** powerfully, and thinking **critically**).

Moreover, these reflections should be archived so that students can use them as evidence of their growth when they are constructing a graduation portfolio defense.

PBL CAN START IN YOUR CLASSROOM

"Project-based learning is great, but it is too hard for teachers to do well." We have heard this belief stated more times than we can count. Is PBL really so difficult that only a select number of masterful teachers, innovative schools, and dynamic school leaders can pull off high-quality projects? We don't think so.

So far in this chapter, we've depicted PBL in rather grand strokes. The Campaign Ad Project is indeed PBL writ large: three disciplines coming together over the span of months, culminating in an all-school evening event.

We are aware of the fine line between generating excitement and creating anxiety. So let us repeat here that large-scale is not a defining feature of PBL. Projects don't have to be as big as the Campaign Ad Project. They don't have to extend for so long or involve so much collaboration or culminate with such a big production. Smaller-scaled projects, whether in terms of timeline or amount of collaboration, are just as legitimate and maybe even more important than the big ones.

Think back to our simple definition: a project is an act of creation over time. This is something that can happen in a day, and often does. Most projects in the world operate on a much smaller scale, often within the walls of a single classroom.

Rather than ask teachers to become master orchestrators of project-based curriculum overnight, we should encourage teachers to tweak or adapt their current work to give it a more project-based flavor.

This section describes some easy ways to start implementing PBL in your classroom, right away and in the context of what you are doing right now, applying a few of our design principles.

Ask, "What's the Creative Next Step?"

PBL is not a radical upending of the educational paradigm. We see PBL quite simply: teachers and students taking the time to finish whatever learning journey they've started. If you accept the principle that creation is the highest form of understanding, then PBL is nothing more than taking learning to its logical conclusion. Figure 3.2 shows some simple examples.

Figure 3.2 The Creative Next Step

Academic Topic	Traditionally Ending with ...	Now Ending with an Act of Creation
Greek drama	a literary analysis of a Greek play	Write a Greek tragedy, embodying the central elements of the genre, on a modern-day issue
Physics: Simple machines	a unit test on simple machines	Design and build a Rube Goldberg device that uses at least four simple machines. The forces for each must be calculated and captioned
A grammar unit	a grammar test	Produce a video, à la *Schoolhouse Rock*, that teaches a grammar concept
Homer's *Odyssey* (or any given literary work)	a plot-based, multiple-choice test and an in-class essay	Interpret the literary work with a piece of art, justifying artistic choices with learned literary terms
Turn-of-the-century immigration	a unit test on immigration: short answer and multiple choice	Interview an immigrant in your community, analyze how the experience compares to that of immigrants 100 years ago, and share findings through a podcast
Constitutional democracy	a unit test on the concepts of constitutional democratic government	Design a constitution for a newly emerged nation, justifying all choices based on the nation's history, demographics, and economic circumstances (see "A Government for Xlandia" on bie.org)

Reverse the Order: First the Challenge, Then the Instruction

Kevin Gant, one of the most talented and inspiring PBL teachers in the country, likes to say that PBL is not so much changing your instruction; it's more about changing the order.

In life, challenges tend to come first; then we learn how to meet them. Yet for some reason, education has fallen into the habit of reversing this order. Teachers give instruction first, and then students are given a challenge (usually a test).

Essentially, PBL is an attempt to restore the natural order of learning. Like life, PBL starts by dishing out a challenge, problem, or question you can't yet answer. The learning that follows now has a purpose.

Try it: Take one of your existing units that provides challenge *after* instruction, and simply reverse the order. Present the challenge first (though you may have to spice it up to make it more provocative or engaging).

After presenting the challenge, have a class discussion on what students think they will "need to know" to meet that challenge. Brainstorm every big or little thing that students feel is a missing piece of knowledge or undeveloped skill that they will need to be successful. Record it all on chart paper. This is now the class's "need to know" list. If you've designed the challenge carefully enough, then the student-generated need-to-know list will closely match what was already on your "need to teach" list.

The unit becomes working through the class's need-to-know list. Most of your original lessons will work perfectly, only now the students are asking for them.

The radical shift in PBL is situated not in the mechanics of teaching but in the mindset of the learner. Teachers tend to overestimate PBL's difficulty and underestimate its power.

Put Your Unit in the Form of a Question

Another way to think about the point made in the previous section is to use inquiry as a driver for almost all projects, units, and lessons. A physics teacher who has a solid lab unit on bridges need only change the focus. Instead of a recipe lab that produces structurally strong bridges, she can ask the students the question, "What is the best structural design to produce the strongest bridge?" She can teach the content as she always has, but now students will need to apply that knowledge to their bridge design. Not all of the bridge designs will be strong, but many will be. Most important, the students will own the content because they applied it.

Get Students Conducting Interviews

Envision students are required to write a college-ready research paper to graduate. This could be a completely academic affair, or it can be an opportunity for one of Adria Steinberg's (1997) six A's of PBL: Adult Connections. For a history paper, for example, require students to interview an adult—not at the school—who was alive during the studied historical period or is recognized as a content expert, such as a college professor.

In addition to learning the research process and the history content, students learn how to locate a source and set up and conduct an interview. We have seen the attention to detail and quality rise significantly with this approach. The students want their interviewee to be impressed by their paper.

PROJECT PROFILE: THE INFERNO MOSAIC RETELLING PROJECT

How do I, as an artist, interpret Dante's Inferno?

[Designed for grades 11–12. Substitute Homer's *Odyssey* for grades 9–10.]

For 700 years, Dante's vision of Hell in his epic poem, *The Inferno,* has captured the imagination of artists. Now it's your turn, as artists with your own individual talents, to continue the tradition of artistically imagining *The Inferno.*

Our reading of Dante's *Inferno* culminates with the Mosaic Retelling Project. The class will divvy up the important scenes and plot events of Dante's journey through Hell. You will analyze your part closely and then create a work of art that "retells" those lines of *The Inferno* in whatever way you are inspired.

In the end, the class will assemble all its artistic retellings into a "mosaic" to be theatrically presented to the school community.

How you retell your lines of *The Inferno* is entirely up to you; any art form is acceptable: drama, music, poetry, painting, sculpture, animation, comics, puppetry, film, radio, dance, the list goes on. Your imagination sets the limits of what is possible.

The major products that you will create for this project are

- a work of art interpreting lines from Dante's *Inferno.*

- a dramatic presentation of your art. You will collaborate with three other students to plan, script, and rehearse an entire "scene" within the larger production.

- an essay of textual analysis on the lines from *The Inferno* that inspired your art-work. This paper is eligible for the graduation portfolio.

For complete details on this project, see http://teacher.justinwells.net/InfernoMosaicRetellingProject.

Watch Video 6: The Inferno Mosaic Retelling Project (referenced in chapter 2) to see examples of the art created for this project as well as scenes from the exhibition.

ANSWERING THE SKEPTICS

Over the years of teaching and leading at schools that use PBL as a key strategy for preparing students for success in college and career, Bob has been questioned by hundreds of educators and parents about PBL's rigor and effectiveness. Many of these questions and statements about PBL reveal powerful misconceptions of teaching, learning, and assessment. These fallacies are impeding students' opportunities to learn and prepare for the world outside of school.

Here are Bob's Fallacies of Teaching, Learning, and Assessment and the common ways they are expressed:

Coverage Fallacy

- If I cover/teach "it," students learn "it."

- Students need to master all the content in a subject area in order to be prepared for middle school … high school … and college.

- How do I know that they learned the content if I do not teach it to them?

- I have too much to cover to spend the time on projects.

Rigor Fallacy

- If students do well on a test of knowledge, that means they know the material and can recall it and apply it in new situations.

- The more homework you assign, the more rigorous your curriculum; time on task = rigor.

- PBL is great at engaging students, but I am worried that it is not academically rigorous.

Demographic Fallacy

- PBL works best for middle-class white students.

- Projects are great for your students but not my students.

Let's address these myths one by one.

Coverage Fallacy

The coverage fallacy takes two forms: (1) students will not learn something unless the teacher tells them what to learn, and (2) students need be "taught" everything in a subject area so that they will succeed at the next level. In fact, research shows that interactive learning triples the learning outcomes for students (Lambert, 2012). The teacher believes that because he has conveyed the information, students have learned the material, but in fact, it is through inquiry, application, demonstration, communication, and metacognition that students learn new materials and skills.

According to David Conley in *College Knowledge* (2005), most first-year college professors assume that students do not know the content of their courses and build their courses to teach the same content that was taught in high school. They would like more students to come prepared by acquiring "key cognitive strategies … like problem-solving skills, conducting research, interpreting results, and constructing quality work products" (Vander Ark, 2012). Employers report the same need and plan on teaching their content to new hires. We have not seen a survey of ninth-grade teachers asked this question, but we bet we would see the same result. Larry Rosenstock and Rob Riordan of High Tech High animate this argument in a YouTube video: "Changing the Subject: Making the Case for PBL."

Rigor Fallacy

A corollary to the Coverage Fallacy, the Rigor Fallacy assumes once again that telling kids challenging content to remember and regurgitate (and a lot of it) is rigor. The amount of homework assigned is often used as a gauge for rigor ("That teacher is really rigorous. She assigns two hours of homework every night!"). However, this type of so-called rigor is poorly aligned with the skills and dispositions students need for success in college and career. As Harvard professor Tony Wagner (2008) explains, "I have yet to talk to a recent graduate, college teacher, community leader, or business leader who said that not knowing enough academic content was a problem. In my interviews, everyone stressed the importance of critical thinking, communication skills, and collaboration."

Demographic Fallacy

When Bob was working at Sir Francis Drake High School in San Anselmo, he served a primarily white, middle-class student body. He had hundreds of visiting educators spend time at his school to learn more about how he employed PBL. Unfortunately, more times than he can count, he heard the statement, "This is great, but it will never work for our students [code for low-income students of color]." The motivation behind the genesis of Envision Schools was to prove those people wrong. We believe that all students should have the opportunity to know, do, and reflect through projects and performance assessment. At Envision Schools, more than 65 percent of our students are low income, more than 85 percent are students of color, and over 70 percent will be the first in their family to go to college. They are producing amazing student work and finding success in college and career. Now, when people come to visit Envision Schools, they see "their students" engaged in rigorous and relevant PBL, and they ask, "How can we do this with our students?"

WHY PROJECT-BASED LEARNING?

Q. Are projects engaging?	A. Yes.
Q. Are projects fun?	A. Yes.
Q. Do students like to do projects in school?	A. Yes.
Q. Is this why we use PBL as a key strategy for success?	A. No.

We employ PBL because PBL is the best way for students to simultaneously

- Learn and master key content knowledge and skills (KNOW)
- Demonstrate and apply the knowledge and skills (DO) and learn how to learn
- Build the capacity to transfer their learning to new and different learning opportunities (REFLECT)

In "Rigor Redefined," Tony Wagner (2008) lays out this challenge to educators, parents, and policymakers:

> It's time to hold ourselves and all of our students to a new and higher standard of rigor, defined according to 21st-century criteria. It's time for our profession to advocate for accountability systems that will enable us to teach and test the skills that matter most. Our students' futures are at stake.

We could not agree more. It is time to let go of the myths and fallacies about PBL and get to work building the capacity of teachers and leaders to redesign classrooms, schools, and districts so that our young people can be ready for a bright future.

WHAT STUDENTS REMEMBER: THE STORY OF THEIR EDUCATION

The best history teacher Justin has ever met happens to be the teacher he was lucky to have back in sixth grade. This was in the early 1980s, and Nancy Tracy taught ancient world history. Much of the course was quite traditional: reading of textbook chapters on Mesopotamia, Egypt, and the Greeks, and tests that required the meticulous recall of historical facts.

She required her students to outline every chapter, drilling down to every sentence, hammering Justin and his classmates to use a ruler to line up the Roman and Arabic numbers of their outlines.

In other words, Nancy's course could be viewed as pretty "old school." But Nancy knew deep down that historical facts about the Egyptians and the Greeks were not what she was teaching; she was teaching both study skills and big ideas about the way that humans construct history from incomplete data. No matter which ancient era of history she taught, Nancy drove home the fact that our conception of ancient peoples is based on the interpretation of incomplete evidence, and neither the evidence nor the interpretations are static.

And Nancy also knew that such an important concept deserved deeper treatment than reading and discussing could provide. So midway through the year, the class embarked on the Archaeological Dig Project. She divided the class into two teams, found them separate spaces to meet, and tasked them with creating a civilization from scratch, applying the criteria for the concept of civilization that they had learned by studying the Greeks, Egyptians, and Mesopotamians. The students were charged with total secrecy.

Then Justin and his teammates had to create artifacts that represented the various aspects of their civilization. They invented an alphabet, deciphered it on a clay tablet, even broke it into pieces — their own Rosetta Stone. All this they scattered and buried in the school's sandbox, clues to a civilization that the other half of the class would uncover and interpret, using authentic archaeological tools and technique: brushes, sand sifters, a grid of string, careful note taking.

After interpreting the data and attempting to fill in the gaps, the student team constructed a vision of the uncovered civilization. All this set up the memorable final day: the interpreters of the culture presented their findings to the creators of the culture, who then unveiled "the truth." And vice versa.

For every hilariously mistaken interpretation there was also spot-on analysis. The project was unforgettable. Of course, Justin doesn't remember the names of the Egyptian pharaohs, but he certainly remembers grasping the significance of what Nancy wanted her sixth graders to understand: our knowledge of history is induced through painstaking work by patient scholars, and they are not always right.

When Justin is asked to recall a powerful learning experience from his life as a K–12 student, this is one of the two or three that always spring to mind. Nancy didn't call it PBL; that term wasn't trendy back in the early 1980s. But when Justin took his first teaching job at Bob's first project-based Envision school, he immediately understood why Bob was asking him to deliver his content through the structure of projects. Nancy had already taught him that a richly designed learning experience — both creative and intellectual — can sear a student's memory and forever alter his understanding of the world.

Video 10. Impact Academy Student: Government Project

Relevance in education is critical! Impact Academy student Rahil talks about reviewing and analyzing immigration law for an AP Government project—a topic meaningful to him as a member of an immigrant family—and reflects on what deeper learning means to him: "internalizing the information."

PROJECT PROFILE: THE BILL NYE AND I PROJECT

How do you teach a difficult scientific concept to someone?

[Designed for grades 11–12]

Many of us are familiar with Bill Nye, the Science Guy, who teaches scientific concepts to kids through his fun-filled television programs. In this project, you will try out what it's like to be Bill Nye, using film to teach science to young people.

Scientific literacy is a requirement for any educated citizen of the 21st century. And to be literate is not merely to know about science; it is to be able to communicate your scientific knowledge to someone who doesn't know what you know.

In this project, you will work in small groups to research and become expert in a focused topic in physics or mathematics. The starting point is one of ten nonfiction books that treat a particular scientific or mathematical concept. After writing independent research papers on the topic, you and your team will collaborate on writing and producing an educational video that teaches your scientific or mathematical topic to elementary school kids. Finally, you must seek out and establish a relationship with a local elementary school class, where you will teach a lesson that incorporates both your film and a hands-on learning activity that your team has designed.

The major products that you will create for this project are

- Scientific research paper—on a topic in physics or mathematics chosen with guidance from the teacher. This paper is eligible for the graduation portfolio.

- Documentary educational film—geared toward elementary school kids, using both film and Flash animation.

- Guest lesson—presenting the film and teaching the concept in a San Francisco elementary school classroom.

For complete details on this project, including the benchmarks and the list of nonfiction books, see http://teacher.justinwells.net/BillNye/.

You can also see video of this project in action. Envision Education worked with the Oracle Foundation to produce a PBL video series that covers the six steps of project implementation. Featuring The Bill Nye and I Project, the series covers planning, doing, reviewing, showing, assessing, and managing a PBL experience. Watch the whole series on Envision Education's YouTube channel: http://tiny.cc/BillNyeandIvideos.

REFERENCES

Allen, D. (2001). *Getting things done: The art of stress-free productivity*. New York, NY: Penguin Books.

Boss, S. & Lamar, J. (2013). *PBL for 21st century success: Teaching critical thinking, collaboration, communication, and creativity*. Novato, CA: Buck Institute for Education.

Conley, D. (2005). *College knowledge: What it really takes for students to succeed and what we can do to get them ready*. San Francisco, CA: Jossey-Bass.

Ferlazzo, L. (2013, January 20). Response: Best ways to prepare our students for CCSS in Language Arts [*Classroom Q & A* blog post]. Retrieved from http://blogs.edweek.org/teachers/classroom_qa_with_larry_ferlazzo/2013/01/response_best_ways_to_prepare_our_students_for_ccss_in_language_arts.html

Lambert, C. (2012, March-April). Twilight of the lecture. *Harvard Magazine*. Retrieved from http://harvardmagazine.com/2012/03/twilight-of-the-lecture

Larmer, J., & Mergendoller, J. (2012). *Eight essentials for project-based learning*. Buck Institute for Education. Retrieved from http://bie.org/object/document/8_essentials_for_project_based_learning

Steinberg, A. (1997). *Real learning, real work: School-to-work as high school reform*. New York, NY: Routledge.

Vander Ark, T. (2012, June 20). Q&A: David Conley on college and career readiness. [Getting Smart blog post]. Retrieved from http://gettingsmart.com/2012/06/qa-david-conley-college-career-readiness/

Wagner, T. (2008). Rigor redefined. *Educational Leadership*, 66(2), 20–25. Retrieved from http://www.ascd.org/publications/educational-leadership/oct08/vol66/num02/Rigor-Redefined.aspx

Chapter 4

Transforming School Culture

Everyone has a strength, and it was utilized.

— Paul Conroy, Envision graduate

In the hands of a master, the simplest tool is the most powerful. Witness the practice of Tony Harris, the very first teacher hired to Envision Schools. Mr. Harris's entire teaching practice and philosophy are embodied in a single, simple artifact: a yellow pencil, tucked behind his right ear.

Let us paint the picture of what surrounds this pencil. Most immediately, it is a mane of brown hair, which swoops into a thick, Grizzly Adams–style beard. Only half of the pencil emerges from this wooly thicket, which somehow hardens and softens the man's presence simultaneously. The contradiction is echoed by the uniform: invariably a button-down shirt and tie (the professor) belted over a pair of jeans and leather work boots (the craftsman). Like a bear, Mr. Harris straddles the line between endearing and intimidating. The students love him for it.

The focal point of the room, the baton that conducts the orchestra, is that pencil, tucked behind the ear. A small group of students approaches Mr. Harris, carrying a storyboard for a documentary (always a required step before they can touch the video camera). The student work is placed on the table. Mr. Harris leans over. The students huddle in. Up goes a hand to the pencil, and all eyes trace the pencil's trajectory as it descends to the paper.

Will the pencil land on the upper right-hand corner? Will they get the coveted check mark? Have they met the expectations for this important benchmark of the project?

The pencil comes down midpage, circumscribing a frame of the storyboard. The students already know what this means. "I told you guys this needs more detail," Mr. Harris says. "This is an improvement, but it's still not there." He elaborates and offers a few suggestions.

Looking disappointed but determined, the students make their way back to their project table. They've been here before. They know that a Mr. Harris check mark is not easy to come by. This last bit of feedback was in fact encouraging. It looks as though they are close. One more revision, and it is likely that Mr. Harris's pencil will come down and sign them off.

ENVISION SCHOOLS CULTURE

Of course, this is not about the pencil but what the pencil represents. Mr. Harris has created a culture in his classroom. He masterfully uses the yellow pencil to help orchestrate a culture of learning through failure, growth, revision, inquiry, coaching, caring, and joy.

So far in this book, school transformation has been described as a structural process. In this chapter, we acknowledge that structural changes are necessary but insufficient for reaching our goals.

Your graduate profile may be inspiring and beautifully wordsmithed, your schoolwide rubrics may reflect all the best practices, and your August professional development may spawn brilliant projects for the school year, but none of this potential will germinate if there isn't a school culture that allows it to grow.

To transform the lives of students—especially those who will be the first in their family to attend college—there has to be a strong and pervasive culture that is promoted and supported by all of the stakeholders. Like many schools across the nation, we have students who enter our schools well below grade level. With only four years to make more than four years of progress and to get these students into college, our school culture *has* to be transformative.

School culture encompasses beliefs, values, and assumptions that drive behavior — what we think, what we say, and what we do. There are certain things that a school's stakeholders — students, teachers, support staff, school leaders, even parents — must *believe* for any of this to work.

At Envision Schools, seven key beliefs drive our design, our direction, our decisions, and our daily actions:

- Ability is not fixed; through effort, it grows.

- Failure is essential to learning.

- Revision is the route to mastery.

- Knowledge deepens and expands through inquiry.

- Teaching is coaching.

- Caring is essential to accomplishment.

- Learning can (and should) be fun.

Let's take a closer look at each of these beliefs and how they can be nurtured.

Ability Is Not Fixed; Through Effort, It Grows

Similar to the nature-versus-nurture debate, the difference between a fixed-ability belief and a growth belief can be summed up in one question: Are our abilities innate, or can they be developed?

It is tragically ironic that fixed-ability attitudes are so pervasive in education, an institution that was born in aspiration. The enormous amount of time, money, and effort that society invests in education suggests a fundamental belief that human beings can expand their capacities.

Yet notice all the commonplaces that serve to undermine this belief. We track students into ability groups from which they almost never leave. We use labels such as "gifted and talented" or "learning disabled," words that describe states of being, not points on a journey. We evaluate student performance with abstract composite scores, letters, and numbers. Most assignments are one-shot affairs: if you don't succeed, then "better luck next time."

It all adds ups, accumulating as softly but inexorably as snow, and it doesn't take long before the implicit message is deep and smothering: your intelligence is fixed, and school's job is to tell you where you stack up.

Yet a growing body of research is telling us that not only is the fixed-ability premise false (the mind is remarkably plastic; IQ is dynamic), its very falseness is detrimental to people's ability to learn, regardless of where they think they lie on the intelligence scale.

Let's start with the people who believe they are smart and were born that way. What they gain in short-run confidence they lose in long-term development. Paradoxically, they distrust effort ("If I am smart, things should come easy") and fear intellectual risk-taking ("If I fail, people won't think I'm smart"). Such attitudes impede growth and limit the potential for education to expand their capacities.

Of course, for people who believe they are not smart, the consequences of a fixed-ability mindset are even more damaging. They distrust effort even more ("What's the point?") and never consider taking intellectual risks ("Why bother?"). These attitudes are particularly devastating for students whose school experience may be the only transformative opportunity in their lives. For kids whose families live in poverty, kids who lack access to enriching learning experiences (music lessons, club sports, travel, and so on), school culture can make them or break them. All too often it breaks them.

Sadly, many of the students who believe they are not smart will say that they know this to be true because their teachers tell them so. How? First, they will mention that teachers give them bad grades. When probed, they don't connect effort to grades; their perception is that teachers are arbiters of grades, doling out letters and numbers that determine intelligence. They will also tell you, with great conviction, that they believe they are not smart because of the way teachers interact with them (which, they will tell you, is quite different from how the teachers act with the smart kids). If you don't believe us, start asking around. Students will tell you.

In her seminal *Mindset: The New Psychology of Success,* Stanford University psychologist Carol Dweck (2006) shares more than three decades of research that unpacks the difference between equally talented people who are successful and unsuccessful.

What determines success? According to Dweck (2006), it is what people believe about their ability to change and improve. Believing that ability is fixed will limit your potential, and believing that ability can change and grow will enable success. The former is what Dweck calls a fixed mindset; the latter, a growth mindset.

A growth mindset is powerful. People with a growth mindset believe that they can improve their abilities through effort and hard work. People with a growth mindset tend to embrace challenges, persist through setbacks, learn from criticism, and be inspired by the success of others. Significantly, Dweck (2006) also tells us that your mindset, like your intelligence, is not fixed; it is influenced by the messages you receive from the people and the culture that surround you.

Video 11. Carol Dweck on Performance Assessment

Carol Dweck, Stanford psychologist and growth mindset researcher, shares her insights on the approach of Envision Education, particularly the positive impact of communicating high expectations to students.

Carol Dweck
Professor of Psychology, Stanford University
Author, "Mindset"

At Envision Schools, we can't afford to have a fixed mindset. The challenge our students face is too big for that. Of our incoming ninth graders, 60 percent read on average at the sixth-grade level; 20 to 30 percent of those read below the fourth-grade level. Statistically, our students have less than a 20 percent chance of enrolling in college, and less than a 30 percent chance of persisting in college. (The term *persistence* refers to a student staying in college, year after year, until graduating with a degree.)

Yet it is our mission to transform our students' lives, which, in concrete terms, means their going to and persisting in college. This may be viewed as no more attainable than No Child Left Behind's goal of 100 percent of students proficient or above by 2014. Arguably, our mission is aspirational, but so far, our record shows that we are defying the odds. Every year, we see remarkable numbers of students, whom others may have considered not smart or who themselves may have believed that to be true, go off to college. Ninety percent of Envision Schools' twelfth-graders enroll in colleges, and 90 percent persist to their second year. We attribute this success, in large part, to our widespread and deeply held belief in growth.

Take Dakarai Griffin, for example, who came to City Arts and Technology (CAT) high school from a tough part of town. He shared stories of people with knives. He has an infectious smile and personality, and quickly became a favorite of adult visitors. (One visitor was so taken with Dakarai that he followed up five years later to find out if Dakarai had graduated from college.)

In ninth grade, Dakarai created an award-winning digital story, "Picture Me Black," for the local public television station, but like most of our students, he arrived at CAT three grades behind in basic math and reading skills. In his junior year, Dakarai excitedly told a visiting panel that he had just finished reading an entire book for the first time.

He had come a long way in two years—he was reading closer to grade level—but he still needed to work hard to get ready for college success.

Video 12. Dakarai's Digital Story: "Picture Me Black"

Through spoken word and video, Dakarai invites the world to look beyond the stereotype of the young black male, to see what he sees for his future and what he is planning to accomplish.

Video 13. Dakarai's Defense

This short clip of Dakarai's portfolio defense in 2008 highlights Dakarai quoting James Baldwin and vowing to make a positive difference as an African American man.

Dakarai successfully defended his portfolio, graduated, and was accepted to multiple colleges. He chose to attend San Francisco State. However, when we did our college enrollment tracking in the fall, we found out that Dakarai had not enrolled. Dakarai's senior-year advisor reached out to him and discovered that he had run into challenges with enrollment, decided not to attend, and found a job instead. His advisor worked with him and his family to get through the paperwork, and he began attending in the spring. Eventually, he transferred to Langston University, a historically black college in Oklahoma, and graduated in 2013. Today, Dakarai is currently a student advocate for the Harlem Children's Zone in New York. He plans to attend graduate school in 2015.

Dakarai's is a feel-good story and a testament to the growth mindset. But it's important to note that it was not solely the teacher's belief in Dakarai or Dakarai's belief in himself that made the outcome possible. It was both. Dakarai's own can-do spirit pulled him through many of his challenges. But other times, Dakarai needed adults who believed in his potential to pick him up when he was down. Dakarai's story reminds us that the growth mindset must live in both the teacher and the student. It must permeate the whole community for it to have any kind of systematic effect.

How can you create a growth-oriented culture? The simple answer lies in Gandhi's quote, "The change begins with me." What do you believe? Do you believe that you have the ability to teach, coach, and mentor students in ways that transform their lives? Can you do it for a few students? Some? All? Do you believe that even if you don't know how to do it, you can learn? Do you have a growth mindset?

If you don't believe that you can transform your own practice, it is highly unlikely that you would have the fortitude to transform the lives of your students. We shape culture through what we say and what we do. All day long, we are modeling what we believe. This is the best place to start.

An honest assessment of the mindset of your students is essential for creating a growth culture. Once you understand the characteristics of Dweck's mindsets, observe your students' work habits and work products. Do they reflect a growth or fixed mindset?

Students with a fixed mindset provide us with important clues about how to help them adopt a growth mindset. They often attribute their intelligence to what teachers tell them through their interactions and grades.

Let's start with interactions. There are two simple things you can do to develop a growth culture. First, give students specific feedback about the effort they put into their work. This means saying things like "I like how you tried different ways of solving this problem" as opposed to "You are smart" or "Good job." Second, provide regular time for students to reflect on their learning. These simple changes help students make the connection between their effort and their results and assume more responsibility for their learning (and their grades).

Teacher feedback plays an important role in a growth culture. Grades can stop students in their tracks. As a composite score (letter or numerical), grades do not provide students with the specific feedback they need to improve. Criteria for grades are opaque to students and vary wildly between teachers. Students can earn an A in one class and a C in another for work of comparable quality. A grade becomes something you *get* from a teacher rather than something you *earn* from your own performance. The traditional practice of grading promotes a fixed-ability culture.

Mr. Harris's check mark, in contrast, is the growth mindset in action. He uses it to help students assess how close or far they are from meeting preestablished criteria. When he withholds the check mark, he is communicating not only his belief in their potential but also the vital message that effort leads to growth. More time, more thought, and more effort can and do lead to a better product. When the students return to their tables to try again, they are enacting that same belief in themselves.

Failure Is Essential to Learning

One of Bob's favorite lines when doing strategic planning is that the plan has a 50 percent chance of success and a 100 percent chance that we will learn from the experience and get "smarter" about how to deliver on our mission.

In other words, failure is not a bad thing. It is an inevitable part of learning, and as a learning organization, we will experience failure, as surely as a toddler will fall while learning to walk.

It is another terrible irony: in education, particularly in this high-stakes accountability era, *failure* has become the term we attach to our persistent challenges. Wholesale problems, such as the achievement gap and the high school dropout rate, are labeled as the "failure of education." We argue over how to "prevent" more failure. In our field, failure has come to mean something terrible.

John Dewey (1933/1998) said it best: "Failure is instructive. The person who really thinks learns quite as much from his failures as from his successes" (p. 142). We also believe that failure is essential to learning. We are not talking about dead-end failure, the kind that results in loss of opportunity, being stuck, or regression. We think about failure as an opportunity to receive feedback on strengths and areas of improvement in order to get better. When reframed as a good thing and essential to learning, failure is a master teacher.

At Envision Schools, failure is an intentional part of the school design and, consequently, the culture. It has to be. The majority of our students enter ninth grade with a very personal and negative understanding of failure, based on a chronic lack of school success. To make the kinds of gains needed to master the Common Core State Standards and Envision's competencies and leadership skills, students have to learn to receive feedback and use it to improve. Failure has to be a close friend on their journey through high school and college.

How do you make failure students' friend? Follow the example of Mr. Harris. Set a high standard and don't be afraid to tell students that they haven't met it. But in the next breath, give detailed suggestions on what can be done to change that. And, most important—though so often given short shrift—allow students the time, space, and support to make the revisions. In such a culture, failure does not mean "You lose"; it means "You can do better. Here is some feedback; revise, and try again."

Tiana Alba is not only the first in her family to go to college but also the first in her family to graduate from high school. She came to Envision as an eleventh grader, but a lack of credits required her to repeat tenth grade. Tragically, at the beginning of her first year at Envision, her mother passed way. Her teachers and advisor visited her at home to make sure she was OK and to support her and her family. She came back to school determined to work hard to succeed. She persisted and reached her senior year with enough credits and a GPA that qualified her for California State University, but she still needed to pass her senior year portfolio defense. In fact, she failed her first attempt, but with support and coaching from the same teachers who visited her at her home, she revised, prepared again, and eventually passed. She is attending Sonoma State and majoring in education so that she can become a teacher.

Video 14. Tiana Fails Her Portfolio Defense the First Time and Revises

In this video, learn how Envision students work with their teachers to prepare for their portfolio defenses and how failure can be an "extremely positive experience" for students on their way to passing. Tiana resubmits a stronger portfolio the second time around and succeeds.

Over time, Envision teachers have come to see that the students such as Tiana, who don't pass on their first attempt, are in fact the fortunate ones; what they learn by persisting and maturing through the failure pays off down the line. And because this reframing of failure is modeled so publicly and systemically by the portfolio defenses, our teachers, convinced of its power, tend to recreate similar cycles of failure and redemption back in the day-to-day of their classrooms, where school culture lives.

Another practice that is vital to reframing failure is reflection. On a daily basis, across subject areas, students regularly reflect on their work, which provides them with substantive opportunities to think about what they are doing and assess the extent to which their work meets (or does not meet) standards. Students need to have built-in time to take a step back and assume the role of assessor, figuring out if their work is good enough. This builds agency and resilience in students, as well as a risk-taking culture.

Revision Is the Route to Mastery

On a visit to her alma mater, a recent Envision graduate remembered how frustrated she had been with her social studies teacher, Paul Koh: "He kept returning my research paper with the rubric and comments and telling me, 'It's not there yet. You can do better. Revise it.'" She lost track of how many versions she created, but she recalled how proud she was when the paper was finally deemed proficient (which was a step below advanced, but still qualified it for her portfolio).

Sheepishly, she admitted to submitting the same paper to a professor during her first year of college, where it earned a B.

"I guess Mr. Koh was right," she said. "It was proficient. More work, and it could have been an A."

Developing grit or resilience has become an important topic in the school reform conversation today (Tough, 2012; Duckworth, 2013). How do we educate students so that they are not only academically prepared for life beyond school but also prepared to persist through the eventual challenges and failures of life—both academic and non-school related?

In our opinion, past attempts by schools to develop student resilience through lessons focused on self-esteem, followed by surveys asking students to identify their feelings about themselves, are flawed. It reminds us of the 1990s self-esteem movement epitomized by Al Franken's spot-on satire. Playing Stuart Smiley on *Saturday Night Live*, in front of a mirror, he chanted the mantra: "I'm good enough, I'm smart enough, and people like me!"

True self-esteem, we believe, comes from working hard and persisting through setbacks to achieve mastery; this is what builds the resilience and the confidence to tackle new and different challenges.

Envision students don't participate in self-esteem lessons. They engage in rigorous college preparatory work aligned to schoolwide rubrics based on Common Core State Standards and aligned to the graduate profile. Through the assessment and reflection processes, students learn what they need to know and be able to do in order to achieve mastery; eventually they do it. That is the essence of a culture of revision.

In a culture of revision, students produce multiple drafts of papers, work products, and presentations that are critiqued by the teacher, peers, and/or outside experts. Students create multiple versions of work products until they meet standards for proficiency or are ready to exhibit.

Across too many schools, the rule of the day is "one and done." Students create products, write papers, or give presentations, and then the work is evaluated and returned to students. Sometimes, students are assessed with rubrics and given feedback on the work, but because the students don't get a chance to respond to the feedback, they pay little attention to it, giving rise to the perennial complaint of hard-working teachers everywhere: "I don't know why I spend so much time leaving comments on students' papers." Kids are smart. Grades are what count, not a teacher's comments. Why would they read the feedback?

Let's face it: in a one-and-done world, the goal of assignments, for both parties, is a grade. Students turn in their assignment, teachers give the grade, and the transaction is complete.

At Envision, students are working to achieve mastery. For this reason, they eagerly await feedback on their work so that they can incorporate it into the next draft on the road to mastery. Grades count too, but what matters most to students is getting the feedback they need to create college-ready work.

At Envision, revision toward mastery is a systematized part of the culture and language. It is systematic because students know when they enter ninth grade that they will not graduate until they have achieved mastery of the core content, the core competencies (inquiry, analysis, research, and creativity), and the four C's (critical thinking, communication, collaboration, and completing projects). When you ask Envision students how many drafts it took to achieve proficiency on, say, a portfolio-eligible research paper, the answer will likely be five to seven, sometimes more.

Most adults in professional careers create multiple iterations of a product before they submit it to a client or for production. Creating a culture of revision puts schools in step with the work world and prepares students for college, where they will need to revise their work independently or with their peers prior to submitting a final draft to a professor.

College is challenging. Many students, even those from privileged backgrounds and those who have achieved excellent grades in high school, struggle to the point of failure on assignments and even classes in their first year. For some, it is their first taste of failure. This is devastating for students who lack strong coping skills to self-manage through failure or the academic skills needed to take the feedback and use it to improve. If students' mental model is one and done, a failing grade means they are done. We believe that this is one reason for our nation's substantial first-year college dropout rate.

Failure for Envision students produces a simple shrug of the shoulders, followed by the question, "What do I need to improve?" By the time our students are in their freshman year of college, they have learned to take feedback (both positive and negative) and use it to get better. A culture of revision prepares them for the transition from high school to college, and from college to career and beyond.

Video 15. Envision Principal's Graduation Message—Revise, Revise, Revise

Allison Rowland, former principal of City Arts and Technology High School, delivers an ode to revision to the 2012 graduating class, describing the rigorous and rewarding process the students went through to earn their spots on the graduation stage.

Here are a few ways to infuse a culture of revision into your practice, whether schoolwide or in a classroom:

Use Rubrics, But Use Them Formatively, Not Summatively

The very nature of rubrics is growth oriented. As road maps to success, rubrics allow students and teachers to engage in side-by-side assessment and identify exactly what students need to do to grow to the next level. But a rubric is no better than a one-and-done grade if it's not used as a tool for dialogue between a teacher and a student *during the production of the work*.

Give Students Tasks That Require Multiple Steps to Complete

And, à la Mr. Harris, don't take the time to "grade" every step. Sign off on student work when it is ready; return it with some manageable feedback when it's not. It's impressive how much revision can be built into one well-planned, multiweek project.

Demand Lots of Public Speaking

A comedian once remarked that people's number-one fear is public speaking. Number two is death. His conclusion: people would rather be the one in the coffin than the one giving the eulogy.

Kids are not any different. Public speaking in front of an authentic audience — not as part of a class activity, but a real audience of interested people and/or experts — is a daunting challenge for young people. Giving a good speech requires tons of preparation — writing and revising the text and then practicing the speech alone and with peers multiple times. When everyone in a class faces the same challenge, then true community builds, because everyone is in the same boat. At the finish line, the feeling of pride won by a successful public presentation is huge and can catalyze a shift to a growth mindset for many students.

Envision schools often begin the school year for ninth graders with the "Who am I?" project. Students read and write a personal narrative in English class. The narratives are grouped by theme (for example, conflict or growth), and students form groups to create a "book." Each student's story is a chapter in the book. The group collaborates in their Digital Media Arts course to create the visual or graphic theme using graphic design software, and the project culminates with them "publishing" their book and inviting parents and community members to a book reading. Each student prepares an excerpt to read and a reflection to share about why he or she chose that selection. Students bond as a class and often report that this project — especially the public speaking — was the most rigorous learning experience of their young lives.

There are so many aspects of public speaking that make it the perfect way to usher students into a culture of revision: the challenge it presents, the way it can disrupt the normal academic pecking order, the way it invites supportive and on-the-fly feedback, the naturalness with which a student can be asked to "try that again," and the tangible progress that the student can make in a relatively short amount of time.

Knowledge Deepens and Expands through Inquiry

As human beings, we respond to our natural curiosity about the world through inquiry. We use our senses (seeing, touching, hearing, smelling, and tasting) to answer our own questions about what surrounds us. Our knowledge deepens and expands through this multimodal approach to learning.

Then we enter school. Learning that takes place in preschool and kindergarten often includes a rudimentary level of inquiry, called hands-on learning. Students learn the alphabet through song, colors through blocks, math through pattern blocks, and life science during a visit to the zoo or the pumpkin patch.

But as students advance through the grades, opportunities to ask curiosity-based questions or engage in hands-on learning get fewer and farther between. The use of inquiry becomes random and sporadic, typically based on an individual teacher's initiative, skill level, or philosophical leaning.

By high school, students are accustomed to looking to the teacher for the right answers to the teacher's own questions. Students ask questions not to satisfy their curiosity but to clarify what it is that the teacher wants them to know. Figuring that out means getting a good grade.

At Envision, we try to reconnect students to their own curiosity. Teachers frame courses, projects, and lessons around provocative essential questions that explore big ideas in subject disciplines and life in general. Through inquiry, students learn to investigate, find solutions, and ask new questions. Inquiry is open ended. There are multiple answers and different sources of information. The focus is on students learning, not on teachers teaching. Students might turn to a teacher as a resource or for guidance, but the teacher does not play the role of Keeper of the Right Answer.

Inquiry-based learning can be designed in a variety of ways, ranging from structured (that is, teacher driven) to guided (teacher designed) to self-directed (student driven). For teachers who are new to inquiry, a good place to start is with structured inquiry, gradually shifting to a more student-driven approach.

But do make the shift. If the goal is for our students to become lifelong learners, then a commitment to inquiry-based education is not optional; it's an obligation. Because when our students are adults, outside the structures of a school or program, curiosity and questions are the only engines of learning.

Teaching Is Coaching

When a colleague at another urban high school commented to Bob that because his students needed more structure, he no longer employs PBL, Bob replied that his decision presumes that PBL is unstructured. Bob's own experience as a teacher, an instructional coach, and a school leader has taught him that effective PBL is highly structured — structured to facilitate student learning — whereas traditional instruction is often structured to support student compliance.

To many educators, the model of teacher as coach implies lack of structure. However, all of Bob's coaches in high school, college, and postcollegiate athletics were highly structured in their approach to their work: they taught him strategies and techniques in a direct manner. They put him through drills and critiqued his performance in practice, with little empathy for his feelings. They inspired him to go further than he thought he could go, both physically and mentally.

When it came time to perform in a game or match, however, he and his team were on their own: they needed to apply what they had learned in real game situations. After each performance, the coach asked the players to review their performance; he gave them feedback, too. Both coach and player used this reflection to adjust their practice and refine their game plan. Often, it meant relearning a skill or tactic. Other times, they needed to fill a gap in their knowledge by learning something new.

The best coaches map backward from a vision of outstanding performance in their sport. Coaches assess their athletes' skills and knowledge and make a plan for the season that will get their team ready for peak performance. In short, coaching requires tons of structure.

So does PBL.

Teachers need to be coaches. As coaches, they are master designers of learning, aligning curriculum and instruction to assessment. They are keen observers of student learning who ask just the right questions to provoke student reflections that lead to improvement. They know how to give specific and timely feedback in a way that motivates each student in his or her own way. They know when to step back and let kids fail and when to step up and catch them before they fall too hard. This is what it takes for students to become self-directed learners who can persist through challenges in school and beyond.

Like the best coaches, Envision teachers create a vision of the students' performance plan first. They design highly structured projects aligned to the plan. With guidance from Envision instructional coaches, teachers plan their assessment first. Working toward desired student outcomes, teachers determine the prerequisite skills and knowledge required to complete a project.

Logically, teachers start by taking stock of what kids already know and can do. They make a plan to teach what students need to learn in order to complete the performance. Teachers create a thorough plan, which includes details on assessments (for example, exhibition, research paper); structures and processes (for example, grouping strategies, roles and responsibilities); identification of key skills needed for success (for example, collaboration skills); and the type of inquiry used (structured, guided, or self-directed).

Envision teachers map clear benchmarks, with deadlines for each task or product, and post these on their walls and websites. The benchmarks scaffold learning toward a high-quality product or performance. They are the road map that students use to get to their final destination on time. People often think that classrooms where PBL is happening are noisy and out of control. In an effective learning environment, there is a healthy buzz, but students are moving around and talking with each other for a clear purpose and are in control of their behavior.

At last, it is *game day*. For Envision students, game day is an exhibition of their work and learning, with an authentic audience. What happens on game day is up to the students. As coaches, teachers can only observe and support their students now. After the game, teachers debrief students' performances with them, assess the outcomes, and adjust plans for the next project. The information students glean from the debrief makes their next project even better.

Teachers who are serious about students' developing deeper learning competencies have to make the shift from teaching to coaching. In order to communicate powerfully, think critically, collaborate productively, and complete projects effectively, students have to engage in authentic, meaningful, and rigorous learning experiences that require them to *use* those deeper learning competencies. This will not happen by having teachers simply teach.

Caring Is Essential to Accomplishment

In a three-part article titled "Emotional Engagement in Education," Edutopia blogger Jim Moulton (2008) provides some concrete ways to respond to student apathy and to rally your school community through PBL. Moulton really drives his point home when he says,

> For any of us, whether student or teacher, child or adult, to do our best, to achieve our highest potential, we have to care. Many of you have, at some point in your life, accomplished something you never thought you could do. Had you not cared enough to try, you would never have accomplished the goal. Your amazing accomplishment began with caring. (para. 2)

The content in this section was written by Kyle Hartung and is used with his permission. It was originally posted on Bob's Edutopia *Social and Emotional Learning* blog in February 2008: "Learning How to Care, Part 1: Celebrating Student Successes" (http://www.edutopia.org/student-accomplishment-part-one) and "Learning How to Care, Part 2: Building Academic Identities" (http://www.edutopia.org/student-accomplishment-part-two).

It is easy to talk about how students don't care about school. Maybe the question isn't whether or not students actually care about school, but whether or not they know *how* to care about their time in school. We think it is the latter.

At Envision, for the majority of our students, school has not been a place of inspiration, improvement, or happiness. School lacks meaning, relevance, and joy. Why would students care about school? How would they know how to care about a place to which they are not connected in a positive way?

How can we teach students how to care? Just as Moulton says, we can begin by providing them with experiences and opportunities to care about, that allow them to shine and excel, that give them a real and deep sense of accomplishment for their hard work. When we ask students to pursue inquiries or questions that only they can answer, they begin to see a reason for the work they do and see that what they do today is relevant to what they will do tomorrow.

Teaching students how to care goes even deeper than the kinds of projects and assignments we ask them to do. We must give careful consideration to the way we act with students and to the way we build community in our schools. Moulton is right. Amazing accomplishments are born from a place of caring, and we must care enough to teach students how to care as well.

At Envision, we teach students how to care through public exhibitions of their work and public celebrations of their accomplishments.

At one of our schools, for example, all of our twelfth-grade students participated in a formal public debate. The students did extensive research and preparation so that they could argue either side of a controversial global issue; they did not know which side they would have to defend at the exhibition.

The morning after, the students and faculty gathered in their weekly community meeting. For forty-five minutes, students individually celebrated one another's achievements and gave props to one another's debate performance. As they relived the excitement and anxieties of the night before, students thanked their partners and teachers for their efforts.

During the meeting, students made comments that reflected a deep level of caring: "You really impressed me with your research." "I know I was skeptical about being your partner at the beginning, but we worked great together." "I never thought I would be able to actually do it." Teachers also took time to celebrate individual students' accomplishments in front of the school community and to thank their teams for their dedication and hard work.

This experience is not an isolated one at Envision Schools. Community meetings and other similar events begin in the first months of ninth grade. For example, at one

Envision school, all the ninth-grade students participated in an alternative-energy trade show, with a culminating exhibition of an interdisciplinary study in mathematics, integrated science, and digital media arts.

To more than three hundred people in attendance, students presented their work through multimedia public service announcements, illustrative models of systems, and informational booths to sell the attendees on their energy proposals. Before leaving, attendees voted for the most viable energy proposal.

In the community meeting the next morning, teachers recognized students' accomplishments in such categories as creative expression, scientific thinking, and persuasion, and they announced the winners. All students felt a sense of pride and accomplishment on a job well done. It was never about who won or lost, but rather about the success of everyone sharing in a tremendous achievement. The students were able to learn as part of a public exhibition, which served to help build a community of caring where students work together because it benefits them all personally.

Public exhibitions and celebrations can also teach parents and community members how to care about school. Carolyn Mathas (2008), a parent of a ninth-grade student who participated in the alternative-energy trade show, posted a blog entry on the *EE Times* website called "Finding Excitement in Science and Engineering"; in it, she compares what she learned in high school to what her daughter learned in the trade show project: "I learned to memorize, study for tests, and for some subjects promptly [forgot] the material the moment the test was complete. In comparison, these students are experiencing education, not attending it."

It is through experiencing education and these community events that our students learn how to care about school. It's not just about their academic achievements but also about the building of their academic identities through the kinds of work we do with them.

As described by a graduating Envision senior,

> Before I came to Envision Schools, I never really cared about my work. I used to turn in my papers and just expect that I would get a decent grade. Now that I've come here, I care about my work. I think about what I want it to say, what I want it to mean to people. I've been able to come to terms with who I am, and how I learn—and what I want out of my education just by doing projects. (Hartung, 2008)

These experiences demonstrate the impact school can have on students. It is not only the adults telling students how to care about school. Students tell one another. They tell their teachers. They tell their parents.

When students care, school becomes personally meaningful and relevant to their lives, and students can paint a portrait of who they wish to be. This is done through our own embodiment of caring in all we do as teachers and leaders. When we act this way, students can truly experience their education. But if we lose sight of our need to care, we lose our reason for doing what we do. This is true in our lives and in our schools.

Learning Can (and Should) Be Fun

Unfortunately and ironically, our schools and districts often stifle collaboration, learning, and fun for adults and kids. Student learning and fun are not mutually exclusive. In fact, we believe that fun and celebration are essential to student and adult learning.

Let's start with having fun with adults. Having fun at school has to start with adults. As models for students, we can shape a risk-taking culture for students by having fun with one another and with students.

Envision Idol is a good example of adults having fun in schools. We did this at one of our All Envision Days, an organization-wide day of professional learning, celebration, and fun.

In order to entertain and inspire our students during community meetings and assemblies, teachers and staff members in all of our schools had produced and choreographed musical productions of current pop hits. Video of these spirited, fun, and sometimes "instructional" numbers began circulating, along with friendly trash talk about who had the most talent. It became clear that we needed to have a competition at an upcoming All Envision Day to determine the true Envision Idol.

And so it was. All of our schools, along with their principals and support office staff members (including Bob, CEO at the time), stepped up to the challenge. We all had a chance to exercise our inner diva and rap/pop/rock star. Across Envision, people were still laughing and bragging about this event almost two months later.

Video 16. Envision Idol

Envision Education staff show their talent at Envision Idol!

Celebrating is another way to have fun, and at All Envision Day, we celebrate our strengths at every meeting.

At the conclusion of each All Envision Day, we give two very special awards. Our principals and our CEO present the "C" Awards to a teacher from each school, as well as a support office staff member, who exemplifies one of the four C's we seek to develop in our students (communication, collaboration, critical thinking, or completing projects). Each honoree is given a special introduction, during which the principal or CEO describes the ways in which the honoree consistently demonstrates these important skills. Next, our special education team gives the coveted MVP of the IEP award. The team nominates one staff member from each school who excels at implementing our intervention strategy through their classroom practice, at IEP meetings, and in their team collaborations. From that group, an All-Envision MVP is named, an announcement that is always accompanied by a standing ovation and wild applause. The winner is presented with a perpetual trophy to be passed on to the next MVP of the IEP at the next All Envision Day.

These awards may sound hokey, but they authentically celebrate our aspirations and our colleagues in ways that resonate with our culture.

Envision students also engage in fun. Fun is incorporated into weekly community meetings, which are organized by division. Lower division students are in one community meeting along with their advisory teachers, and upper division students are in another. At community meetings, students learn about upcoming clubs and events, and they engage in hokey fun.

Enter the Impact Academy auditorium. It is 1:00 p.m. on a Wednesday; time for the lower division community meeting.

More than two hundred ninth and tenth graders are seated (and partially standing), laughing and yelling out their friends' names. Teachers are laughing too. Some are standing. Some are sitting. None are disciplining students. It is amazingly controlled by an assistant principal and a lead teacher who share a microphone (from time to time when they are not just projecting their voices).

Ten students are on stage, one from each advisory. Standing shoulder to shoulder, they play Chubby Bunny. Each student is given one marshmallow to wedge into his or her mouth and immediately says, "One chubby bunny." At first, it is a competition, with kids and teachers in the audience cheering on the student from their advisory class. The more marshmallows the kids eat, the funnier it is. Watching a kid say "Twenty chubby bunnies" with twenty marshmallows in his mouth is nothing short of hilarious. The hooting and hollering continue until the last student wins with twenty-two marshmallows. As the reigning Chubby Bunny winner exits the stage, the assistant principal simply asks students to quiet down (and they do). He announces the three winners and moves on to important announcements on a PowerPoint slide.

Kids like to have fun. We would argue that adults do too. Surprisingly, schools don't capitalize on students' natural proclivity for fun. Instead, kids have fun outside of school, while in-school time is exclusively about being serious. Creating ways to have fun (the kind of fun kids like) makes school a real place for students where they can express themselves the way they do outside of school with their friends and family.

WHICH CAME FIRST?

Culture and structure are like the chicken and the egg. Every time you start to think that one causes the other, you see the holes in that theory and you change your mind. Does a belief in a growth mindset give rise to a portfolio defense system? Or is it vice versa: Does working with a portfolio defense system convince you of students' capacity to grow?

Answers vary. We've seen school structures change teachers' beliefs about kids. We've also seen teachers with unwavering belief in student potential persevere against seemingly insurmountable structural barriers.

The only practical way forward is to leave the chicken-and-egg question open and pay equal attention to both. Implement the structures; nurture the beliefs. Never be tempted to turn on the autopilot for either. Never trust that one side of the equation will take care of the other on its own.

This book gives all sorts of reasons why the adults in a school building need to be in constant dialogue with each other, but none is more important than this: teaching is emotionally exhausting work. The school year is long. Morale will hit its lows. Optimism and faith are impossible to sustain at every turn. Who hasn't labored through a late-night stack of student papers and been numbed into concluding that ability is fixed after all?

The collaboration demanded by PBL and schoolwide performance assessment has a side benefit that may well be the primary benefit: ongoing, supportive dialogue between teachers who are on the same team. This dialogue is vital to nurturing a culture that aligns with transformative structures. The beliefs we've outlined in this chapter cannot be taken for granted, nor can they be forced. Teachers and school leaders need constant opportunities to speak to these beliefs, live them out, and buck each other up in times of doubt.

If the adults at a school don't collectively believe in the students, then we can't expect the students to believe in themselves.

REFERENCES

Dewey, J. (1998). Analysis of reflective thinking. In L. A. Hickman & T. M. Alexander (Eds.), *Essential Dewey* (Vol. 2, pp. 137–144). Bloomington: Indiana University Press. (Original work published 1933)

Duckworth, A. L. (2013). The key to success? Grit [Video file]. Retrieved from https://www.ted .com/talks/angela_lee_duckworth_the_key_to_success_grit

Dweck, C. S. (2006). *Mindset: The new psychology of success*. New York, NY: Random House.

Hartung, K. (2008, February 29). Learning how to care, part 2: Building academic identities [Blog post]. *Edutopia*. Retrieved from http://www.edutopia.org/student-accomplishment-part-two

Mathas, C. (2008, January 28). Finding excitement in science and engineering [Blog post]. *EE Times*. Retrieved from http://www.eetimes.com/author.asp?section_id=36&doc_id= 1283611

Moulton, J. (2008, January 30). Emotional engagement in education, part one: Should teachers care about student apathy? [Blog post]. *Edutopia*. Retrieved from http://www.edutopia.org /emotional-engagement-education-part-one

Tough, P. (2012). *How children succeed*. Boston, MA: Houghton Mifflin Harcourt.

Chapter **5**

Transforming School Systems

Advisory allowed us to connect what we learned in school to the outside world, and to start preparing for our futures.

— Kyle Zunino, former Envision student

When Bob was a teacher at Sir Francis Drake High School, the school created a new schedule. The project included an essential question: "How does it feel to be a student in a traditional bell schedule?"

To answer the question, four teachers volunteered to shadow students for an entire day and then report back to the faculty. They embarked on a day that is typical for high school and middle school students all across the country and has been for decades: six to nine classes over six to seven hours, each class fifty-five minutes or less.

The teachers reported that it was very difficult to stay focused as the day wore on, and that they found the experience exhausting and lacking any coherence. One teacher was so overwhelmed, he "cut" class after lunch because he couldn't take it anymore.

Eventually—though it took over a year to get there—the faculty voted over-whelmingly to change to a ninety-minute rotating "block" schedule, with classes alternating days. The schedule included an advisory/tutorial period that occurred twice per week.

The new schedule was a game changer for Sir Francis Drake High. Students reflected that it felt as though someone had waved a magic wand and changed the culture of the school from frenetic to calm.

STRUCTURE MATTERS

We don't tell this story because we think that a ninety-minute block schedule is some kind of structural panacea. Without making deeper changes to teaching, learning, and assessment, changing the schedule will result in a schedule change, not transformation. If students are just sitting, listening, and taking notes, then ninety minutes is twice as alienating as forty-five.

But the example does speak to a point we made at the end of the previous chapter: structure and culture are interdependent. If you can initiate a change in a critical structure under the right conditions, you can make a tangible impact on your school's culture.

The bell schedule is one of many aspects of today's schools that look alarmingly similar to schools at the start of the 20th century, a time when schooling went to scale to meet the mass-production needs of the Industrial Revolution. Others include the academic calendar, bells, desks in rows, teachers in front of classrooms, students grouped by ability, and the letter grading scale. They are all legacies of an era long gone.

One-hundred-year-old structures seem ill-suited to helping people become knowledge workers in a digital revolution. Frankly, they're not even good at preparing people for today's "blue-collar" jobs, most of which now require a college diploma or rigorous postsecondary training accompanied by a high level of technical knowledge and skills.

It is time for school structures that are expressly designed for our present and our future, structures that enable and promote learning that aligns with our goals. The reason to change a school schedule, for example, is to accommodate a deeper approach to learning based on a schoolwide graduate profile. If we want students to develop communication and critical thinking skills, to collaborate, to create, and to manage long-term projects, we need to provide structured time for this to happen. It is virtually impossible to do deep work in fifty-five minutes or less.

PBL and performance assessment aligned to Common Core standards cannot survive (let alone thrive) in the traditional school structures that have been handed down to us. At Envision, we have worked hard over the years to build school structures that facilitate our goals and live up to our values. Because we believe that learning is deepest when it is creative, we structure time and space to promote creativity. Because we believe that every learner deserves individual attention, we try to create small, personalized learning environments. Because we believe that learning is a social act, we work hard to build community.

Remember the coach who spurred you on to athletic achievement that you never thought you could attain by yourself, or the teacher for whom you would do anything because he or she understood you so well? We believe that schools need to be intentionally designed to create more of these experiences for kids. School must be a nurturing, caring, high-expectation place where students feel well known, well supported, and well connected to their peers and teachers.

In this chapter, we describe the structures we believe are most crucial for a school-wide performance assessment system to "stick":

- Student cohorts and teacher teams
- Project-based scheduling
- Teachers as advisors
- Student-parent-advisor conferences
- Common planning time
- Professional development
- Community meetings
- Integrated classrooms (no tracking)
- Workplace learning
- Grading

Before we jump in, a caveat: new structures alone won't produce better results. Structure and culture are interdependent. Indeed, structures can be understood as *artifacts* of an organization's culture (Schein, 1985). They are culture made tangible. When you visit our schools, you can see students in advisory or teachers engaged in common planning. What you cannot see are the underlying beliefs, assumptions, and values that were the basis for their creation.

This is important, and a point we made in the previous chapter on culture. Creating structures without tending to culture will result in new structures, but not in transformation. Cultural changes are needed for structures to endure. School transformation always requires a comprehensive and integrated approach.

Still, you can choose structure as a point of entry into the transformation process. Changing the bell schedule at Sir Francis Drake High demonstrates how a new structure can provide space and time for a new culture to take hold. Let's take a closer look at how this and other structural changes can deepen the learning at school.

STUDENT COHORTS AND TEACHER TEAMS

At Envision Schools, we group students into cohorts and teachers into teams to create the conditions for personalized learning.

Teams of core subject-area teachers, including instructors in art and digital media, share the same group of roughly one hundred students for two years. Generally, a student's ninth-grade teacher becomes his tenth-grade teacher, and his eleventh-grade teacher goes on to teach him in the twelfth grade. After a teacher's twelfth graders (or tenth graders) leave her, she "loops" back to a new cohort of eleventh graders (or ninth graders). By teaching the same students for two years, teachers get the opportunity to know their students well. This approach is especially helpful in jumping off to a fast start in the second year.

Teams of teachers have common planning time, which they use to develop projects, coordinate curricula, look at student work together, and discuss the learning and engagement of individual students. (A teacher leader plans and facilitates this effort.) Teachers can then collectively target students for more support within the classroom and possibly plan for other interventions outside of the classroom experience (such as tutoring or counseling).

In addition, the teacher team helps students build their own learning-community teams, each of which has a name. For instance, one school has four teams: Earth, Air, Fire, and Water. The students take courses, work on projects, go on field studies, visit colleges, and solve problems together.

Creating learning-community teams for students can have a big impact on students' connection to school and their learning. Many of the students describe their school friends and teachers as family. One student explained to Bob, "It is not as if we always get along. We are like a family. We might have disagreements, but we know that we will always be there for one another."

When students are known and supported as learners and people, they will strive for excellence and eagerly engage in rigorous learning. The strong connection that they have to their teachers and peers is a safety net that keeps them from falling. They don't want to let down their peers or teachers. The move from individual accountability to community accountability for learning is a cultural shift.

Having students feel supported is a good outcome, but we don't think it is enough. If we don't use these strategies and structures to increase student learning, we have just made kids feel better without pushing them to their potential or preparing them for college and career.

PROJECT-BASED SCHEDULING

Larry Rosenstock, founder and CEO of High Tech High, tells a great anecdote about his attempt to change the school's traditional schedule to a block schedule during his tenure as principal of Rindge School of the Technical Arts. In an all-staff meeting to address the matter, a veteran teacher stated, "We can't change the schedule; the schedule won't let us." And so it went: there was not enough time in the schedule to choose an appropriate schedule, resulting in no time to develop teachers' capacity to teach in longer periods of time.

Sooner or later, a school needs to adjust its school day to accommodate deeper learning. A new, well-designed schedule can't create time, but it can help an organization prioritize time in a way that matches its goals and values. Longer classes make it possible for students and teachers to engage in a workshop style of learning. Students have time to get into a creative or focused zone and stay there before the inexorable bell sweeps everyone off to the next class. A good schedule can also reprioritize time for professional development, collaboration, and structures such as advisory and community meeting, which support personalization, relationship building, and community building.

Of course, every bell schedule reflects the tension between aspiration and reality. We've been playing with our schedules for a decade; the perfect solution is always just around the next bend. The point is that there are many ways to improve a school schedule, but no one right way that works for everybody. Still, it doesn't take much to come up with a schedule that serves our learners better than the traditional forms that have been handed down to us. (See the Envision Sample Daily Schedule in the appendix.)

ADVISORIES

Often, the difference between a student who graduates from high school and goes on to college and one who doesn't is a relationship with a caring adult at school who knows him well, believes in his ability to succeed, and will not let him fail.

This type of student-teacher relationship is especially important in the first years of high school. It's so important, in fact, that we've built a structure into our school design that promotes this relationship: the advisory system.

Almost every teacher in Envision Schools serves as an advisor to twenty to twenty-five students. Students stay with the same advisor for two years. Students in grades 9 and 10 have a lower division advisory. When they move to grade 11, students get a new upper division advisor, who stays with them through senior year.

Advisories at Envision begin with teachers greeting their students at the door, often with a handshake or a hug. Inside the classroom, students sit in one large circle facing one another. Norms or agreements are posted prominently in the room (for example, "Respect each other" and "Listen"). They are not just words on a poster; teachers and students hold each other accountable to them daily.

Before each lesson, teachers and students check in by sharing how they are feeling, even if with just a thumbs-up or thumbs-down. Then teachers explicitly teach collaboration skills that help groups working on projects to be more successful and simultaneously build community. Teachers also facilitate group discussions and activities to confront issues of diversity, race, and class in the context of their curriculum.

We have established goals for our advisory system that promote success for all students. Specifically, students will

- Know and demonstrate deeper learning skills in critical thinking, project management, problem solving, collaboration, communication, and creative expression

- Create and maintain a safe, respectful learning community

- Investigate and experience the process of researching, preparing for, and applying for college

- Know and demonstrate the practices and attitudes necessary to be successful in college and the workplace

Schools provide advisors with extensive guidelines and distribute weekly agendas for their meetings. Bob collaborated with Envision teacher leaders to create a job description to help teachers who are advisors for freshman and sophomore students understand this important role. It reads:

> Advisors meet at least once a week with their advisees. Teachers will receive support in the form of professional development and a curriculum. However, the key to being an advisor is "owning" one's students. That is, the advisor should know each student extremely well and be able to rally support, intervene, and acknowledge when needed. If the Envision advisory system is working well, no student will fall through the cracks.

(See the 9th Grade Envision Schools Advisory Curriculum in the appendix.)

Social-emotional interventions can be implemented through advisories. During the first two years of the program, every student develops a wellness plan that includes goals around self-regard, self-regulation, relationships, and future orientation. These plans help alert advisors to students who may need more formal outside help, and because every student has a plan, it is easier to reduce the stigma sometimes attached to receiving psychological services.

Video 17. Advisory: Check-In and Support

At Envision Schools, the advisory is one concrete way we build a culture of support for students. In this video from the Teaching Channel's Deeper Learning series, an Envision teacher talks about creating a positive culture through advisory and describes how advisory benefits both students and teachers.

PARENT-STUDENT-ADVISOR CONFERENCES

At least twice a year, elementary parents meet with their children's teachers to set goals, to review progress toward these goals, and to collaborate on how to best support their children's learning at home and at school. Why is it that after elementary school, this important practice often comes to an end?

As students get older, especially as they begin high school, they yearn for a sense of independence and maturity. In this struggle, there is often a disconnect between students and their parents, particularly in regard to school performance. Because older kids and parents often talk less and less about school, we think parent-teacher conferences are imperative. By requiring this interaction, we are telling parents that it is *OK* to get involved with their teenager's high school education. For students, we give them some cover; they really do want their parents involved.

At Envision Schools, advisors schedule a conference two or three times a year for each student. These meetings, which students lead, also include parents and significant mentors.

More than 90 percent of our parents take advantage of this opportunity, so we know that parents generally want to stay engaged when their kids are in high school. There is an incentive: we hand out report cards at the meetings rather than mail them home. If you don't attend a conference, you will not receive a report card. Each advisor follows up with each parent until they attend.

At these conferences, students reflect on what they've learned, what they consider to be areas for growth (for example, grades or skills they can improve), and long-term goals (such as what college they plan to attend). Advisors review student transcripts and highlight any concerns about progress toward graduation. At this time, advisors also review key benchmark assessments in language arts and math and plan any interventions that may be necessary to address learning gaps or credit deficiencies. Parents become aware of current benchmarks or graduation portfolio work so that they can see progress firsthand and become a part of this very important process side by side with their children.

A powerful student-led parent-teacher conference focuses on setting student learning goals based on examining the student's work. It is not a passive look at a folder of assignments. It is an active event in which the learner and those responsible for supporting her education identify her strengths and areas of growth and make plans to address these areas.

Many parents are unsure how to support their children in school, particularly if they were unsuccessful in their own schooling. The conference is one tool to help parents support their child's success. And teachers benefit greatly from the conferences because they get to know their students and their families better.

PROFESSIONAL DEVELOPMENT

"We are crew, not passengers." This quote from experiential education pioneer Kurt Hahn projects brightly onto a large screen in the school auditorium. This is the start of an Envision Schools professional development (PD) session.

After a brief welcome, thirty-five new teachers at Envision Schools are asked to respond to the quote in their journals. Then, following some quiet reflection time, the teachers meet their fellow group members. Teachers are put in heterogeneous groups. They come from different schools and content areas and have varying levels of technical expertise. In their new groups, teachers discuss their responses to the quote and how they think it could inform the way they work together over the next two days.

The Envision Schools facilitator then leads an activity on the attributes of high-quality stories. She projects the graph shown in Figure 5.1. "What could these data

Figure 5.1 Mystery Chart

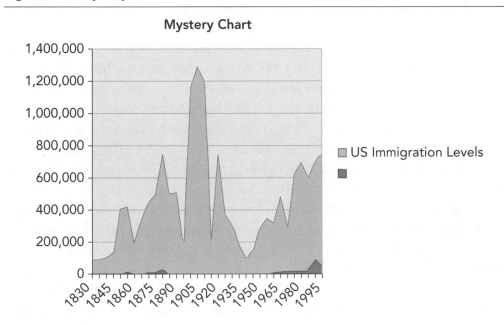

possibly be describing?" she asks, challenging this group of teacher learners. "Together, we will explore the essential question 'Why do we exclude people?' by exploring the Angel Island Immigration Station," she explains. "Each group will propose an answer and share their findings through a digital story and free-verse poetry. Hopefully, your curiosity is piqued. Let's go—we have a boat to catch!"

The teachers and the facilitator catch the next ferry to the Angel Island Immigration Station, a facility on an island in the San Francisco Bay that detained Chinese immigrants in the early 1900s. There they spend the day learning about immigration and exclusion. Teachers learn from expert docents, explore primary source documents, read and write free verse (the walls of the Immigration Station are covered with the immigrants' original poetry), study challenging historical documents using literacy strategies from the Strategic Literacy Initiative (SLI), and look for answers to their questions in the Angel Island museum.

After a long day on the island, the facilitator gives teachers their homework assignments: *Consider the question of why humans exclude others and create a response using evidence gathered on Angel Island.* The next day, teachers return to school early and work diligently and frantically through the morning to meet the noon deadline. In the afternoon, it's show time: every group presents its digital story and its poetry to the entire Envision Schools professional learning community.

This two-day PD session is an example of the types of learning experiences teachers at Envision Schools have on a regular basis. We try to make sure that teachers' own professional learning mirrors students' learning, dramatically increasing the likelihood that teachers will apply what they've learned to their classroom practice. In the Angel Island project, teachers experience what a PBL classroom feels like: managed chaos. They also learn the power of a scheduled exhibition to motivate younger and older learners alike.

It is no secret that dedicated time for teachers to learn together matters. Countries like Finland and Singapore, which outperform the United States on the Programme for International Student Assessment, better known as the PISA, have significantly more professional learning time for teachers than we do (among other factors that lead to their success). PD is an essential strategic lever for improving day-to-day teaching and learning.

Expert organizations, such as the National Staff Development Council (NSDC), have defined what effective PD is and created standards to guide the field (http://learningforward.org/standards-for-professional-learning). But if we know what it is and why it matters, why is effective PD not happening in all schools? One huge reason is lack of time. Time was at the heart of the scheduling dilemma that impeded the Rindge faculty from even discussing a block schedule. It is *the* obstacle to PD.

At Envision Schools, we have pushed through the challenge of finding time for PD and created structures in our schools that support and promote professional learning as part of the school schedule and calendar. We don't send teachers out to conferences and workshops (as a general rule). Instead, teachers, instructional coaches, and principals codesign and collaboratively deliver PD that is aligned to what and how we teach Envision students. Teachers have ten or more days of student-free PD time annually, three-and-a-half hours of collaborative time weekly, and monthly classroom mentoring. (This is good, but teachers actually need much more time. We're always looking for ways to increase it.)

To wrap up the Angel Island project, the facilitator asks folks to reflect in three ways: as individuals, as a work group, and as a large group. As great as the learning is during the *doing* stage of PBL, the real learning occurs during reflection. Teachers quickly move from making generalizations about the experience and its implications to applying what they learned to their classrooms, their integrated project-based teams, and their schools as a whole.

The facilitator shares the tools used for designing the project and teaches how to use them. (See the Six A's of Designing Projects in the appendix.) Teachers leave the session as members of a crew, ready to change lives and prepare students for success in college and beyond.

COMMON PLANNING TIME

Do your teachers agree on what constitutes college-ready work? If your answer is yes, please share your story with us! If your answer is no, then you are among friends. Defining performance standards that describe how good is good enough is a sticky problem. We see this challenge manifested in two common ways in schools: (1) uneven (kids would say unfair) grading practices across classrooms and (2) disputed criteria for student recognition awards.

Teachers need common planning time to solve sticky problems of practice and answer such questions as "What constitutes college-ready work?" Structured time is needed for common planning above and beyond professional development. This is dedicated time for teams of teachers to look at student work and engage in structured dialogue to develop common language, calibrate teachers' performance standards, and share effective practices.

A team from Envision Schools (comprising Bob, the chief academic officer, a teacher, and a partner from Stanford University) designed a professional development session for an institute for the annual California Early College High School Conference in San Diego. On the basis of what happens during common planning time at Envision Schools, they designed the session around the essential question "Do college instructors and high school teachers agree on what constitutes college-ready work?"

In the session, college faculty and high school educators scored an Envision student's work from an ELA performance task focused on literary/textual analysis.

Here's a brief description of the task from our guidebook:

> Through the study of language and literature, we expect students to develop the appropriate skills and tools necessary to be confident critical readers and thinkers, as well as effective and persuasive communicators. We expect students not only to show an understanding of the concerns and implications of literature in its varied forms and styles (fiction, nonfiction, genre, and author, etc.) but also to use literature as a tool to investigate and discuss topics and concerns that are relevant to

students' lives today. To demonstrate their mastery of the discipline, students must select a writing sample that demonstrates the ability to read and think critically and to communicate effectively and persuasively.

After discussing the rubric, the Envision team presented a paper that had been created as part of an integrated American history and American literature project unit. In the unit, students selected an American author to research and were required to read at least five lengthy pieces from this writer. Students were asked to write a seven- to ten-page paper comparing the various pieces of literature in the context of the historical and cultural times in America. The student work submitted for the session analyzed the writings of Flannery O'Connor.

The college faculty and high school teachers engaged in a rich discussion about whether or not the student work was college ready. Even though the student work chosen for the session had produced a contentious debate about college readiness among Envision teachers, all the teachers (college and high school) in the session ultimately agreed that on the basis of the piece of work they reviewed, the student *was* ready for a freshman-level English course at a university.

Agreeing on college-ready work is essential to improving student learning and strengthening teaching across a school. Teachers have to have dedicated (and facilitated) time to engage together in deep dialogue and reflection about student learning and their practices. At Envision Schools, teachers have three hours of common planning time each week with content-area colleagues. They also have three-and-a-half hours of facilitated collaboration time with their interdisciplinary team or family colleagues.

Common planning time, professional development, and collaboration are essential ingredients for teacher success in achieving deeper learning outcomes. (See the Project Sharing Protocol in the appendix.)

COMMUNITY MEETINGS

Each week at Envision Schools, students and teachers participate in community meetings. In their advisory groups, students in grades 9 and 10 go to the lower division community meeting; students in grades 11 and 12 go to the upper division community meeting.

Community meetings, sometimes known as town halls, are a vital structure for creating the space for whole-school learning and community building. Each school has developed its own rituals and formats. Some are facilitated by a school leader; others are run entirely by students. Some start with a chime and an inspirational reading; in others, students choose music for the opening soundtrack.

Once they are running, community meetings can serve all kinds of purposes; they offer an opportunity to

- Celebrate successes
- Train students to plan and facilitate meetings
- Address a critical school issue (A school leader often heads these types of meetings.)
- Distribute important and/or mundane information in an engaging way
- Explicitly teach values, such as integrity
- Showcase student performance, both academic and artistic
- Inspire people through insightful readings or videos
- Reflect (Moments of silence can be powerful.)
- Have fun (for example, holding a hula hoop contest for advisories)

When implementing community meetings, it is important to balance creativity and fun with a sense of order. We have learned that community meetings work best when

- They happen regularly at a scheduled time.
- They are well planned and have a specific agenda.
- Teachers and advisors sit with the students.
- Expectations for audience behavior are clear and are consistently enforced.

Although every school's community meeting looks different, the ultimate outcome is the same: students and teachers feel more connected and part of something bigger than themselves. Over the course of four years, this experience encourages Envision students to create and lead communities wherever they go. We believe that once you have been privileged to experience true community, you feel both the obligation and the motivation to create it.

INTEGRATED CLASSROOMS (NO TRACKING)

At Envision Schools, there is no tracking. All Envision Schools students take the required courses for freshman admission to both the University of California and California State University systems. By not tracking students and by having heterogeneous classrooms, we have systematized our belief that *all* students can achieve success in college.

Tracking is a pervasive school structure that seems to be another sticky problem of practice. It simplifies master scheduling challenges that consume hours of counselors' and school leaders' time. While it solves administrative challenges, it also creates a structure that sorts and selects kids by ability, test scores, or grades and communicates and institutionalizes a fixed mindset about students' ability to learn and grow. Schools and teachers often say that all kids can go to college, but when they don't place some students in academically rigorous courses, these students (and their parents and guardians) learn to believe that "all" does not include them, that they cannot go to college. Teachers and students lower their expectations. This is detrimental to all kids, in our opinion, but it is even more so for underprivileged students who are living in poverty and/or who will be the first to go to college in their families. These students need the system to tell them, "Yes! You can do it!" Tracking says "Yes!" to some and "No!" to others.

At Envision Schools, we say "Yes!" to every student who enters our doors, even students who enter ninth grade reading at an elementary level. As at every other school serving a diverse student population, our students have a wide range of skills. Integrating them into heterogeneous classes is challenging. It is, without a doubt, harder to integrate students than to track them, but it is better.

Integrated classrooms are better for all students. How do we know? Because 100 percent of Envision students complete California's college preparatory course work, and over 90 percent of seniors enroll in college and persist to sophomore year.

Integrated classrooms make a big difference for traditionally underperforming students because in such classrooms they learn to adjust to higher expectations and can see the connection between success and effort. Students who have not been in academically rigorous classrooms have not had exposure to high expectations from their teachers. They don't understand the effort that high-performing students make in and out of class. They believe that those students are simply "smart," and they really do not make the connection between effort and grades. For underperforming students, this is a wake-up call. Although that call can be very frustrating to low-achieving students at first, it also can inspire them to work toward the standards set by their peers.

High-performing students in integrated classrooms push their teachers to create challenging and fast-paced lessons and projects. Without these demanding voices, a teacher just might lower his or her expectations for students. That's much less likely to happen in a class with well-prepared students, so teachers learn to keep high standards for all the kids.

A universal concern of parents and educators about integrated classrooms is that struggling students consume teachers' time, taking away from what higher-performing students need. At Envision, we have observed that this is more of a fear than a reality. High-performing Envision students apply and are accepted to competitive colleges and universities, similar to their peers in other high schools.

Integrated classrooms provide *all* students with a diverse learning space to develop deeper learning skills that transfer to college and the workplace. By learning to collaborate and communicate with students with backgrounds different from their own, students will be more prepared to succeed in an increasingly diverse workplace.

Educators who are interested in dismantling tracking are frequently apprehensive about including all students in college-prep courses, and they typically have these three questions in common:

- Will we dumb down the curriculum?

- Is it fair to put so much pressure on students who are not prepared? Can't we prepare them in remedial classes and then have them take college-prep courses?

- Isn't all of this difficult for the teacher?

After ten years of persisting through ongoing challenges associated with integrated classrooms, we have answers to these questions. It is important to note that you cannot just create integrated classrooms and assume that the structure is self-sustaining. These classrooms need to be nurtured and adjusted to meet the dynamic challenges of changes in teacher and student assignments. The answers we offer in this section are not intended to be *the* answers, but rather to provoke your thinking about how you can liberate your students from the shackles of tracking.

Curriculum in integrated classrooms is not dumbed down at Envision Schools. As we have noted elsewhere, teachers use rubrics that align to Envision's graduate profile and the Common Core State Standards. Well-designed projects offer multiple entry points into the curriculum for students performing at all levels.

Of course, not all students enter ninth grade academically prepared for these academically rigorous courses. This means that Envision teachers need to differentiate and scaffold their curriculum, using PBL and other teaching methods. They use teacher-created formative assessments and diagnostics to identify students who will require specific interventions in reading, language, or math to accelerate their learning.

We believe not only that it is fair to push underperforming students but also that it is our moral obligation to hold all students to high standards and provide targeted support to help them through high school and beyond. Envision's mission—to transform the lives of students—drives our organizational energy and resources. We also believe in a growth mindset, which is why we created integrated classrooms that explicitly and tacitly communicate to students and their families that all students can do it. We think it is unfair *not* to push students.

Finally, integrated classrooms do pose challenges for teachers. Like teachers in tracked classrooms, Envision teachers have to have a high level of content knowledge and pedagogical prowess, and a deep understanding of what motivates students. In other words, teachers have to be at the top of their game. Other Envision Schools structures enable integrated classrooms, and integrated classrooms would not work at Envision without teacher teams, cohort scheduling, advisories, professional development, common planning time, and parent-student-advisor conferences.

In California, only 35 percent of students graduate from high school having taken the required UC and CSU courses. The percentages are much lower for poor students and African American and Latino students. At Envision Schools, 100 percent of students graduate having taken the required courses. Contrary to the statistics and some people's expectations, it is possible for all students to be college-prep kids.

WORKPLACE LEARNING

Video 18. The Workplace Learning Experience at Envision

Five Envision students prove that they can make it in the real world, as they describe their twelve-week Workplace Learning Experience internships. Because of their preparation at Envision, these students were able to contribute in meaningful ways to their work sites, in addition to learning valuable workplace skills.

At Envision Schools, junior and senior students have an extended Workplace Learning Experience (WLE) at a location of their choice. This internship-type experience offers students a chance to measure their knowledge and skills against what will be required of them in the future, understand how successful adults operate in the world of work, and obtain information about a job or field of interest. Envision students have a semester-long WLE one day per week for five to seven hours per day. Typically, the WLE takes place September through December.

Commonly, young adults lack access to and relationships with successful adults outside the home or classroom; WLE provides students with personalized learning from a successful adult mentor. This is important for so many students, for whom this will be their first real-world work experience. The role of the workplace mentor is to act as a role model and trainer, assisting students in making the connections between the world of work and the importance of doing well in school.

During the WLE, students do real work, solve real problems, and are offered continual challenges. Throughout the WLE, students document their experience and learning in a journal that is accessible to mentors, parents, and advisors. They also design and complete research or a project that is relevant and meaningful to the workplace. At the conclusion of the WLE, students present their project or research to their mentor and staff as the culminating exhibition of learning in the WLE.

Like any learning experience, for the WLE to be meaningful and relevant, it must be student centered. Specifically, this means matching the WLE to a student's interests and including a student-driven project that corresponds to a specific need of the sponsoring organization. The WLE can happen in just about any industry or organization. Examples include science centers, arts organizations, hospitals, medical centers, nonprofits, marketing agencies, banks, law offices, newspapers, and radio stations. Examples of WLE projects include organizing a benefit concert, editing and publishing an article in the local newspaper, designing a website, and creating a technical guide.

The following are key elements that make WLEs rigorous, relevant, and meaningful while ensuring that students develop professional skills and gain exposure to careers of interest:

- The WLE is related to one or more of the classes the student is enrolled in and/or the educational goals and career interests of the student.

- The high school advisor (or counselor), the student, and the mentor codesign the experience. The work is grounded in the student's capabilities, interests, and goals, and results in a "product" that is presented by the student at the workplace.

- The scope of the WLE is sufficiently extensive as to require no less than several weeks to reach competence.

- At the work site, the student has an immediate supervisor/mentor who provides direction or instruction and close supervision initially, then supervision as necessary.

- There is periodic evaluation by the mentor and the advisor, who will also visit the work site.

WLEs are mutually beneficial to students and industry. They provide workforce training prior to placement, alleviating some of the burden of future training costs to create a pool of potential applicants. They also influence the kinds of skills students develop based on industry needs. For employees, the WLE is an opportunity to act as mentors, refining and honing their interpersonal, training, and supervisory skills, which boosts employee morale. The WLE also creates positive exposure in the community for both schools and employers.

GRADING

One of the most entrenched features of American education is the grade scale. You remember it well: 90–100 percent is an A, 80–89 percent is a B, and so on. There is hardly a movie about high school that doesn't include a student receiving back a graded paper with a large *F* printed in red. Most colleges and high schools include plus/minus systems that provide additional ranges and options to teachers when assessing student performance. Furthermore, in most high schools, each teacher has the flexibility to design and implement his or her own grading policy. Usually, grading policies either take a simple ratio of total points earned over total points possible to arrive at a percentage score, or break up work into categories that are then weighted according to the priorities set by the teacher.

At Envision Schools, we believe that these traditional approaches to assessment reinforce a belief in students that knowledge and academic performance are static. In other words, students who are "smart" get good grades, while students who are "dumb" perform poorly. As we discussed in the culture chapter, this epitomizes what Dweck (2006) calls the fixed mindset. In the classroom setting, this plays out when students receive graded work back with a percentage score that often equates in their minds to a measure of intelligence. At Envision, we seek to instill in students what Dweck calls the growth mindset, helping students understand that "basic qualities are things you can cultivate through your efforts" (p. 7).

We have therefore developed a holistic grading system designed to hold students accountable for their academic performance while also developing a growth mindset in students (and teachers). Our grading policy can be difficult to learn for those who are new to our school, and it certainly requires additional work as teachers constantly consider how their assignments will be reflected in students' final grades. In any case, we believe firmly that what is most important is student learning and growth, taking into account where students arrive as a result of the educational experience we provide.

Envision created a balanced assessment approach to grading that uses weighted formulas together with a holistic approach to assessing individual assignments. This approach also integrates the four C's as explicit outcomes that we want to measure as students develop as leaders. (See the Envision Course Grade Rubric in the appendix.)

Our holistic approach to grading requires that teachers use a 4-point scale when assessing student performance. This is sometimes a big shift for teachers and students who are used to the traditional 100-point scale. The 4-point scale not only makes sense, as it directly corresponds with the 4-point GPA scale, but it also allows us to use a common language for student performance that encourages a growth mindset. Students are assessed on a 1–4 scale for every assignment as follows:

The 4-Point Holistic Approach Grading Scale

1.	Emerging
2.	Developing
3.	Proficient
4.	Advanced

Using this language reinforces for students that knowledge and performance are not static and that even proficient work contains room for growth. These categories work particularly well in a performance assessment context, such as when grading with a rubric. They do, however, require that a teacher define for students what the terms *emerging*, *developing*, *proficient*, and *advanced* mean for every assignment. These categories easily translate into the traditional letter grades of the 4-point GPA scale as follows:

Traditional Letter Grade Translations

1	Emerging	No credit
2	Developing	C
3	Proficient	B
4	Advanced	A

Notice that at Envision Schools we do not assign D grades, as they are not accepted by colleges. Therefore, a student must earn a C– or higher to pass and earn credit for a class.

Figure 5.2 is designed to help our teachers determine which of the three categories applies for each assignment. Many of the assignments in the Application of Knowledge and Metacognition category require more in-depth assessment, often a rubric, for evaluation. Decisions are largely left to individual teachers and teams to determine the most appropriate category for any given assignment.

This system does create the challenge to design assessment over the course of a quarter and semester in a way that provides the teacher with enough evidence to defend his or her assessment decisions. In most cases, this requires a variety of assessments within each category.

As we've mentioned elsewhere, commonly folks ask, "Do I have to grade everything?" Our answer is, "No!" We suggest you grade major benchmarks, projects, assessments, and so on, but not every assignment. Many teachers like to randomly choose which smaller assignments will be graded, as well as to randomly choose to grade some assignments for completion and others for quality and accuracy. But teachers do need enough graded material to defend their decisions on final grades.

What does grading look like for students with exceptional needs? If a student has an IEP, accommodations must be taken into account when assigning final grades. A student with an IEP cannot earn an NC if he did not receive the "necessary" accommodations. The teacher has to work closely with our learning specialists in order to understand what those necessary accommodations are for any particular student. It is very important for teachers to be in constant communication with the learning specialist in cases where a student with an IEP is in danger of receiving an NC.

We manage our grading system using Powerschool, which is web-based student information management software. It allows students, teachers, and parents to track academic performance and progress. Although Powerschool can compute grades for students, you have to check regularly to make sure that the Powerschool system is weighting assignments to reflect your holistic approach to grading. Specifically, teachers may want to value major projects higher, as well as assessments toward the end of the semester that reflect growth. Powerschool will not do that for you automatically.

Weighting assignment grades is complicated, but it is also essential for understanding how to use our holistic grading approach effectively and appropriately.

To close, we must acknowledge that as a charter management organization (CMO), we have had the freedom (and challenge) that comes with creating schools from

Figure 5.2 Envision Schools Grading Criteria

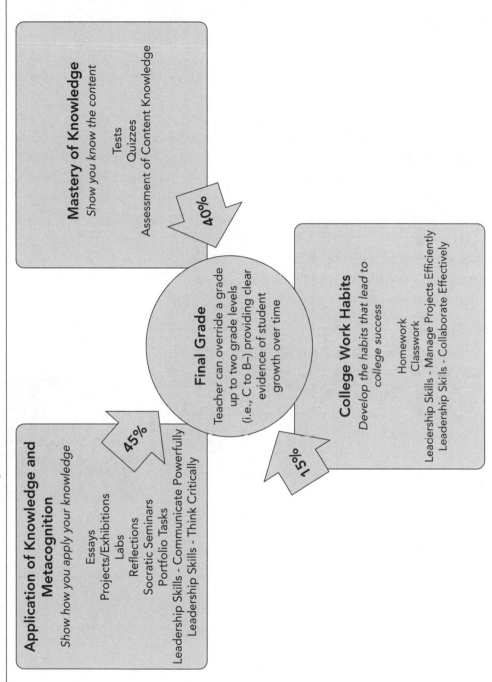

Mastery of Knowledge
Show you know the content

Tests
Quizzes
Assessment of Content Knowledge

40%

Final Grade
Teacher can override a grade up to two grade levels (i.e., C to B−) providing clear evidence of student growth over time

College Work Habits
Develop the habits that lead to college success

Homework
Classwork
Leadership Skills - Manage Projects Efficiently
Leadership Skills - Collaborate Effectively

15%

Application of Knowledge and Metacognition
Show how you apply your knowledge

Essays
Projects/Exhibitions
Labs
Reflections
Socratic Seminars
Portfolio Tasks
Leadership Skills - Communicate Powerfully
Leadership Skills - Think Critically

45%

scratch, with new students, teachers, leaders, culture, and structures. This has also given us the ability to "play" with structures over the years. We know that's a blessing, and although that freedom has led to many mistakes, we've also stumbled into some things that really work.

With or without this advantage, you *can* transform the lives of your students. In fact, Envision Schools grew out of innovative changes that Bob helped lead at Sir Francis Drake High, a comprehensive district school.

We encourage teachers who are reading this chapter to reflect on our school structures and consider ways in which you might adapt them to your classroom on a smaller scale. For example, if you don't have schoolwide advisories, how might you integrate advisory strategies into your practice? Are there local business folks who might be willing to serve as mentors to your students?

Change has a ripple effect. The changes that Bob made in his classroom spread to his department, to his school, to Envision's first school, then to two other Envision schools, and now to hundreds of schools through the work of Envision Learning Partners. Small changes can have a big impact.

Video 19. Teacher Collaboration

Sticky note collaboration! Teachers and learning specialists work together at the beginning of each year to map out curriculum plans and ideas. Because they are collaborating, they can see and make connections across disciplines and then create projects that achieve multiple content and skill learning targets.

Video 20. Calibration: Assessing Portfolio Defenses

In order for Envision teachers to make sure they have a common understanding of the expectations and requirements of the portfolio and defense and that they are all using the assessment tool in the same way, teachers need to calibrate their assessment of student work. This video offers a window into that process.

REFERENCES

Dweck, C. S. (2006). *Mindset: The new psychology of success*. New York, NY: Random House.

Schein, E. (1985). *Organizational culture and leadership: A dynamic view*. San Francisco, CA: Jossey-Bass.

Chapter 6

Leadership for Deeper Learning

PDO: Persistence and Determination are Omnipotent.

— Bob Lenz quoting Erin Brockovich quoting
Calvin Coolidge

Bob's leadership journey started with a question: How do I get my students to own their learning the way Sarah just did?

What Sarah, a high school student, had just done was exhibit a video documentary that she had cocreated on the 1930s. When the documentary ended, she turned to the audience and explained how she had collaborated with her team to create the video. Then she gave a commanding lecture on Franklin Roosevelt, arguing that he was the greatest president of the 20th century.

Bob was a teacher and Sarah a student at Sir Francis Drake High School, in San Anselmo, California. Sarah wasn't Bob's student. She attended a small learning community within the school called Communications Academy. It was clear to Bob that what was happening at Communications Academy—an integrated curriculum, PBL, and a career-themed smaller learning community—was allowing students to go deeper with their learning than he had previously thought possible. He decided to find colleagues and students who would work with him to create another small learning community within the school, called Academy X.

Step by step, Bob moved from a question to a shared vision to an action plan. Eventually, Bob led Drake High School in a whole-school redesign, which resulted in major improvements in student learning and garnered the school national recognition as a New American High School. Drake was featured in a story on high school improvement in *US News and World Report*.

As news of the school's success spread, hundreds of people began to visit Drake High School, wanting to learn how they might replicate some of the strategies that had worked so well. Over and over, Bob heard the same comment from these visitors: "This is great, but what are the demographics here?" They could see that the students were mostly white and middle class. The question was often followed by "because I don't think our students [i.e., low income and/or students of color] can do work like this."

So Bob was incited to take action once again.

Bob knew that all kids could learn deeply. Again, he found colleagues, students, parents, and other community and business partners to create a shared vision of not simply a redesigned high school but a redesigned high school system whose mission was college success for all students. That is the mission of Envision Education today.

Leading for deeper learning can start—must start—with small steps that lead to big changes. This book outlines many ways to start leading the change. The next step is to share that vision and implement the change, no matter how small.

LEADING WITH "HOLONOMY"

In the introduction to this book, we explained how our school transformation model (Figure 6.1) is premised on the concept of *holonomy,* the theory that for learning to go deep, an organization's parts must work harmoniously toward the whole (Costa & Garmston, 2002; Costa & Kallick, 1995; Koestler, 1974).

Leaders occupy a special place in our transformation model. It's not simply that they are the outermost of the nested circles. Significantly, they are the only people who operate outside the layers of culture and systems. All the other people, students and teachers,

Figure 6.1 The Envision Schools Transformation Model

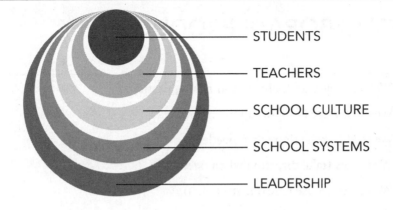

STUDENTS

TEACHERS

SCHOOL CULTURE

SCHOOL SYSTEMS

LEADERSHIP

live inside the cultural and structural forces. The diagram represents why true leadership demands both responsibility *and* humility. No one but the school leader is positioned to see across all organizational layers, but that vantage point is attained by being the farthest removed from what matters most—the students.

When asked, many school leaders will say that their job is to serve students and their learning. But in general, leaders don't serve students directly; they serve them *through* various organizational layers. What the model reminds us is that for leaders to truly serve students, they must attend to all the organizational layers that wrap those students: the teaching, the culture, and the systems. To neglect any one of these, or to ignore an inconsistency within any layer, means that the leader is not serving the students to the degree that he or she can. As stewards of a school's mission, leaders should see themselves as *stewards of consistency* across all levels of the organization.

Pick something that your school is asking of your students—a goal that you have identified for your students—and then ask, "Are we supporting this goal at every level of the organization? Are we expecting this of *all* members of the community? What do we need to do make this a value that is enacted consistently throughout the entire organization? Is the organization practicing what it preaches?"

At Envision Schools, one of the deeper learning skills announced in our graduate profile is the ability to *collaborate productively*. And we go on to tell our students what we think it means to collaborate productively, offering a list of criteria:

COLLABORATE PRODUCTIVELY

- We plan together (actively contribute, participate).
- We encourage (support all members).
- We lead (take action when needed).
- We follow (take direction when needed).
- We use expertise (use our strengths).
- We share responsibility (distribute work).
- We do our part (our individual responsibility).
- We network (seek additional expertise, go beyond what's in front of us).

It's one thing to define a value or goal for students; it's another for an organization to live it out. If we want students to succeed at collaborating productively—a challenging and complex goal—then our school leaders must scrutinize collaboration at every level of the transformation model.

Start with the teachers, the first layer surrounding the students. Our teachers, like our students, should be collaborating productively: planning together, encouraging each other, leading, following, using expertise, sharing responsibility, doing their part, and networking. We have to answer the questions that then emerge: How prepared are our teachers to collaborate productively? How much time do they have to collaborate? How much psychological space do they have to focus on planning, encouraging, and leading? Do our teachers know how to collaborate? If not, are we giving them opportunities to learn? In our experience (and probably yours too), honest answers to these questions point to the need for change.

But don't stop there. Move outward to the layers of culture and structure. What does a school culture look like when teachers are collaborating productively? What core beliefs drive the culture? What are our norms for collaboration? Does our school culture embrace and promote teacher learning? Teacher leadership? A growth mindset? Shared responsibility? We ask similar kinds of questions of our structures and systems. Do the school calendar and the bell schedule provide dedicated time for collaboration? When do students and teachers learn to collaborate productively? *Where* can they collaborate productively?

Our leaders must also collaborate productively *and* lead others in the development of that deeper learning skill. Do our leaders know how and when to step up to lead teachers or step back to follow? To what degree are school leaders sharing their decision making? Are our leaders seeking out others when they need support and guidance?

Considering this example of just one deeper learning skill, you can see that leading a holonomous organization requires rigorous inquiry, resolute courage, and sustained commitment. This is hard work, and it is the right work to create the schools we need and deserve.

KEY LEADERSHIP VALUES

We have divided the rest of this chapter into two sections. The first is a set of big-picture insights into leadership that we've learned along our journey and that we believe will help you in yours. Then we move into some practical advice for school leaders.

Leading for change requires …

- Vision and courage
- A mission with a moral purpose
- A persistent learning stance
- The power of staying

Vision and Courage

Vision and courage are at the heart of leading deeper learning. In *Leading Minds,* Howard Gardner (1996) explores the characteristics of influential 20th century leaders. He found that the most successful leaders, whether leading a country, a movement, or a school, have the capacity to communicate a vision for the future that motivates their constituents to move toward that vision.

Educators leading deeper learning need to declare—and repeat over and over again—a vision for student outcomes, teaching, and learning that compels students, teachers, parents, and community members to redesign and transform their learning, their classroom, and the school.

Unfortunately, vision is not enough. Leading change is messy and hard work. Leaders need to summon courage to act and to persist through the inevitable challenges, missteps, and opposition that accompany change. Leading with courage means implementing change that not everyone agrees with and some actively oppose. To provide common planning time for teachers, for example, a leader might have to rearrange the school schedule in a way that disadvantages the scheduling of singleton honors courses. The vision, if it's clear, is a place to draw courage.

Vision without courage is a great story with no conclusion, and courage without vision results in changes that are disruptive but not effective. Leadership is the exercise of both vision and courage.

Reflecting on your leadership for deeper learning, you can ask yourself these questions: How clearly does my vision paint a picture of the future? To what extent does it compel others to lead and follow? How willing am I to do whatever it takes to realize the vision?

A Mission with a Moral Purpose

Missions matter. Mission statements describe organizational goals and the philosophy underlying them. They signal to the world what you are all about. For deeper learning, mission statements have to reflect broad goals and deep philosophies. Schools and districts have to live and breathe missions with moral purpose.

One of our favorite educational leaders, Michael Fullan (2002) describes moral purpose as social responsibility beyond our own organizations. According to Fullan,

> School leaders with moral purpose seek to make a difference in the lives of students. They are concerned about closing the gap between high-performing and lower-performing schools and raising the achievement of—and closing the gap between—high-performing and lower-performing students. They act with the intention of making a positive difference in their own schools as well as improving the environment in other district schools. (p. 17)

Our mission at Envision Education is to transform the lives of our students—particularly those who will be the first in their families to attend college—by preparing them for success in college, in careers, and in life. Our mission is an accurate reflection of the depth and breadth of our purpose. It has helped us maintain a focus for over ten years on what matters most: college, career, and life readiness.

Do you have a clear and compelling mission for your classroom? School? School system? How does your mission describe your moral purpose? In what ways can you use your mission to help you fulfill your purpose?

A Persistent Learning Stance

Learning is the core purpose of schools. In most schools today, we are focused on student learning. Adult learning tends to be sporadic, superficial, and often planned haphazardly. This represents a lack of commitment to learning for our teachers and leaders.

To achieve deeper learning outcomes, educators absolutely must create a learning community in which all members (students, teachers, parents, leaders) engage in learning. Leaders have to assume a persistent learning stance. Persistent learning means *sticking with it,* even when things get difficult.

At Envision Education, one of our four core values is persistent learning. Persistent learning means that we are determined and deliberate, and we learn from our successes and failures. Our learning makes us consistently smarter and stronger. We innovate. We never give up.

Through all the times we have faced challenges related to enrollment, budget, and retention, we have never given up. We believe that our persistent learning stance has created organizational resilience and contributed to our remarkable student outcomes.

What stance do you take? How engaged are you in learning? How do you respond to challenges and sticky problems?

(See Envision Core Values in the appendix.)

The Power of Staying

Leaders come and leaders go. The revolving door of principals and superintendents continues to turn, while fewer and fewer teachers consider school leadership a viable career option. Thus the shortage of leaders in our nation's schools and district continues to grow.

School leadership is considered an impossible job. In 2003, the Center for Reinventing Public Education (Fuller, Campbell, Celio, & Harvey, 2003) published a survey of urban superintendents describing the job as just that: impossible.

Achieving deeper learning outcomes takes time, and we need leaders with staying power who lead changes through all the phases of implementation. Unless leaders see changes through the institutionalization phase (that is, embedded within the structures and culture of an organization), it is highly likely that schools and districts will regress to old patterns and practices. This is the risk we run with the Common Core.

A big part of Bob's legacy at Envision Education is his staying power. Unlike many other CEOs, Bob has stayed with Envision since its inception and weathered many storms. Why? Because he is committed to Envision's mission, *not* just for our students but also for students across the nation. Across the years, he has redesigned Envision to adapt to the economic, political, and social landscape and the changing needs of our students, families, teachers, leaders, and communities. Part of these redesign efforts included adapting his own contribution to Envision. Over the years, he has transitioned from being a teacher to a principal to a consultant/trainer/coach to the CEO to the role he is in today, working to bring the Envision model to schools across the country as Envision Education's chief of innovation.

Bob's leadership journey has been full of expected and unexpected challenges, missteps, and opposition. Bob and Envision have persisted, leading to thousands of students going to college and finding success—most of them the first in their family to attend college.

Urging people to stay in an impossible job is not sound advice. The way around this problem is to leverage your leadership position toward designing a job that is not only *possible* but also a dream job. What would a school look like where you would want to learn, teach, and lead for a lifetime? Let that be your vision.

PRACTICAL ADVICE FOR LEADING FOR DEEPER LEARNING

It's time to get down to some brass tacks. These leadership tips have served Envision well over the years.

Pay as Much Attention to the How as to the What

Too often we spend too much time in schools paying attention to the technical aspects of a proposal for change—for example, the schedule, the project and unit plan templates, the advisory handbook. It isn't that the technical aspects are unimportant—they are critical; however, leaders need to bring their constituents along with them. When people feel that they have participated in the creation of change, they own the change. Leaders often shy away from large-scale participation because they want to avoid the messy and sometimes diluting process of seeking consensus. We have found that there are protocols and processes for change that not only make the outcomes better but also widen the circle of ownership.

Use RAPID Decision Making

At Envision Education, we use a decision-making process called RAPID, developed by the Harvard School of Business. RAPID stands for

Recommend. Some person or group makes a recommendation for change.

Agree. A designated leader has to agree with the potential decision or can veto the idea. This is often the most senior leader and/or group (for example, the superintendent or the board of trustees).

Perform. It is important to identify who will execute the work that will be generated by the decision. (How often do we forget to gather input from the people who will actually do the work?)

Input. If there is an opportunity for authentic input, people will relax their shoulders and provide their thoughts to their leaders. The leaders must be forthright that this is for input and be clear about who has the "D," or decision. Envision often uses a process called Fist to Five to gather input after laying out the implications of a possible change. At the conclusion of a presentation and discussion, constituents are asked to represent their level of support through the number of extended fingers on a raised hand:

Five: Total support

Four: Strong support

Three: Support

Two: Reservations

One: Strong reservations

Fist: Will actively oppose the change

Although this process does not require consensus, the leader might think twice about implementing a change — at least as currently imagined — when a significant number of the people are rating it at a two or lower. On the other hand, given an imperative for change, she might go forward, but at least she knows clearly where people stand.

Decide. It is vital to be clear about who has the "D"—who makes the decision. At Envision we try to push the D down as close as possible to where the work will happen. Ironically, we've discovered that people often don't want the D. They'd rather have someone else higher up be responsible for the D so that when there is a problem, they don't need to own it; the higher-up will deserve the blame. The hard part of leadership is not making decisions but working to empower others to make decisions. (See Decision Making at Envision Education in the appendix).

Establish Norms and Use Ground Rules

We believe that it is critical for groups to establish norms for meetings (and in classrooms). The Envision norms are

- Listen and be respectful
- Be present: no other devices or work
- Silence equals agreement (so voice your concern in the meeting)
- Step up or step back—we need to hear all voices

We have also found that our "ground rules"—adopted from the consultant Susan Edsil—have been instrumental in helping us conduct more productive meetings. (See Ground Rules for Meetings in the appendix.)

Plan Every Meeting as a Well-Designed Lesson

Every meeting and interaction—no matter how big or how small—is an opportunity to move a school's vision forward. Leaders can tend to look only to the big meetings or high-profile events as the times to communicate about changes at the school. The fact is that every team meeting in the conference room, every one-to-one appointment in an office, every interaction in the hall, and every visit to a classroom is an opportunity to move a school's vision forward. Leaders must know their message and repeat their mantras ("We go slow to go fast," "We are about the mission—college success," and so on). They must also *live* the message, and one easy but often overlooked way to do this is to make sure that all meetings and interactions model the mission and values of the organization.

This means no more "sit and get" or "spray and pray" professional development. No more PowerPoint stand-and-deliver staff meetings that could be replaced by an email update (and are treated by staff members as an opportunity to get updated on their email). A leader for deeper learning is the school's lead teacher. If the school is to be holonomous, then adult learning must reflect what we want to see happen for student learning. Every meeting, big or small, should be mapped to explicit outcomes and structured like a good lesson — that is, learner centered, inquiry based, and engaging. Meetings are one of the leader's best leverage points for establishing holonomy. (See our Meeting Agenda Template in the appendix.)

We are huge fans of the National School Reform Faculty (NSRF) and its resources at the Harmony Education Center (www.nsrfharmony.org). When we need to facilitate a meeting, we go to its resource guide to find the right protocol or process for the outcome we seek. We train all of our staff to use these protocols.

One process that is a staple for us is the Tuning Protocol, which we use to vet project drafts, schedules, professional development agendas — just about anything that we want feedback on. We often find that the process itself provides new insights to the presenters and those giving feedback. (See the NSRF Tuning Protocol Guidelines in the appendix.)

Go Slow to Go Fast

Visionary leaders have a strong sense of urgency — as they should. But this can be a huge pitfall if the leaders are too far in front of their constituents. Many leaders move too fast, and their reforms fail. Initiating the same change a second time is next to impossible. Paradoxically, these leaders' sense of urgency has doomed the change they hoped to make. By taking time to build capacity and widen ownership, leaders strengthen the chance of the change taking root; and, to borrow an analogy from Jim Collins's seminal business leadership book, *Good to Great* (2001), once the flywheel is spinning, the rate of change speeds up and is hard to stop. Going slow to go fast can feel counterintuitive, but all great change leaders know how to balance urgency with capacity building.

Keep It Simple

The Envision Education three-year strategic plan is three pages long. We believe that organizations spend way too much time creating long and complex strategic plans that are almost incomprehensible to any but the small committees that created them. Once again, we applaud the urgency that leaders bring to implementing change, but attacking all parts of a system at the same time can result in no change at all.

We think of change as a river of good outcomes that has been blocked by the dam of unintended consequences or institutional inertia. There's a choice: we can take down the dam stone by stone, or we can be strategic — thus the name "strategic plan" — and pick out three to five stones whose removal will unleash the energy of the river and move the entire organization forward. These become the focus, the message, and the mantras.

The collective energy of the organization, school, and even classroom gets focused on a few powerful keystones for change.

Leaders also need to scaffold change. When changing the schedule of a school to longer blocks, successful leaders have already built the capacity for teachers to use that time with project-based learning and performance assessment—they do not wait until after the schedule is implemented to begin professional development. When implementing deeper learning assessment, successful leaders start with one outcome and build the capacity for teachers and schools to implement that one outcome well. Once they have one down, they can add another, and so forth.

Hold a Vision of Success *and* Plan for Every Pothole

As we noted earlier, strategic plans have a 50-50 chance of success. They are just that—a "plan." But no matter what happens, we have a 100 percent chance of learning and adjusting the plan as we go. It's the great odds of the latter that ultimately bring success.

When planning for a deeper learning transformation, create a clear and compelling picture of the successful outcome—both for yourself and for those you lead. Tell the story of the future with clarity, detail, and joy. But also figure out everything that can go wrong—every pitfall, every detour, every curmudgeonly obstacle—in your control and outside your control.

We like to use Edward de Bono's Thinking Hats ("Six Thinking Hats," 2014) to leverage the power of a group—its multiple points of view—in planning for the worst while expecting the best. Learn more about this protocol at www.debonogroup.com /six_thinking_hats.php

Don't Forget to Have Fun

Heed the advice of Bruce Springsteen (Bob's musical hero):

> So rumble, young musicians, rumble. Open your ears and open your hearts. Don't take yourself too seriously, and take yourself as seriously as death itself. Don't worry. Worry your ass off. Have ironclad confidence, but doubt—it keeps you awake and alert … And when you walk on stage tonight to bring the noise, treat it like it's all we have. And then remember, it's only rock and roll. (2012)

Of course, education—the work of transforming lives—is not rock and roll. But educators, just like musicians, must live this paradox: to achieve success in this serious work, we can't take ourselves too seriously—the leaders most of all.

The following are some of the techniques that we at Envision use to keep it fun (and poke fun at ourselves):

- Use art with your team to make meaning. (It can be finger paint.)
- Sing songs.
- Play hokey games to start meetings or as energizer breaks — the leader needs to model these. (Picture Bob leading a conga line while wearing a banana suit.)
- Tell personal stories as a team — the leader needs to tell his first.
- Have meals together.
- Make meals together.
- Go off-site.
- Go on a retreat.

If we take ourselves too seriously, people will not follow. If we don't have fun along the way, we'll give up before we reach our goals.

REFERENCES

Collins, J. (2001). *Good to great: Why some companies make the leap — and others don't*. New York, NY: HarperBusiness.

Costa, A. L., & Garmston, R. J. (2002). *Cognitive coaching: A foundation for Renaissance schools* (2nd ed.). Norwood, MA: Christopher-Gordon.

Costa, A. L., & Kallick, B. (1995). Systems thinking: Interactive assessment in holonomous organizations. In A. L. Costa & B. Kallick (Eds.), *Assessment in the learning organization: Shifting the paradigm* (pp. 3–7). Alexandria, VA: Association for Supervision and Curriculum Development.

Fullan, M. (2002). The change leader. *Educational Leadership, 59*(8), 16–20.

Fuller, H., Campbell, C., Celio, M., & Harvey, J. (2003). *An impossible job? The view from the urban superintendent's chair*. Seattle, WA: Center for Reinventing Public Education.

Gardner, H. (1996). *Leading minds: An anatomy of leadership*. New York, NY: BasicBooks.

Koestler, A. (1974). *The roots of coincidence*. London, England: Pan Books.

Six thinking hats. (2014, May 23). The de Bono Group. Retrieved from http://www.debonogroup.com/six_thinking_hats.php

Springsteen, B. (2012, March 28). Exclusive: The complete text of Bruce Springsteen's SXSW keynote address. *Rolling Stone*. Retrieved from http://www.rollingstone.com/music/news/exclusive-the-complete-text-of-bruce-springsteens-sxsw-keynote-address-20120328#ixzz3DQFJB

Chapter 7

A Call to Action

> I used to feel forced to learn. Now I feel privileged.
>
> — Stazanea Tidwell, Envision graduate, reflecting on her
> deeper learning education

Doctor and writer Atul Gawande (2013), in an article he wrote for the *New Yorker* magazine, describes how two 19th-century innovations transformed the practice of medicine, one rapidly and the other slowly. Anesthesia using ether spread quickly. Its initial use was first documented in October and November of 1846, and by June 1847, ether was being used to anesthetize patients throughout the entire world. By contrast, a Scottish surgeon determined in 1867 that surgeons could stop the spread of sepsis — the infections that often occurred following surgery — by washing their hands. Sepsis was a serious problem: it was a leading cause of death in the late 19th century. Yet it took over a generation for hand washing to become standard practice among doctors. Gawande reflects:

> In our era of electronic communications, we've come to expect that important innovations will spread quickly. Plenty do: think of in-vitro fertilization, genomics, and communications technologies themselves. But there's an equally long list of vital innovations that have failed to catch on. The puzzle is why.

He proposes that although both changes benefited patients, the use of anesthesia benefited doctors as well, and the positive effects were immediate: Who wants to perform surgery on a screaming and writhing patient? Ether transformed the surgical process from one of chaos to one of order. By contrast, hand washing demanded that doctors radically change their practices and think differently about their profession, all for the sake of a change whose effects would not be immediately apparent. They resisted, so the change was slow.

If we think of deeper learning as a "treatment" for what ails education in this country, then the history of hand washing suggests the challenges we face. Transforming schools through performance assessment and PBL requires more work by educators (at least initially) and a significant change in practice at all levels, with the positive effects of this treatment not readily visible. But like a surgeon washing her hands, this investment of time, resources, and commitment will save lives.

Deeper learning isn't new. Many of the principles and strategies discussed in this book have been around at least since John Dewey advocated for more engaged and democratic learning over one hundred years ago. In the 1980s, Ted Sizer rekindled and advanced the cause of deeper learning with his book *Horace's Compromise* (1985) and his founding of the Coalition of Essential Schools. And since the 1990s, educational organizations around the country, including Envision Education and our Deeper Learning Network colleagues—High Tech High, Big Picture Learning, Expeditionary Learning, Internationals Network for Public Schools, New Tech Network, EdVisions, Asia Society, New Visions, and ConnectEd—have been redesigning schools, employing deeper learning strategies, and achieving positive results.

Given its one hundred years of history, it seems clear that deeper learning is on the hand washing—not the ether—timeline. On first take, this is disheartening. When we know what's right, we want the doors of potential flung open for all children all at once. Anything less feels tragic.

But we mustn't be demoralized by the pace of change. On the contrary, the hand washing story should provide hope and inspire commitment. Because they never gave up, proponents of hand washing ultimately persuaded a massive change in medicine across the industrialized countries of the world, effectively transforming surgery from a game of Russian roulette into a practice that saves millions of lives.

That social process continues today, because antiseptic hygiene is still not widespread practice in many parts of the world. "Person-by-person" efforts are slowly changing how nurses deliver babies in remote parts of India. It takes "sandals on the ground," as

Gawande puts it: repeat visits by disciplined emissaries whose social skills are as important as their technical training.

This is also at the heart of our efforts to spread deeper learning far and wide. Technology, social media, big message campaigns, incentive programs for teachers—all of these have their place in this social change movement. But real change will happen when teachers talk to teachers, when principals talk to principals, and finally when superintendents and other decision makers join the conversation. When personal connections are made, personal choices follow; to transform education, the deeper learning movement needs these personal connections. Like Gawande, we cite Everett Rogers (1995), the great scholar of diffusion, who concludes that "people talking to people" is how innovation spreads (Rogers, 2002, p. 990).

We encourage everyone who believes in deeper learning to talk and keep talking. Tell the story of that one student who changed the way you teach or whom you were able to help because of a deeper learning strategy you tried. Find out what your colleagues are doing: listen to them, learn from them, and support them in the challenges they face. Ask lots of questions. Nurture a wide range of relationships. Remember that teachers share the same goal: to give students what they need to imagine and achieve bright futures. Foster those conversations that will help you and your colleagues improve classroom practices and redesign schools so that students can do exactly that. The greatest strategy we have for transforming education is to develop strong relationships through which we can share the deeper learning story.

TAKING ACTION: TIME TO START A MOVEMENT

This book has tried to make a case and serve as a guide for transforming your classroom, your school, and your school system. But let's concede: easier said than done.

If you are feeling the way we have often felt at various stages in our work, you are wondering, "Where do I begin?" As is so often true with any long journey or challenging undertaking, the hard part is not imagining the destination but figuring out how to take that first step.

Here are three suggestions. Depending on your role and your context, pick one of these as a starting point that could work for you:

- Set a goal of creating at least **one deep learning experience per year** for your students.
- Initiate the development of a **graduate profile** with your school community.

- Spearhead **one structural change** to your school that could help shift the school culture.

Where to Begin Idea #1: Ensure at Least One Deep Learning Experience per Year

Our colleague from Expeditionary Learning, Ron Berger (2014), tells a story of his parents' trip to Europe. Using train passes, they visited fourteen countries in twelve days. Ron wishes that his parents had stayed in one country for three or four days. That would have still given them eight days for eight or nine other countries, but they would have had one deeper experience, an opportunity to immerse themselves in one country's culture, food, and people.

Ron believes, and so do we, that travelers and learners benefit when they slow down and go deep, at least for part of the journey.

If you believe in deeper learning, there isn't a more fundamental way to begin than this: give students at least one deep learning experience per year. You do not have to wait for your school to be redesigned or for all colleagues to buy in. A single teacher and her students can step off the train and spend some time going deep with at least one project or complex performance assessment.

Here are some examples:

- Build a class website on a particular topic.
- Hold an evening symposium where students present their papers.
- Participate in a science fair — local or online.
- Have a debate.
- Hold a poetry slam.
- Make something and participate in a Maker Faire.
- Learn to code and create an app or game.
- Put on a play dramatizing something learned.
- Conduct an experiment outside the school's walls.
- Curate an exhibit of photographs.
- Create lesson plans for younger students, then go teach them.

> For more ideas on how to design deeper learning experiences for your students, see chapter 3 on PBL.

Do not underestimate the power of just doing it and hoping it catches on. Bob's deeper learning journey started when he was inspired by the work of a colleague. A pocket of deeper learning is often the starting point for school transformation. It's hard to build the case for deeper learning if it's not happening somewhere in the building. If you are a teacher, start in your classroom. If you are a school leader, start by encouraging at least one of your like-minded teachers to make this commitment.

Just remember: taking on depth, even a little, means sacrificing some breadth. It means seeing fewer countries. Accepting this trade-off can be difficult, but refusing to accept it makes deeper learning impossible.

Where to Begin Idea #2: Develop a Graduate Profile for Your School

If your school doesn't have a graduate profile, then another good place to start the deeper learning journey is to appeal to the school community to develop one, a collective pronouncement of what every student will know and be able to do by the time he or she graduates.

> See chapter 1 for our in-depth discussion of graduate profiles.

If people ask why a graduate profile is needed, what it offers beyond the school's already existing motto or mission statement, cite the converging forces — the new century, the new economy, new state standards — that challenge us to set goals for our students that are more specific and more up-to-date.

Assemble voices from across the community — students, teachers, and parents — for this dialogue on what is needed to prepare students for their futures. The process of developing a graduate profile is as powerful as the product. Developed thoughtfully and collaboratively, a graduate profile can be the North Star for everyone in the community, pointing self-evidently and steadfastly to the need for deeper learning.

Where to Begin Idea #3: Spearhead One Structural Change at Your School

This book has argued that for learning to go deep and stay there, schools need wholesale changes in culture and in structure.

> Pick one of the school structures discussed in chapter 5 and then organize a movement to make that structural change.

Sometimes it's easier to change a structure than it is to change everybody's mind, at least at first. Indeed, it often works that a structural shift is what creates the possibility for a shift in culture, because the new arrangement of time and space opens new ways of seeing. An advisory program, for example, allows students and teachers to relate to and view each other differently, laying the groundwork for subsequent changes.

Other structures that can be leveraged for deeper learning include a block schedule that would facilitate PBL, weekly time for teacher collaboration, or any kind of organized student internship opportunity. Choose one for which you think your school is ripe.

You don't have to be a school leader to implement a structural change. An enterprising teacher (or student or parent) is often the catalyst behind a successful internship program, an annual learning exhibition, or an innovative bell schedule.

Whenever spearheading change, be ready to communicate the why and the how. Rehearse a persuasive explanation for why this change will deepen learning for students. Prepare a detailed plan for how it could work logistically.

"IS IT SCALABLE?"

Whether seeing our schools firsthand or hearing us talk about them, educational leaders, after expressing admiration, usually voice their doubt in the form of a question: "This is impressive, but is it scalable?"

Translation: "This looks hard. Isn't there an easier way?"

What people mean by "scalable," we've come to believe, is the desire for a solution that feels easier, simpler, automatic, even "human-proof."

We hear it's the same in medicine. Writing about the work of teaching lifesaving childbirth practices in India, Gawande observes, "The most common objection is that, even if it works, this kind of one-on-one, on-site mentoring 'isn't scalable.'" He counters that scalable is the "one thing it surely is," pointing to comparable sea changes in medicine, farming, and education (namely, improvement in the world's literacy rate) that have been achieved only through massive societal investment and hundreds of thousands of foot soldiers. These campaigns remind us that scalable is not synonymous with inexpensive or effortless.

If one school can transform the lives of a few hundred students, then two schools can transform twice that, and three schools can triple the number. And if a district can transform the lives of thousands of students, then two districts can … you get the idea. We don't have to wonder if deeper learning is scalable; look to the organizations that have already proven it: Expeditionary Learning, Asia Society, High Tech High, New Tech Network. All of them have scaled deeper learning; none of them would say that it has been easy or that it ever will be.

Gawande writes:

> In the era of the iPhone, Facebook, and Twitter, we've become enamored of ideas that spread as effortlessly as ether. We want frictionless, "turnkey" solutions to the major difficulties of the world—hunger, disease, poverty. We prefer instructional videos to teachers, drones to troops, incentives to institutions. People and institutions can feel messy and anachronistic. They introduce, as the engineers put it, uncontrolled variability.

If there is any field that should be accepting of "uncontrolled variability," it's education. We are in the business of developing human potential. We can't—and shouldn't ever try to—avoid the messiness that comes with a focus on human beings. "Growing adults," as John Merrow (2012) pithily sums up the purpose of education, will always be hard work.

So is it scalable? Our answer to the explicit question is "Yes."

Our answer to the implicit question is "No, there isn't an easier way."

PERFECT STORM

To acknowledge that our movement requires effort, patience, and perseverance is not to say that the pace of change can't or won't accelerate. Margaret Wheatley and Deborah Frieze (2006) argue that large-scale changes do not happen from the top down. Instead, they happen through small local actions, which become connected across systems through sharing and learning. This process, which Wheatley and Frieze call "emergence," can gather tremendous collective power to change a large system.

These small local actions can eventually converge into a "perfect storm" (Wheatley & Frieze, 2006). We cannot predict when they will converge, nor can we estimate the magnitude of the storm's power. When the storm hits, though, we feel its tremendous power. Previously incremental, change becomes suddenly sweeping.

Signs abound that deeper learning is gathering energy for such a perfect storm. For the last twenty years, we have had small local actions in classrooms, schools, and districts promoting the integration of deeper learning skills, performance assessment, and project-based instruction aligned to standards. Increasingly, we are sharing and learning across systems. The Deeper Learning Network is a notable example. EdLeader21 has created another network of over 130 districts committed to teaching 21st Century Skills. The Buck Institute for Education, dedicated to promoting PBL across the world, is growing by leaps and bounds.

Meanwhile, the Common Core and next generation assessments have accelerated the emergence of deeper learning. Despite their political volatility, the Common Core standards, by redefining for our nation what it means to be "college and career ready," have shifted America's pedagogical emphasis from knowing to doing and ratcheted performance assessment into the mainstream. States that opt out of either the Common Core or the testing consortia aren't going to dust off and reinstate their No Child Left Behind–era content standards. Expect cosmetically modified, state-branded versions of the Common Core or, promisingly, standards and assessments that push beyond the Common Core, swinging the pendulum farther toward performance assessment.

Deeper learning is emerging at the university level as well. The Degree Qualifications Profile, which defines what college graduates are expected to know for work, citizenship, global participation, and life, is being piloted across the nation. Colleges such as Alverno and Sarah Lawrence are using performance assessments in lieu of standardized tests. Other colleges are challenging the hegemony of the SAT test. Lewis and Clark College accepts applicants based on submitted portfolios of college-ready work. Bard College has its own performance-based entrance examination that measures applicants' research writing skills. In teacher education programs all over the country, aspiring teachers must demonstrate their readiness to run a classroom through a portfolio-based performance assessment known as the edTPA, which not only increases the rigor of credentialing but also models deeper learning to thousands of young educators. In 2014, California State University's CalStateTEACH program incorporated into its curriculum *PBL in the Elementary Grades* (published by the Buck Institute for Education, 2011) and will require its elementary teacher candidates to create and implement a project-based unit as part of their training.

All of these pockets of deeper learning are spreading and connecting. The more they do, the more we can anticipate a moment when deeper learning tips from emergence to convergence—the perfect storm. We must continue to treat this as a gritty, long-term campaign. But what has so far been changing at the pace of hand washing could suddenly start spreading like ether.

Let the promise of a deeper learning storm help motivate us.

A STORY TO CLOSE ON

While writing this book, we sometimes used Facebook to reach out to Envision alums and gather their reflections on their Envision school experience from their post–high school perspective. Far and away the most thoughtful and often flattering responses to these posts consistently came from a former student named Kyle Zunino.

"College was where I discovered just how much [Envision] impacted my life," Kyle writes, a recurring theme in his posts. In another, he says, "Overall, I am glad I [was there] to attain those project-based skills. It is something that I wish I had appreciated more at the time because [Envision] highly resembled the classroom structure of many of my college courses."

Kyle's posts delighted us. They also surprised us. Kyle did not graduate from an Envision school. A member of Envision's very first cohort of students, he was a decent if sometimes distracted student for his first two years of high school. Then, in his junior year, he checked out. Apathy deteriorated into truancy. Concerned, we tried a number of interventions, but before the year was out, Kyle stopped coming to school completely.

We learned years later, while interviewing Kyle for this book because we were so intrigued by his Facebook posts, that we were right to be worried about him. After dropping out of high school, Kyle spent a couple of years in a dark place. He dealt drugs, got arrested, and was convicted of a felony.

The judge gave him a stark choice: three years of prison or a probation requiring attendance at a community college. Kyle was glad to avoid prison, but he recalls that he wasn't thrilled about the prospect of going back to school, which he considered "not applicable" to his life. Still, he showed up and turned in assignments, if only to meet the requirements of his probation.

Then one day, an anthropology professor, Michelle Markovics, asked Kyle to stay after class. "I've read some of your stuff, and I appreciate how you think and write," she said. "I am wondering if you'd like to be a TA for this class."

"That moment changed my life," Kyle recalls. "It was like she held up a mirror to me, and suddenly I saw myself in a different way."

From then on, Kyle cared about school. He read what he was assigned. He wrote essays in advance so he had time to edit them. He started talking to his professors. He started getting A's in everything. After a couple of years of this, he sent a Facebook message to Justin, his high school English teacher, and asked him to review an application essay he had just written. Kyle was applying for a transfer from his community college into UC Berkeley.

The essay told the same story we are telling you here, and it was compellingly written. Between that and his stellar grades, Kyle had a strong application. UC Berkeley accepted him as a junior. Obsessed with social theory, he poured himself into his studies at Berkeley. At the end of his first semester there, he proudly posted to his Facebook page a screenshot of his grades: straight A's.

Dedicated teachers everywhere love to tell stories like Kyle's, the story of the comeback kid, that student whom you didn't think you reached but later makes good and returns to thank you for it. "I will say that the seeds sown by [Envision] really flowered later in my life," Kyle wrote to us in one of his posts, and of course it makes us proud that he thinks so.

But we are not telling Kyle's story to take credit for his success. Let's be honest: Kyle is an anomaly. We all know what the prospects are for the vast majority of high school dropouts; making a comeback and landing at a prestigious university aren't the norm. Statistically speaking, Kyle represented a failure for us. He was part of our dropout rate, and as soon as he went into that column, he was never tracked again. His later success never belonged to us (nor do we think it should).

Kyle's story reminds us that statistical measurements can't tell the entire story of deeper learning. We say that even though we have enormous pride in our statistics, especially the ones that matter most to us. Hardly any students drop out of our schools, 100 percent of the students who graduate are eligible to attend university, and the college persistence rates for Envision's low-income students of color are seven times their peers and equal to middle-class whites. We believe that Envision Education exemplifies a model of schooling that achieves remarkable results through the integration of performance assessment and PBL. We hope that this book has communicated our passion for our school design and made the case for why we think it works.

We also hope that you don't mistake our passion for overconfidence. Empirical evidence can mask both successes and failures. Our failures have been many. Our vision is still evolving. Our schools are works in progress. The successes we've had can be frustratingly impermanent. The quality of our PBL ebbs and flows. School culture can feel healthy, then you turn your attention to the next thing and it falters. The work is hard, and it's never done.

The reality of this impermanence is what makes deeper learning so important and so powerful. When learning is deep, it is buffered from the stormy and changeable surface of things. That's why it stays with you, and why it can resurface again still intact, as it did for Kyle. What has been consistent at our schools through all the highs and lows — and ultimately the key to our success — is that when asked about their academic experience, our students have stories to tell: about memorable projects, the challenge and triumph of graduate defenses, eye-opening internships, relationships with teachers that they were able to build over multiple years. "Deeper learning is learning you can tell a story about": for us, this continues to be as useful a definition as any.

By Kyle's analysis, the deeper learning at Envision gave him a lot before he left, and came to serve him well later. But Kyle never defended a graduation portfolio at an Envision school. He left Envision before he got what he needed most: a belief in himself. He would need some other deeper learning experiences to forge his academic identity. Fortunately for Kyle, a professor took notice of him, respected his intellect, and held up that mirror.

Transformative learning doesn't have to be a function of fortune. Schools can be designed to transform lives.

Video 21. Sha'nice—Nasty Attitude to Bright Future

One student's transformation from having a "nasty attitude" to having a bright future! Sha'nice talks about coming to Envision "not ready for life" and then graduating ready to take on new challenges.

REFERENCES

Berger, R. (2014, April 7). Getting off the train in Italy [Blog post]. *Education Week*. Retrieved from http://blogs.edweek.org/edweek/learning_deeply/2014/04/getting_off_the_train_in_italy.html

Gawande, A. (2013, July 29). Slow ideas. *New Yorker*. Retrieved from http://www.newyorker.com/reporting/2013/07/29/130729fa_fact_gawande

Merrow, J. (2012, March 2). Digital natives, or digital citizens? [Blog post]. Retrieved from http://takingnote.learningmatters.tv/?p=5629

Rogers, E. M. (1995). *Diffusion of innovations* (4th ed.). New York, NY: Free Press.

Rogers, E. M. (2002). Diffusion of preventive innovations. *Addictive Behaviors, 27,* 989–993.

Sizer, T. R. (1985). *Horace's compromise: The dilemma of the American high school.* Boston, MA: Houghton Mifflin.

Wheatley, M., & Frieze, D. (2006). How large-scale change really happens—Working with emergence. Retrieved from http://www.margaretwheatley.com/articles/largescalechange.html

Appendix

Supplementary Material

1. Envision Schools Course Syllabus Template

2. Envision Schools College Success Portfolio Performance Task Requirements: Scientific Inquiry

3. Envision Schools College Success Portfolio Performance Task: English Language Arts Textual Analysis

4. What Is the Most Effective Method for Cleaning Oil, Dispersants or Absorbents?

5. Envision Schools College Success Portfolio Performance Assessment: Creative Expression

6. Performance Assessment Planning Template

7. SCALE Performance Assessment Quality Rubric

8. Envision Project Planning Template

9. Envision Sample Daily Schedule

10. 9th Grade Envision Schools Advisory Curriculum

11. The Six A's of Designing Projects

12. Project Sharing Protocol

13. City Arts and Tech High Shool Holistic Grading Rubric

14. Envision Core Values

15. Decision Making at Envision Schools

16. Ground Rules for Meetings

17. Meeting Agenda Template

18. NSRF Tuning Protocol Guidelines

ENVISION SCHOOLS
COURSE SYLLABUS TEMPLATE

Course Title:

Teacher:

Email:

School Phone:

Course Overview: This is a short narrative that explains the general scope and ideas behind the class.

Essential Questions/Themes of Course: Here you will list the overarching essential questions and/or themes that the course will cover during the year.

Outcomes & Alignment with CA Content Standards: This is where you list the outcomes that students will be able to have completed by the end of the course. Outcomes are both **skills** and **content** that students will work towards mastery over the course of the year. Think of this as academic skills that students need to master AND the academic goals/content that students are expected to master. You should use the Envision Schools Graduation Portfolio Outcomes as a guide for this.

You may want to set this up in a table that shows the specific skills and related CA content standards related to your course outcomes. When outlining these outcomes, include the skill and the ways in which students might demonstrate that skill; however, you do not need to input every assignment, assessment, or project you will assign during the year. In some cases, the CA standard will tie directly with the expressed outcome. Other times the related CA content standards might be the area within the sequence of your curriculum where students will work toward the specific outcome.

For example:

Outcomes (Know and Do)	Related CA Content Standards
Analyze a historical event using a documentary or written essay	History 10.2-4: short recap of standard narrative

ENVISION SCHOOLS
COURSE SYLLABUS TEMPLATE

Graduation Portfolio Alignment/Leadership Skills: This is where you will specifically address the components of the Envision Schools Graduation Portfolio that can be met within the course work. You want to be as specific as possible as to which outcomes in the course will align with the required portions of the portfolio. Within this category, you will want to also consider which Leadership Skills your course will highlight. As these are included in the Graduation Portfolio, you want to be explicit about how Leadership Skills will fit into the work that students do.

Assessment, Exhibition, and Reflection: This section provides information related to how students will be assessed in the course. You want to provide examples of assessment, exhibition, and reflection connected to the Outcomes (listed above). However, you may also want to list "general" examples of assessment and/or exhibitions (essays with topics listed, documentaries, etc). You can refer to rubrics that exist or that will exist. You also want to explain ways in which students will reflect on their learning, since this is directly connected to the Envision Schools philosophy of Academic Rigor.

Grading System: This section should outline your specific grading system. *(You may decide to combine or incorporate this section with the Assessment, Exhibition, and Reflection section.)* You will want to outline the Envision Schools Grading Philosophy, explaining the three different grades that students will receive at each quarter (Academic Achievement, Leadership Skills, and Student Work Skills). You should then want to specifically explain how your projects, demonstrations, tests, quizzes, "homework", etc., within the course align to the ES grading system. You'll want to explain your policies related to late work, extensions, and classroom expectations. This is not necessarily the place to include percentages/breakdowns unless you have a system that uses these within the three different grading areas.

Course Outline: This section consists of a brief outline of the major units of study included within the course. You can be as specific as you'd like, but be sure to remember that although the outline will give a general sense of the course and sequence of the class, it is not set in stone.

Course Materials/Texts: This section can be used to provide students and parents with information about specific materials, texts, and other items that will be used within the class.

Other: This section is for you to add items to the Syllabus that have not been covered above. Of course, you'd want to change the title "other" to reflect the section more accurately.

Envision Schools
Course Syllabus Template

Parent/Guardian Sign Off

Directions: Parents/Guardians, please sign below to acknowledge that you've read and understand the above course syllabus. If you have any questions, please feel free to contact the teacher listed at the top of the page.

Parent/Guardian Printed Name _____

Student Printed Name_____

Parent/Guardian Signed _____

Date_____

To demonstrate their mastery of the Inquiry competency in science, students must select a project that that embodies the following performance outcomes:

INITIATING THE INQUIRY:

What is the evidence that the student can formulate questions that can be explored by scientific investigations as well as articulate a testable hypothesis?

- Asks empirically testable, scientific questions
- Constructs drawings, diagrams, or models to represent what's being investigated
- Explains limitations and precision of model as representation of the system or process
- Formulates a testable hypothesis that is directly related to the question asked

PLANNING AND CARRYING OUT INVESTIGATIONS:

What is the evidence that the student can design and perform investigations to explore natural phenomena?

- Designs controlled experiments (with multiple trials) to test the suggested hypothesis
- Identifies and explains the independent and dependent variables in the hypothesis
- Clearly communicates the details of the procedures so that they can be replicated by another group of students
- Creates a detailed and clear data collection method for all trials
- Conducts multiple trials

REPRESENTING, ANALYZING, AND INTERPRETING THE DATA

What is the evidence that the student can organize, analyze, and interpret the data?

- Organizes the data in tables and/or graphs
- Expresses relationships and quantities (units) using mathematical conventions
- Explains mathematical computation results in relationship to the expected outcome
- Analyzes and interprets the data and finds patterns
- Draws inferences from the data
- Suggests strengths or weaknesses in inferences from which further investigation could result

CONSTRUCTING EVIDENCE-BASED ARGUMENTS AND COMMUNICATING CONCLUSIONS

What is the evidence that the student can articulate evidence-based explanations and effectively communicate conclusions?

- Constructs a scientific argument, explaining how data and acceptable scientific theory support the claim
- Identifies a counter-claim (possible weaknesses in scientific argument or in one's own argument)
- Provides multiple representations to communicate conclusions (words, tables, diagrams, graphs, and/or mathematical expressions)
- Draws conclusions with specific discussion of limitations
- Uses language and tone appropriate to the purpose and audience
- Follows conventions of scientific writing, including accurate use of scientific/technical terms, quantitative data, and visual representations

REFLECTION

What is the evidence that the student can deeply reflect on performance, growth as a learner, and ability to apply this in the future?

- Knows: Explains goals, purpose, and academic skills of artifact
- Does: Explains process, decisions, and Leadership Skills used
- Reflects: Describes impact of artifact on self, future, and growth as a scientist

Envision Schools College Success Portfolio Performance Assessment: *SCIENTIFIC INQUIRY*

Scoring Domain	Emerging	E/D	Developing	D/P	Proficient	P/A	Advanced
INITIATION OF THE INQUIRY *What is the evidence that the student can formulate questions that can be explored by scientific investigations and articulate a testable hypothesis?*	• The inquiry question is stated in general terms • Background information is limited or irrelevant • The student articulates a prediction, but it has limited relationship to the question under investigation		• The inquiry question is stated in specific terms • Background information is relevant to the question, but is not well organized • The student articulates a relevant prediction of the expected results, but with no explanation		• The inquiry question is specific and testable. • Background information is relevant and well organized. • The student articulates a prediction to the investigated question, with some description of the involved variables ("if…then…" hypothesis)		• The inquiry question is specific, testable, and challenging • Background information is relevant and well organized and provides insight into the inquiry. • The student articulates a possible explanation to the investigated question and a clear description of the expected relationships among the involved variables (*"if…then…because…" hypothesis*)

Scoring Domain	Emerging	E/D	Developing	D/P	Proficient	P/A	Advanced
DESIGN OF EXPERIMENTAL PROCEDURES *What is the evidence that the student can design and perform investigations to explore natural phenomena?*	• The experimental design is not relevant for the stated question • The lab procedures are vague and difficult to follow • The data collection methods are vague and difficult to follow • The inquiry design doesn't allow control of the independent variable		• The experimental design is partially related to the stated question • The lab procedures are detailed but incomplete • The data collection methods are detailed but incomplete • The inquiry design allows for control of one variable and measurement of one dependent variable		• The experimental design matches the stated question • The lab procedures are detailed and clear • The data collection methods are detailed and clear • The inquiry design allows for control of all involved variables and measurement of the dependent variable		• The experimental design matches the stated question and shows innovation • The lab procedures are detailed, clear, and logical • The data collection methods are detailed, clear, and logical • The inquiry design allows for control of all involved variables and valid measurement of the dependent variable

Scoring Domain	Emerging	E/D	Developing	D/P	Proficient	P/A	Advanced
DATA COLLECTION, ANALYSIS, PRESENTATION, AND INTERPRETATION *What is the evidence that the student can organize and analyze the data?*	• Data are based on one trial only • Data tables are limited and graphs contain inaccuracies • Data analysis and interpretation are inaccurate or irrelevant		• Data are based on one trial only • Data tables and graphs are presented, but they may be poorly organized • Data analysis and interpretation are relevant, but not necessarily accurate		• Data are collected from several repetitions of the experiment • Data tables and graphs are accurate and appropriately organized • Data analysis and interpretation are accurate and relevant to the inquiry questions		• Data are collected from several repetitions of the experiment and are consistent within a reasonable range • Data tables and graphs are accurate and expertly organized and presented • Data analysis and interpretation are thorough and directly related to the inquiry question

Scoring Domain	Emerging	E/D	Developing	D/P	Proficient	P/A	Advanced
Conclusions and Discussion *What is the evidence that the student can interpret the data, draw conclusions, and assess the validity of the conclusions?*	• The conclusions are not consistent with the data • Limited sources of experimental errors are identified • New relevant questions are not posed		• The conclusions are based on the data • Sources of experimental errors are identified, but their impact is not discussed • New questions are posed but are not relevant		• The conclusions are clear and consistent with the data • The impact of possible sources of experimental errors on the results is discussed • New relevant questions are posed		• The conclusions are clear, consistent with the data and compared to data from professional literature • The impact of possible sources of experimental errors on the results is discussed and solutions are offered to minimize future errors • New relevant questions and suggestions for further research are developed

Scoring Domain	Emerging	E/D	Developing	D/P	Proficient	P/A	Advanced
CONVENTIONS *What is the evidence that the student can accurately use scientific conventions to communicate ideas to others?*	• Language and tone are inappropriate to the purpose and audience • Attempts to follow the norms and conventions of scientific writing with major, consistent errors, for example in the use of scientific/ technical terms, quantitative data, or visual representations		• Language and tone are appropriate to the purpose and audience with minor lapses • Follows the norms and conventions of scientific writing with consistent minor errors, for example, in the use of scientific or technical terms, quantitative data, or visual representations		• Language and tone are appropriate to the purpose and audience • Follows the norms and conventions of scientific writing including accurate use of scientific/ technical terms, quantitative data, and visual representations		• Language and tone are appropriate to the purpose and audience • Consistently follows the norms and conventions of scientific writing, including accurate use of scientific/ technical terms, quantitative data, and visual representations

Scoring Domain	Emerging	E/D	Developing	D/P	Proficient	P/A	Advanced
REFLECTION *What is the evidence that the student can deeply reflect on performance, growth as a learner and ability to apply this in the future?*	• Know: Explains the topic of class when artifact was assigned • Do: Explanation of process, decision-making, and Leadership Skills is incomplete or unclear • Reflect: States what was done well and what could be improved upon		• Know: Describes some context of class (learning goals, purpose of artifact, or necessary skills) • Do: Briefly explains process, decision-making, and Leadership Skills used during the task • Reflect: Explains how artifact impacted self as a learner		• Know: Clearly states general learning goals and purpose of artifact, including academic skills needed to be successful • Do: Thoroughly explains process and decision-making, including Leadership Skills used during the task • Reflect: Describes how artifact impacted self & own future, including growth as a scientist		• Know: Explicitly ties context of class to content and skill goals as well as purpose of artifact • Do: Explains process, decision-making, and Leadership Skills with detail and through lens of thinking like expert in field • Reflect: Describes and analyzes how artifact impacted self & own future, including growth as a scientist

To demonstrate their mastery of Textual Analysis in English Language Arts, students must select a writing sample that demonstrates the ability to read and think critically, communicate powerfully, and that embodies the following expectations, which are aligned to the Common Core State Standards for English Language Arts:

Critical Thinking

Argument
What is the evidence that the student can develop an argument?
- Responds to the texts with a controlling idea or argument that demonstrates engaged reading and critical thinking
- Acknowledges and responds to key questions, concerns, or alternative claims relevant to the controlling idea/claim
- Makes insightful connections, raises implications, and/or draws meaningful conclusions as a result of the reading and analysis

Evidence & Analysis
What is the evidence that the student can support the argument with evidence? What is the evidence that the student can analyze evidence?
- Examines one or more significant works of fiction and/or non-fiction
- Examines and analyzes the ideas and points of view presented in the texts and the author's language used to convey those ideas (e.g., figurative language, literary elements, rhetorical devices, etc.)
- Provides relevant textual evidence to support ideas and claims

Communicating Powerfully

Organization
What is the evidence that the student can organize and structure ideas for effective communication?
- Presents the controlling idea/argument in a way that is clear and guides the paper's organization
- Demonstrates a coherence and an internal structure that supports the argument
- Consistently uses transitions that relate and connect one idea to another
- Develops ideas and claims in appropriate depth

Conventions
What is the evidence that the student can use language skillfully to communicate ideas?
- Uses grammar, language, and techniques that are appropriate to the student's purpose and audience
- Observes appropriate language conventions

- Engages the reader with a strong voice and rhetorical technique (e.g. anecdotes, "grabber" introductions, repetition, sentence variety, parallelism, etc.)
- Cites textual evidence accurately and consistently

Reflection

What is the evidence that the student can deeply reflect on performance, growth as a learner, and ability to apply this in the future?

- Knows: Explains goals, purpose, and academic skills of artifact
- Does: Explains process, decisions, and Leadership Skills used
- Reflects: Describes impact of artifact on self, future, and growth as a writer

Envision Schools College Success Portfolio Performance Assessment: *ENGLISH LANGUAGE ARTS*
TEXTUAL ANALYSIS

SCORING DOMAIN	EMERGING	E/D	DEVELOPING	D/P	PROFICIENT	P/A	ADVANCED
ARGUMENT *What is the evidence that the student can develop an argument?*	• Argument is unclear or underdeveloped • Makes unclear or irrelevant claims • One claim dominates the argument and alternative or counter-claims are absent • Draws superficial connections or conclusions		• Makes a somewhat clear, but general argument that reflects passive reading or thinking • Makes relevant claims • Briefly alludes to questions, counter-claims, or alternative interpretations when appropriate • Draws general or broad connections or conclusions		• Makes a clear and well developed argument that demonstrates engaged reading and critical thinking • Makes relevant claims that support the argument • Acknowledges questions, counter-claims, or alternative interpretations when appropriate • Makes specific connections and draws meaningful conclusions		• Makes a clear, well developed, and convincing argument that demonstrates engaged reading and original critical thinking • Makes relevant and significant claims that support the argument • Acknowledges and responds to questions, counter-claims, or alternative interpretations to sharpen the argument when appropriate • Makes insightful connections, draws meaningful conclusions, and raises important implications

Scoring Domain	Emerging	E/D	Developing	D/P	Proficient	P/A	Advanced
EVIDENCE *What is the evidence that the student can support the argument?*	• Relies on one or two reasons, examples, or quotations relevant to argument • Makes no reference to the author's point of view or purpose in a text		• Refers to limited textual evidence (reasons, examples, or quotations) relevant to argument • Briefly notes the author's point of view or purpose in a text		• Refers to sufficient and detailed textual evidence (reasons, examples, and quotations) relevant to argument • Determines the author's point of view or purpose in a text and its impact on overall meaning		• Refers to most important textual evidence (reasons, examples, quotations) relevant to argument • Evaluates the author's point of view or purpose in a text and its impact on overall meaning and credibility of ideas

SCORING DOMAIN	EMERGING	E/D	DEVELOPING	D/P	PROFICIENT	P/A	ADVANCED
ANALYSIS *What is the evidence that the student can analyze evidence?*	• Demonstrates minimal understanding of text(s) • Summarizes but does not analyze or evaluate ideas or claims • Makes no reference to author's choices to support central ideas or claims		• Demonstrates basic understanding of text(s) • Summarizes and attempts to analyze the central ideas or claims • Briefly refers to author's choices (e.g., language use, literary/rhetorical devices, organization) that support central ideas or claims		• Demonstrates comprehensive understanding of text(s), including both explicit and inferred meanings • Analyzes the central ideas or sequence of events and their development over the course of the text(s) • Analyzes how author's choices (e.g, language use, literary/rhetorical devices, organization) support central ideas or claims		• Demonstrates comprehensive and critical understanding of text(s) including both explicit and inferred meanings • Analyzes and evaluates complex ideas or sequence of events and explains how individuals, ideas, or events interact and develop over the course of the text(s) • Analyzes how author's choices (e.g., language use, literary/ rhetorical devices, organization) support central ideas or claims and the effectiveness of the text

Scoring Domain	Emerging	E/D	Developing	D/P	Proficient	P/A	Advanced
ORGANIZATION *What is the evidence that the student can organize and structure ideas for effective communication?*	• Argument is unclear or not evident throughout the text • Ideas are disorganized, underdeveloped, or loosely sequenced • No transitions are used		• Argument is evident but not consistently present throughout text • Ideas are organized but not sufficiently developed or logically sequenced • Transitions connect ideas with minor lapses		• Argument is presented clearly and consistently throughout text • Ideas are developed and logically sequenced • Transitions connect ideas		• Argument is presented clearly and consistently throughout text, and drives the organization of the text • Ideas are fully developed and logically sequenced to present a coherent whole • Transitions guide the reader through the development and reasoning of the claim

Scoring Domain	Emerging	E/D	Developing	D/P	Proficient	P/A	Advanced
CONVENTIONS *What is the evidence that the student can use language skillfully to communicate ideas?*	• Has limited control of syntax and vocabulary • Has an accumulation of errors in grammar, usage, and mechanics that distracts or interferes with meaning • When appropriate for the task, textual citation is missing or incorrect		• Has control of syntax and vocabulary • Has some minor errors in grammar, usage, and mechanics that partially distract or interfere with meaning • When appropriate for the task, cites textual evidence with some minor errors		• Demonstrates varied syntax and effective word choice; uses rhetorical techniques • Is generally free of distracting errors in grammar, usage, and mechanics • When appropriate for the task, cites textual evidence consistently and accurately		• Has an effective fluent style with varied syntax, precise word choice, and skillful use of rhetorical techniques • Is free from errors in grammar, usage, and mechanics • When appropriate for the task, cites textual evidence consistently and accurately

SCORING DOMAIN	EMERGING	E/D	DEVELOPING	D/P	PROFICIENT	P/A	ADVANCED
REFLECTION *What is the evidence that the student can deeply reflect on performance, growth as a learner, and ability to apply this in the future?*	• Know: Explains the topic of class when artifact was assigned • Do: Explanation of process, decision making, and Leadership Skills is incomplete or unclear • Reflect: States what was done well and what could be improved upon		• Know: Describes some context of class (learning goals, purpose of artifact or necessary skills) • Do: Briefly explains process, decision making, and Leadership Skills used during the task • Reflect: Explains how artifact impacted self as a learner		• Know: Clearly states general learning goals and purpose of artifact, including academic skills needed to be successful • Do: Thoroughly explains process and decision-making, including Leadership Skills used during the task • Reflect: Describes how artifact impacted self & own future, including growth as a writer		• Know: Explicitly ties context of class to content and skill goals as well as purpose of artifact • Do: Explains process, decision-making, and Leadership Skills with detail and through lens of thinking like expert in field • Reflect: Describes and analyzes how artifact impacted self & own future, including growth as a writer

What Is the Most Effective Method for Cleaning Oil, Dispersants or Absorbents?

Background

The company British Petroleum, otherwise known as BP, had a fairly sizable catastrophe take place on one of its drilling rigs 50 miles to the south-east of the Mississippi delta, the Deepwater Horizon, on the day of April 20th, 2010. An explosion and subsequent fire took place, killing eleven people out of the 126 workers on the drill. The fire lasted for two days, and on the 22nd of April, the Deepwater Horizon sank into the ocean, dousing the fire and thus allowing the oil to flow freely from the oil well 5,000 feet below, and reach/remain on the surface. Though initial and governmental estimates of the amount of crude oil released were low, the Macondo well, a five-story-high structure that allows access to the subterranean deposits of crude oil, is thought to have released around 4.2-5 million barrels into the Gulf of Mexico. This amount of oil covered around 75,000 square kilometers, reaching the coastline of at least four states, Louisiana, Mississippi, Alabama, and Florida.

Of course among the major concerns revolving around this oil spill is the ecological impact that this oil spill could have. It has been established that exposure to crude oil is extremely hazardous to all forms of life that come into direct contact with or absorb it. It can cause many problems in the natural functions of organisms, interfering with natural processes of or physically damaging various cells, and can lead to health complications up to and including death. *"Birds can be exposed to oil as they float on the water or dive for fish through oil-slicked water. Oiled birds can lose the ability to fly and can ingest the oil while preening. Sea turtles such as loggerheads and leatherbacks can be impacted as they swim to shore for nesting activities. Turtle nest eggs may be damaged if an oiled adult lies on the nest. Scavengers such as bald eagles, gulls, raccoons, and skunks are also exposed to oil by feeding on carcasses of contaminated fish and wildlife."*[1] These species are only a few of the coastal and aquatic life forms that interact with or come close to the surface of the water, meaning that they will be in direct exposure to the crude oil. The unfortunate event that crude oil was

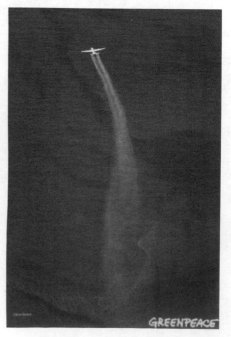

released into one of the most bio-diverse regions in the world could have some very dire consequences. In addition, there is significant concern about the chemical dispersants that are being used, as *"Oil spill dispersants do not actually reduce the total amount of oil entering the environment. Rather, they change the inherent chemical and physical properties of oil, thereby changing the oil's transport, fate, and potential effects. Small amounts of spilled oil naturally disperse into the water column, through the action of waves and other environmental processes. The objective of dispersant use is to enhance the amount of oil that physically mixes into the water column, reducing the potential that a surface slick will contaminate shoreline habitats or come into contact with birds, marine mammals, or other organisms that exist on the water surface or shoreline."*[1] The use of dispersants, should this information be correct, would then affect not only the coastal habitats, but virtually all aquatic life forms within the Gulf of Mexico. In its essence, the use of dispersants on crude oil is a conscious compromise between the effects the dispersed oil has upon the surface and coastal organisms, and the effects that it will have upon the species that live underneath the Benthic zone, creating an inverse relationship between the harm that comes to one as compared to the other. However, the magnitude of the spill is such that the oil has already done great harm to the biotic environment of the Benthic zone, and the future and present use of dispersants would come to affect life within various if not all levels of the water column. The full effects of these dispersants along with the crude oil are not fully known, but it is believed that they may have physiologically negative effects that could be transferred from one generation of organisms to the next. Thus, various members of a species could be affected, not only those who came in direct contact with the oil and dispersants. In addition, there has been some concern that the dispersant-encased oil will enter the Thermohaline Circulation, also known as the Global Conveyor Belt. It is a submerged current of water that travels all around the world and surfaces at various regions with nutrients brought up from the bottom of the ocean, and so these regions are intense with bio-diversity. *"Scientists estimate that it takes one section of the belt 1,000 years to complete one full circuit of the globe. However slow it is, though, it moves a vast amount of water—more than 100 times the flow of the Amazon River,"*[2] meaning that these ecological concerns could still exist within the next millennium, and be transferred into other regions with a relatively high level of bio-diversity.

It is often the case that there is an inverse relationship between the economic gain that resource extraction procures and the ecological effects that it has. However, the extraction of crude oil from the Macondo Well, and the subsequent BP Oil Spill, has transformed into a situation that does not benefit coastal communities economically, and much less environmentally. *"In a preliminary assessment of the economic damage released on May 17, 2010, Moody's Investors Service suggested that while Louisiana, Mississippi, and Alabama may experience short-term economic booms related to clean-up efforts, that will give way to longer-term deteriorating revenue for coastal communities. Cities and counties in those Gulf states are likely to experience a decline in property tax values, which will mean a reduction in services or a necessary increase in revenue to maintain current credit rating levels."*[1] One can then conclude that these coastal communities will be severely affected in terms of the economic opportunities and resources available to them. As their property will no longer be considered a pristine location for urban residence as a direct result of the health hazards of crude  oil/dispersants, so will it no longer be considered prime real estate for commercial development. These communities could be affected through the loss of visitors and investors. As time goes on, these issues could come to grow exponentially, as one by one communities become commercially stagnant. However, the economic effects of the BP Oil Spill might be more significant than we believe them to be. *"The economic impacts from the spill originate in the communities affected by the spill, but then ripple throughout the entire nation. Commercial fishermen in the Gulf harvested more than 1 billion pounds of fish and shellfish in 2008. In addition, there are approximately 5.7 million recreational fishermen in the Gulf of Mexico region who took 25 million fishing trips in 2008. Fishermen in areas closed to fishing, or whose catch are harmed by the spill, feel the immediate effects, as do hotels, restaurants, and other businesses that are tied to tourism, conventions, and recreation in the Gulf Coast. The reduction in the harvest of oysters, shrimp, and other seafood caused prices to rise sharply in the weeks following the spill, which in turn caused food prices to rise in restaurants as far away as New York City. The mere threat of oil caused thousands of hotel cancellations in the run-up to the usually hectic Memorial Day weekend."*[1] Hence, not only are the communities of the Gulf affected, but by the loss of the availability of sea-fish and other aquatic organisms that reside within the Gulf of Mexico, the most culturally or at least most culinarially diverse communities would also perceive the rise in prices of various dishes. The southern coastal communities may become a dead zone for tourism and investing, creating a large dip in their exports of consumable goods, which then could cause the United States to import more of their material goods from other nations, thereby lowering the amount of money within the U.S. I believe that it is quite logical to assume that the interconnectedness of our economic prosperity is of a more significant nature than most are aware of, as exemplified by the fairly broad impact of the most recent recess in our economy due to the housing market crash, among other things.

As the quality of the environment along with the availability of the most important resource in our society, money, decreases, so does the lifestyle of the people who live in the regions most directly affected by the oil spill. *"Public officials have failed to sound an alarm about the public health threat because three federal agencies—DHHS, EPA, and OSHA—cannot find any unsafe levels of oil in air or water. Perhaps the federal air and water standards are not stringent enough to protect the public from oil pollution. Our federal laws are outdated and do not protect us from the toxic threat from oil—now widely recognized in the scientific and medical community. BP is still in the dark ages on oil toxicity. BP officials stress that, by the time oil gets to shore, it is "weathered" and missing the highly volatile compounds like the carcinogenic benzene, among others. BP fails to mention the threat from dispersed oil, ultrafine particles (PAHs), and chemical dispersants, which include industrial solvents and proprietary compounds, many hazardous to humans. If oil was so nontoxic, then why are the spill response workers given hazardous waste training? Our federal government should stop pretending that everything is okay. What isn't safe for workers isn't safe for the general public either."*[3] Thus is the statement made by Riki Ott, a marine toxicologist, who is also a published author of two books related to the Exxon Valdez Spill. As she points out, crude oil and the chemicals used to 'clean' the oil are of significant concern for the health of the coastal population. It is agreed that direct and even indirect contact with these substances can cause various health complications to marine biology, and are also of significant concern to the health of the human population that is exposed to said chemicals. *"Corexit 9500 is known in prior scientific studies to pose a high level of toxicity to primary producer biota in the water column; in addition, it has been shown to accelerate the*

uptake of certain likely carcinogenic minority components present in petroleum such as naphthalene. The dispersants used are approximately 10,000 times more lethal to biota than crude oil itself. Corexit 9500 and Corexit EC9527A, manufactured by an Illinois company, both contain 2-butoxyethanol, a chemical known to cause respiratory and skin irritation effects in humans. These dispersants have been banned for use by the United Kingdom, due to known biological effects on people and natural systems."[1]

    The ultimate and specific consequences of the largest ecological disaster to happen in relation to the extraction of natural resources are yet to be fully known. However, what is known is that they will be negative, and they will be dire. What this will do to accelerate the degradation of our environment must become one of our most important concerns in the present age and thus should be extensively investigated, and all available methods to revert the damage made by the BP Oil Spill must be employed in order to slow or stall if not outright stop the downward spiral that is the condition of our environment. Though some efforts have been made to control the reach of the crude oil, like the use of booms, absorbent pads, or dispersants, we must come to a solution to this problem that is far more effective. This brings us to the education of the generation(s) soon to inherit these responsibilities, such as my generation, and so we come to study the BP Oil Spill in AP Environmental Science. In an experiment representative of the various clean-up methods employed by various agencies and entities, we will compare two different methods of cleaning in order to discern which would be the most effective.

End Notes

1. Cutler Cleveland (Lead Author); C Michael Hogan PhD., Peter Saundry (Topic Editor) "Deepwater Horizon oil spill." In: Encyclopedia of Earth. Eds. Cutler J. Cleveland (Washington, D.C.: Environmental Information Coalition, National Council for Science and the Environment). [First published in the Encyclopedia of Earth December 5, 2010; Last revised date December 10, 2010; Retrieved January 9, 2011]. http://www.eoearth.org/article/Deepwater_Horizon_oil_spill?topic=50364
2. Horton, Jennifer. Deep Ocean Currents (Global Conveyor Belt). How Stuff Works. http://science.howstuffworks.com/environmental/earth/oceanography/ocean-current3.htm
3. Ott, Riki. The Big Lie: BP, Governments Downplay Public Health Risk From Oil and Dispersants. CommonDreams.org. http://www.commondreams.org/headline/2010/07/07-4

Images

http://www.flickr.com/photos/greenpeaceusa09/4628052424/lightbox/
http://www.flickr.com/photos/greenpeaceusa09/4778286681/sizes/o/in/photostream/
http://www.flickr.com/photos/adamhilton/4733280887/sizes/z/in/photostream/

Hypothesis

If we use the liquid-based detergent and cotton balls to clean oil, then the liquid-based detergent solution dispersant will have the best result in cleaning oil from the surface of the water because the cotton balls will interact with water along with oil, whereas the detergent will only cause the oil to clump into denser particles, effectively causing the condensed chemical-encased oil particles to sink and disperse along the water column.

Materials (per trial)

(Detergent)
Liquid-based Detergent - 30 milliliters
Water - 300 milliliters
Oil - 50 milliliters
Tray - 1
Funnel - 1
Coffee Filter - 1
Graduated Cylinder - 1
Scale - 1

(Cotton Balls)
Cotton Balls - 6
Water - 300 milliliters
Oil - 50 milliliters
Tray - 1
Funnel - 1
Coffee Filter - 1
Graduated Cylinder - 1
Scale - 1

Procedure (3 Trials per Cleaning Agent)

Detergent
1. Prepare working space and chart for recording information.
2. Attain water and measure 300 milliliters using graduated cylinder, and pour into tray.
3. Attain the initial oil level of 50 milliliters, and weigh using scale, making sure to compensate for the weight of the graduated cylinder. Then pour into tray.
4. Attain 30 milliliters of liquid-based detergent.
5. Record information of initial water level, initial oil level, and initial level of cleaning agent.
6. Add cleaning agent to tray and wait for 3 minutes.

7. Place the coffee filter in the funnel, and use it to isolate the liquid oil remaining on the surface of the water that is inside the tray, carefully avoiding the clumped oil at the bottom of tray by carefully pouring surface oil from tray to funnel.
8. Remove the coffee filter from funnel, keeping the amount of retained oil intact, and measure weight using the scale.
9. Record the weight of the remaining oil.
10. Clean materials and work space, and dispose of remaining oil and residue.
11. Repeat steps 1-10 for 2 more trials.

Cotton Balls
1. Prepare working space and chart for recording information.
2. Attain water and measure 300 milliliters using graduated cylinder, and pour into tray.
3. Attain the initial oil level of 50 milliliters, and weigh using scale, making sure to compensate for the weight of the graduated cylinder. Then pour into tray.
4. Attain the 6 cotton balls.
5. Record information of initial water level, initial oil level, and number of cotton balls.
6. Add cleaning agent to tray and wait for 3 minutes.
7. Remove the cotton balls from tray if present, place the coffee filter in the funnel, and use it to isolate the liquid oil remaining on the surface of the water that is inside the tray by carefully pouring it from tray to funnel.
8. Remove the coffee filter from funnel, keeping the amount of retained oil intact, and measure weight using the scale.
9. Record the weight of the remaining oil.
10. Clean materials and work space, and dispose of remaining oil and residue.
11. Repeat steps 1-10 for 2 more trials.

Cleaning Agent	Initial H$_2$O Level	Initial Oil Level	Initial Cleaning Agent Level/ Amount	Initial Oil Weight	End Oil Weight	Percentage of Oil Remaining
Detergent (liquid-based)	300 mL	50 mL	30 mL	42.7 g	34 g	79.625 %
	300 mL	50 mL	30 mL	42.7 g	31 g	72.599 %
	300 mL	50 mL	30 mL	42.7 g	33.5 g	78.454%
Average						**76.892%**
Cotton Balls	300 mL	50 mL	6 balls	42.7 g	33 g	77.283%
	300 mL	50 mL	6 balls	42.7 g	33.8 g	79.156 %
	300 mL	50 mL	6 balls	42.7 g	35.8 g	83.840%
Average						**80.093%**

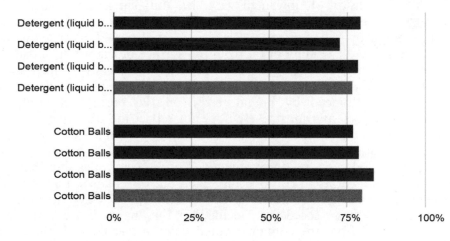

Conclusion

It actually was relatively difficult to discern which cleaning method was best, on account of the similarity of the results between the two cleaning agents, the cotton balls and the detergent. On the first trial of the two cleaning agents, we found that the percentage of oil remaining was larger in the trial corresponding to the detergent, by around 2.342% , a number that in a scale of millions of barrels could make an enormous impact. In the second trial, we found that the amount of remaining oil was larger in the cotton balls than in the detergent's trial, by around 6.557%, thereby proving the initial belief that the detergent would work better as a cleaning agent. In addition, the third trial once again proved that the detergent works best as a cleaning agent by cleaning a higher percentage of oil in comparison to the cotton balls, by 5.386%. Therefore, one can conclude that the cleaning agent that works best is the detergent, which if one takes the average of all trials one finds the detergent to to be 76.892% ineffective, lower by 3.201% than the 80.093% ineffectiveness of the cotton balls. I suppose that this would mean that my initial hypothesis that the detergent would be more effective would be correct, as the cotton balls, according to our trials, are slightly less effective. However, it is difficult to prove this theory if one takes the scale of the experiment fully into account. There is nowhere near enough data to come to a final verdict, due to the minuteness of a high school experiment compared to the real world. The 3.201% difference in the averages of the cleaning agents is not a significant enough difference to be of much consequence outside of a science classroom. Had the experiment been more extensive in its exclusion of unwanted variables and had a more substantial amount of trials, this conclusion may have been more accurate. Those variables could be anything from the unintentional inclusion of dispersed oil mixed within the water column, to the spilling of oil from the surface of the water outside of the coffee filter, to the methodology of how the cleaning agents were introduced in terms of consistency (or lack of it). The trials we did could have been (and most likely are) influenced by human error on the part of a group of inexperienced teenagers, and most likely does not reflect the true magnitude of the difference in the effectiveness of these two cleaning agents. One significant factor that could have influenced the data is the interaction of the oil with the items that hold it. Oil has a relatively high level of viscosity, meaning that it is 'sticky.' This means that as the oil is being taken out of its container, some oil remains behind. This could potentially throw off the data by removing a certain amount of oil that was supposed to be included in the final measurement. Also, as the water poured from the container could have interacted with the coffee filter in such a way that it is possible that it affected its ability to filter. This could have allowed some of the oil to go through the filter, removing a certain amount of oil from the final measurement and affecting the accuracy of our data. Any number of these unintended influences could have been avoided if we were to use a more controlled environment, like a professional lab, rather than a high school level classroom/lab. As part of a controlled environment is the controlled measurement of all the substances used in the experiment, including consistent pouring rates and the use of identical measuring tools. We also did not use a control, meaning that the experiments we did comparing the efficiency of dispersants versus absorbents were not compared to a third set of experiments measuring the average amount of oil that did not **naturally** disperse. Additionally, as part of the controlled environment we did not use materials that would allow for the unhindered movement of the oil from one container to the next.

Of course, certain questions arise out of the experiments, mostly as to the nature of the two cleaning agents. We know, of course, that absorbent pads essentially soak up the surface oil slick, thereby removing it from the environment once the absorbent pads themselves are removed. Dispersants, on the other hand, do not physically remove the oil from the environment. Instead, it disperses the oil along the water column, and that causes one to question if dispersants should be used at all, since they do not seem to effectively 'clean' the oil, as it is not removed from the environment. Wouldn't that just mean that the dispersants do nothing to change the amount of oil floating within the oceans? What is the rate of efficiency of the removal of 100% of the surface oil by the dispersant Corexit as a ratio of oil quantity versus dispersant quantity? Was the use of dispersants by the EPA really an effort to clean up the oil, or was it merely a P.R. campaign, one meant to soothe the concerns of the general population but not really deal with the problem?

Science Reflection

It has always been the case that human society uses its environment to humanity's advantage. For the better part of our evolutionary history, that has only amounted to consuming basic resources that are present on the surface or close to the surface of the earth's crust. However, as our technology has advanced, so has our reach in terms of what resources we can access. This has led to our consumption of hydrocarbons for the production of practically all material artifacts that we today possess, which is a serious cause of concern. Any set of individuals who are so dependent upon such a solitary method of procuring energy and material possessions must reflect upon their situation and critically analyze their relationship between both the system that they are a part of and the rest of the world. It is important to understand the frailty of the conditions on Earth that made life possible, and in doing so, we may come to understand how we may preserve not only the Earth, but ourselves as well.

Part of this self-reflective practice that people should partake in is started and perpetuated by education. Education in human society is meant to create a collective social awareness. It is a means to an end in the way that a covalent bond holds two atoms together. It is the glue that allows us to avoid the Tragedy of the Commons; a dilemma arising from the situation in which multiple individuals, acting independently and in their own interests, will ultimately deplete a shared limited resource, even when it is clear that it is not in anyone's long-term interest for this to happen. However, after the Industrial Revolution - a period of rapid societal change due to the incorporation of machinery to improve the production methodology of material possessions - education has not been all that strong as it too was affected by the assembly-line mindset. As a whole, human society has made some very poor choices, choices that will eventually bring about consequences we would have otherwise liked to avoid. However, the comfortable lives that people lead today are too precious for the majority of the human population to give up, lives led with ignorance or disregard of their effects upon the Earth. This is a major fault in our society, one that has been really brought into focus by our studies of the natural world.

One particular incident we studied that portrayed the faults of our society was the BP Oil Spill. This particular incident really exemplifies the poor choices that we as human beings consciously make, yet are only too willing to blame upon each other as opposed to working to change ourselves. The maxim 'if you are not a part of the solution, then you are a part of the problem' best portrays the attitude we should have towards environmental conservation. My scientific inquiry of the BP Oil Spill has a lot of information regarding the unethical and immoral practice of using chemical dispersants on petroleum, in such a sensitive area. Basically, the authorities in charge of cleaning up BP's corporate irresponsibility knowingly introduced an agent known to be, particle for particle, 10,000 times more lethal to biotic entities, in an area of high biodiversity, close to the Thermohaline Circulation which will eventually spread this toxin all around the globe. Not only were studies on the responses to the BP

Oil Spill informative, but so was the context information on modern society's dependence upon fossil fuels. It really brought into focus the precarious situation we are in when it comes to the sustainability of our society, of which there is virtually none.

My scientific inquiry of the BP Oil spill exemplifies my knowledge of the scientific aspects of that disaster very accurately. In my paper I have various examples of how the economy, society, and environment we have are affected by the spill of 5 million barrels of crude oil. I include information on the effects of the dispersant upon biotic entities, as well as explain very thoroughly what the dispersant does. Additionally, I cover the possibility that the area that is affected by the dispersant could be increased significantly because of the Thermohaline Circulation. As the chemical-encased oil submerges from the surface oil slick it disperses along the water column, effectively creating multiple tiers that the dispersant Corexit resides within. The area affected by the Macondo well spill resides within the Gulf of Mexico, an area relatively close to a current of the Global Conveyor Belt. This proximity to the Thermohaline Circulation is a problem that could perpetuate the negative effects of the dispersant by transporting that dispersant to other areas around the world that possess high bio-diversity.

The background information in my scientific inquiry is very detailed, demonstrating my understanding of the natural world's aquatic environment as well as the effects of anthropogenic chemicals that are introduced into the natural world. It shows my understanding of sustainability, of bio-diversity, of hydrological interactions, and of the immoral practices of modern society. It also portrays my understanding of the scientific method, in two ways. The first is obvious. I used the scientific method to create my groups experiment and to assess what form of cleaning method was best. As a group we had to come to understand what exactly it was that we were attempting to analyze through a scientific lens. In other words, we needed to know what question we were trying to answer. In order to make the question into something measurable through scientific methods, we had to create a detailed hypothesis using the 'If...then...because' format. This meant that we would then be able to design an experiment that could effectively measure the difference in the efficiency of the two cleaning methods we decided to use, dispersants and absorbents.

The second is something that is not so clear at first, but that one can come to understand as valid. In analyzing the scientific method, I came to understand that the methodology of measuring change through a scientific lens, at its basics, was only a process of observation, interpretation, analysis, and synthesis. At first it was a challenge to understand how I would be able to connect the 'big picture' with a relatively short science experiment, yet it was in writing my thesis that I came to realize how the scientific method is only a fancy term used for such a basic intuitive human faculty. The scientific method is something that I used throughout my project, unknowingly yet willingly. This is something that I have done all throughout my four years as a science student at CAT. Although freshman year's is a little sketchy to my memory, I remember learning about and working on a Rube Goldberg machine. I believe that the basic lesson we were taught there is that every action has a reaction, and that a single missed step can be responsible for the downfall of everything else. In Sophomore year, I remember studying different methods of acquiring electricity, more specifically my research of Tidal Power. This was the start of our investigation of sustainability, and the faults of our society's methods of procuring energy. I came to learn in that year of how our society is so focused upon innovation that we no longer concern ourselves with preservation. Junior year was slightly different, in that we were studying biology. However, that taught me a valuable lesson as well. In researching any number of infectious diseases, I came to understand the persistence of life. I came to understand that every living organism is living in a very precarious environment, and that the smallest changes in the environment can have very serious consequences. This year, the BP Oil Spill lab taught me that we really need to understand what it is we do to our environment, because something that is seemingly beneficial can in actuality be very harmful. It is only in reflection that I came to realize how thinking critically plays a significant role in the interpretation of a scientific perspective. It is through reflection that I came to understand that as human beings we never cease to use the scientific method, as we constantly assess our own environment, and how it will affect us personally.

Yet, all throughout the four years I have spent as a science student at CAT, there has been a single recurring message. In its most basic form, the scientific method is observation, analysis, and synthesis, all faculties innate to human beings. This is something that has constantly been reinforced by my studies as a science student here at CAT, yet has been augmented by the instillment of moral values along with the knowledge I have gained. It is this ability to efficiently assess our natural world that the scientific method allows, an ability that is refined both in theoretical and empirical studies. In understanding the natural world, I have come to understand my own methodology of inquiry. As Albert Einstein said, "The whole of science is nothing more than a refinement of everyday thinking."

Envision Schools College Success Portfolio Performance Assessment: CREATIVE EXPRESSION

Through the study of visual and performing arts, we expect students to think critically and creatively and communicate their ideas effectively, persuasively, and artistically. We expect students to demonstrate an understanding of *artistic thinking* and *artistic practice*. Students shall use the arts as a tool to investigate and discuss topics and concerns that are relevant to artistic traditions and their lives.

The Creative Expression Performance Task includes a work of art in a visual or performing arts discipline, English language arts, or world language AND a written or oral (recorded) artist statement.[1] The artist statement may take the form of a log, journal, or essay. A successful statement is worked on during and after creating the work of art so that it can reflect the student's thinking throughout the creative process.

To demonstrate mastery of a visual or performing arts discipline, the selected work and artist statement together must meet the following expectations:

TECHNIQUE
What is the evidence that the student has command of the craft of the artistic discipline?
- creates a piece that reflects substantial craftsmanship
- employs specific techniques and methods to produce intended results
- identifies and apply the tools, materials, and artistic conventions of the specific arts discipline (e.g., drama, dance, 2-dimensional, 3-dimensional visual art) to create a work of art

PROCESS
What is the evidence that the student is envisioning, exploring, and persisting with an aesthetic idea?
- Sets goals and trajectory of the process of creating the work of art
- Demonstrates focus and perseverance during the creative process
- Incorporates feedback, reflection, and research into the creative process

POINT OF VIEW
What is the evidence that the student is constructing and making a work of art with personal meaning and intent?
- Creates a work of art that communicates a personal message, viewpoint, or idea
- Communicates point of view to audience or viewer through the work of art itself, and the artist statement

---

[1] *The Artist's Statement is a __required__ component of this performance task*

CONTEXT AND CONNECTIONS

What is the evidence that the student understands the connections of the work of art to artistic and cultural traditions (contemporary and/or historical)?

- Demonstrates how relevant events, ideas, and experiences from historical and contemporary times inform the work of art
- Demonstrates knowledge of major aesthetic questions/issues (e.g. role of the body, abstraction, audience/creator relationship) and their relation to the work of art
- Demonstrates knowledge about the aesthetic traditions that influence the work of art

REFLECTION

What is the evidence that the student understands how to question, discuss, and judge her own work?

- Describes and analyzes the process of making the work of art as well as the work of art itself
- Uses reflection in the process of making the work of art
- Evaluates the work of art using emotional response, cultural information, art practice conventions, and arts standards

ARTWORK: The Conventions scoring domain is used to assess the art piece itself

SCORING DOMAIN	EMERGING	E/D	DEVELOPING	D/P	PROFICIENT	P/A	ADVANCED
CONVENTIONS *(Technique) What is the evidence that the student has command of the technique of the artistic discipline?* "Tools": e.g., brushes, cameras, choreography, dialogue, improv techniques; "Materials": e.g., charcoal, the body, sound "Artistic conventions": e.g., perspective, color mixing, musical scales, rhythm "Artistic medium": e.g, acrylic painting, modern dance, documentary theater	• The work of art is characterized by an incomplete and limited application of the tools, materials, and artistic conventions of its particular artistic medium • The student has not experimented with tools, materials, or artistic conventions.		• The work of art is characterized by a basic application of the tool, materials, and artistic conventions of its particular artistic medium • The student has experimented in limited ways with tools, materials, or artistic conventions in order to better express a point of view, an idea, or a personal meaning.		• Customize this column using words such as: The work of art has a skilled application of the tools, media, materials, techniques, skills, and conventions. The work of art shows a general experimentation with tools, media, materials, techniques, skills, conventions, etc		• The work of art is characterized by a masterful application of the tools, materials, and artistic conventions of particular artistic medium • The student has experimented in specific ways with tools, materials, and artistic conventions in order to better express a point of view, an idea, or a personal meaning.

ARTIST STATEMENT: The rest of these scoring domains (Argument, Evidence, Organization, and Reflection) are used to assess the artist statement

SCORING DOMAIN	EMERGING	E/D	DEVELOPING	D/P	PROFICIENT	P/A	ADVANCED
ARGUMENT (Point of View) *What is the evidence that the student is constructing and making a work of art with personal meaning and intent?*	• The work of art is a representation of already existing information or works of art. • The student's articulation of point of view is unclear or vague. • The work of art's intent is unclear. • The student's explanation of point of view, meaning, and intent in the artistic statement is vaguely reflected in the work of art.		• The work of art presents a generalized point of view. • The student articulates the intent of the work (orally or in written form) in a basic way. • The work of art expresses an idea or emotion at a schematic level. • The student's explanation of point of view, meaning, and intent in the artistic statement is generally reflected in the work of art.		• The work of art presents a specific point of view. • The student can clearly articulate the intent of the work orally or in written form. • The work of art reflects some consideration of non-literal (e.g., moods, metaphors, etc.) properties. • The student's explanation of point of view, meaning, and intent in the artistic statement is reflected in the work of art. The work of art in relies somewhat on the artist		• The work of art presents a clear a nuanced point of view, conveying an idea, a feeling, or a personal meaning. • The student articulates a clear and specific intent of the work orally or in written form and gives evidence that supports the intent. • The work of art clearly expresses moods, metaphors, and/or other properties that aren't literally present. • The student's explanation of point of view, meaning, and intent in the artistic statement

SCORING DOMAIN	EMERGING	E/D	DEVELOPING	D/P	PROFICIENT	P/A	ADVANCED
					statement to communicate point of view.		is clearly reflected in the work of art. The work of art itself is able to communicate point of view.
EVIDENCE (Context and Connections) *What is the evidence that the student understands the connections of the work of art to artistic and cultural traditions (contemporary and/or historical)?*	• The student describes a personal connection to the work without connecting the work of art to aesthetic or cultural traditions. • The student refers to aesthetic movements that are irrelevant to the work of art.		• The student briefly notes the aesthetic or cultural traditions that inspired the work of art. The work relies primarily on personal interests. • The student demonstrates a cursory understanding of aesthetic movements and/or issues to which the work relates.		• The student generally describes the aesthetic, personal, and cultural inspirations for the work of art. • The student describes how the work relates to aesthetic movements and/or issues.		• The student specifically describes and demonstrates the aesthetic, personal, and cultural inspirations the work of art. • The student clearly addresses relevant issues within the art work. The student demonstrates a comp nuanced understanding of how the work relates to contemporary and historical aesthetic movements or issues.

SCORING DOMAIN	EMERGING	E/D	DEVELOPING	D/P	PROFICIENT	P/A	ADVANCED
ORGANIZATION (Process) *What is the evidence that the student is envisioning, exploring, and persisting with an aesthetic idea?*	• The student relies on others to set goals and provide direction in developing and creating the work. • The student is overwhelmed or discouraged by difficulties in the creative process. The student is not open to feedback from teachers and peers.		• The student has difficulty articulating the trajectory of the process of developing or creating the work • The student makes efforts to overcome difficulties in the creative process but is not entirely successful. Choices appear haphazard. • The student is open to feedback and critique from teachers and peers but there is little evidence that s/he has incorporated it into developing and creating the work.		• The student articulates a general trajectory of the process of developing and creating the work • The student has some strategies and uses some effort to move through difficult moments in the creative process. • The student is open to feedback and critique from teachers and peers and there is evidence that s/he has incorporated it into developing and creating the work.		• The student articulates specific trajectory and states his/her own clear goals in the process of developing and creating the work. • The student demonstrates focus, perseverance, and commitment in the development and creation of the work. S/he is able to learn from mistakes and accidents. • The student welcomes and incorporates feedback and critique from teachers and peers, as well as research to propel the work.

SCORING DOMAIN	EMERGING	E/D	DEVELOPING	D/P	PROFICIENT	P/A	ADVANCED
REFLECTION *What is the evidence that the student understands how to question, discuss, and judge his/her own work?*	• The student describes her/his technique and method in a basic way. • The student evaluates the work using personal emotional responses.		• The student uses everyday vocabulary to describe the work of art and the process of developing and creating the work. • The student draws briefly on external conventions, but relies mostly on personal emotional response to evaluate the work.		• The student uses simple art-specific vocabulary and principles to describe the work of art and the process of developing and creating the work. • The student evaluates the work using emotional response as well as cultural information, art practice conventions, and/or arts standards.		• The student skillfully uses vocabulary associated with the work's particular area of discipline in reflecting on the process of developing the work and in evaluating the work. • The student evaluates the work using emotional response as well as cultural information, art practice conventions, and/or arts standards.

ENVISION
LEARNING PARTNERS *Inspiring Results*

Performance Assessment Planning Template

A **performance assessment** is a form of assessment that requires students to demonstrate what they can do; that they apply the skills of a discipline (i.e., enact the work of historians, scientists, writers, mathematicians, artists, etc.), not just show what they know.

A complete performance assessment has three parts:
1) Pre-determined outcomes
2) A task (product or performance) through which students can demonstrate what they know and can do
3) Criteria that describe what meeting the outcomes looks like

Performance Assessment Title: _____

which is part of **Project Title:** _____ (if applicable)

| Grade level(s): | | Duration: | |
| Discipline(s): | | Authors: | |

The Outcomes

1. Skills/Standards To Be Measured

What is the targeted skill or skills that student and teacher are working together to develop and assess?

Derived from content standards, Common Core standards, 21st Century skills, and/or stated course or school outcomes.

Include a rationale: Why are these outcomes important?

1a. Learning Targets

Next, translate what you put into Box 1 into the student-friendly language known as <u>learning targets</u>: "I can" statements that are clear and measurable.

Long Term Add rows as needed (but not too many; less is more)	Supporting Break down the long-term target to manageable chunks of learning, think at the level of the lesson plan		
I can . . .			

Performance Assessment Planning Template

The Task

2. Prompt – What are students asked to do? (Description of product or performance)
How will students be invited to demonstrate what they can do? Introduce and explain, in language addressed to the student, all three dimensions of the performance assessment: outcome, task, and criteria.

Performance Assessment Planning Template

The Criteria for Success

3. Describe what success looks like

Describe a successful student product or performance that might emerge from the task explained above, in Box 2. Use your imagination and/or actual experience to get specific. Pick a student in your mind and imagine—in detail—what he or she would produce or perform.

3a. Rubric and domains

What rubric(s) will measure the student's level of proficiency within the Performance Assessment? The rubric(s) describe what it means to meet each learning target that you identified in Box 1a. If the rubric already exists, name its dimensions. If it doesn't yet exist, summarize what it should look like.

Note: Be careful that you are not evaluating something different from, or more than, what is targeted or taught.

Performance Assessment Planning Template

3b. Meeting the needs of diverse students

Accommodations, language supports, reading supports

Performance Assessment Planning Template

ENVISION
LEARNING PARTNERS *Inspiring Results*

Journey to Success

After designing a complete performance assessment (parts 1, 2, & 3 above), think through how to guide the student to achieving success.

4. Narrative

Tell the story of the learning process. Describe how students will learn and practice the skills they will need to succeed on this performance assessment.

4a. Resources

What resources will you use to create an authentic experience and maximize the learning?

Fieldwork	
Expert(s)	
Text(s)	
Video(s)	
Website(s)	
Other	

4b. Sequence of Learning and Assessment

Reminder: Assessment does not need to be 'formal.' Think collecting evidence. How do you know what students know? What is 'efficient and effective'? Also, one assessment could measure multiple learning targets, e.g., a writing piece—both skills and content

Date	Long-Term Learning Target	Supporting Learning Targets	Learning Activities/Experiences (That provides knowledge and skills for students to meet the learning target)	Formative and Summative Assessments (How students will demonstrate what they know and can do)

Performance Assessment Quality Rubric (May 2014 version)

1. CLEAR AND WORTHWHILE PERFORMANCE OUTCOMES

Criteria	Work in Progress	Ready For Use	Exemplary
Alignment to Standards	• Segments of the performance assessment **partially address** content or skills relevant to standards. • Scoring criteria **focus on task-specific requirements or surface level features** of the work, with little relationship to standards.	• The performance assessment is **aligned** to content and skill standards. • **Most** of the scoring criteria are aligned to and **reflect grade level expectations** of the content and skill standards, and represent an **appropriate level of challenge.**	• The performance assessment is designed to **integrate** the measurement of key content and skill standards in a **coherent way.** • Scoring criteria are **tightly aligned to grade level expectations** of key content and skills standards, and represent appropriately **high standards of performance.**
Deeper Learning Outcomes	• Completion of the performance assessment requires students to apply some higher order thinking skills OR a 21st century skill, but there may be **limited evidence of it in the work product.**	• Student product provides **some evidence** of higher order thinking skills and/or 21st century skills, such as critical thinking, problem solving, effective communication, collaboration, and meta-cognition.	• Student product provides **clear evidence** of higher order thinking skills and/or 21st century skills, such as critical thinking, problem solving, effective communication, collaboration, and meta-cognition
Big Ideas/Strategies with Transferability	• Builds student understanding with **unclear or questionable importance** within the discipline(s)	• Builds student understanding of key facts, concepts, or strategies with **limited transfer** within and/or across the discipline(s).	• Deepens student understanding of key facts, concepts, and strategies that have **broad transferability** within and/or across the discipline(s).

SCALE
Stanford Center for Assessment, Learning, & Equity

Performance Assessment Quality Rubric (May 2014 version)

2. PERFORMANCE ASSESSMENT FOCUS, CLARITY, & COHERENCE

Criteria	Work in Progress	Ready For Use	Exemplary
Task Prompt Focus and Clarity	• Task prompt for students is **unclear** or attempts to address **too many or confusing goals or objectives.** • Expectations for quality are **unclear, implied, or not communicated.**	• Task prompt for students is **clear** and addresses a **focused set of content objectives** • Expectations for quality or proficient performance are **broadly stated.**	• Task prompt for students is clear and addresses an **explicitly defined and focused set of objectives that require application of content AND higher order thinking within the discipline.** • Expectations for quality or proficient performance are **clear and specific.**
Coherence of Performance Assessment Components with Purpose	• Task prompt for students, resources (texts and materials, if provided), and student product are **misaligned** and provide **limited support** for the purpose of the performance assessment.	• Task prompt for students, resources (texts and materials, if provided), and student product are **supportive** of the purpose of the performance assessment.	• Task prompt for students, resources (texts and materials, if provided), and student product are **tightly aligned** to the purpose of the performance assessment.

Performance Assessment Quality Rubric (May 2014 version)

3. STUDENT ENGAGEMENT: RELEVANCE AND AUTHENTICITY

Criteria	Work in Progress	Ready For Use	Exemplary
Relevance & Authentic Purpose and Audience	• Has **little connection** to students' lived experience, interests, or prior knowledge. • Context for completing the performance assessment is **not provided.** • The audience is the teacher or **not defined.**	• **Makes a connection to** students' lived experience, interests, or prior knowledge. • **Simulates a real-world context** for engaging in and completing the performance assessment, and makes connections to the work of adults in the real world. • Audience for final product includes **the teacher and other students in the class.**	• **Builds on** students' lived experience, interests, and/or prior knowledge. • **Provides a real-world context** that establishes a clear "need to know" purpose for engaging in learning and completing the performance assessment. • Audience for final product includes **individuals beyond the teacher and classroom.**
Authenticity to the Discipline(s)	• Topic/question has **marginal relevance** to the discipline(s); the performance assessment engages students in an activity/product with **little connection** to the discipline(s).	• Topic/question has a **clear connection to the discipline(s);** the performance assessment engages students in an activity/product that is **clearly connected to work in the discipline(s).**	• Topic/question is **key to the discipline(s);** the performance assessment engages students in an activity/product that is **central to work in the discipline(s).**

S C A L E
Stanford Center for Assessment, Learning, & Equity

Performance Assessment Quality Rubric (May 2014 version)

4. STUDENT ENGAGEMENT: CHOICE AND DECISION-MAKING

Criteria	Work in Progress	Ready For Use	Exemplary
Diverse Responses & Opportunities for Choice/Decision-making	• Task prompt for students and resources **bias students toward a particular response; or there is only one acceptable response.** • Provides **no decision points** for students.	• Task prompt for students **allows for diverse ways of responding** to the prompt, but resources **predetermine or limit the ways in which students can respond.** • **Provides a limited set of decision points, like topic or resources.**	• Task prompt for students and resources **allow for diverse ways of responding to the prompt.** • Provides students **explicit opportunities to make key content and strategic decisions** for how to complete the task and **to extend their own learning by introducing new resources or strategies.**

Performance Assessment Quality Rubric (May 2014 version)

5. STUDENT ENGAGEMENT: ACCESSIBILITY

Criteria	Work in Progress	Ready For Use	Exemplary
Developmentally Appropriate	• Most elements of the performance assessment (task prompt, content, context, resources) are **overly complex and demanding,** OR **oversimplified** for the grade level of the students, OR **inappropriate for the socio-emotional stage of students.**	• **Most elements** of the performance assessment (task prompt, content, context, resources) are appropriately challenging for the grade level and **appropriate for the socio-emotional stage of students.**	• **All elements** of the performance assessment (task prompt, content, context, resources) are **appropriately complex and challenging** for the grade level of the students and appropriate for the socio-emotional stage of students.
Accessibility of Resources/Text Complexity (Apply only when present)	• The preponderance of resources is **inaccessible** OR • The preponderance of resources is **too easy for most students** • Resources **do not vary in format,* complexity, or challenge,** and are **unlikely to be engaging to students.**	• Resources are generally appropriate, engaging, and accessible for **most students; one or more sources may be inaccessible** for the grade level. • Resources are grade appropriate and **vary in format,* complexity, or challenge, and may be engaging for some students.**	• Resources are **carefully selected, excerpted, or adapted to improve engagement** and accessibility for all **students, including those with reading challenges and learning disabilities.** • Resources are grade appropriate, vary in format,* complexity, and/or challenge, and are **likely to be engaging to most students.**

* Vary in format: Resources that vary in format provide multiple ways for students to engage with content, and thereby provide multiple entry points into the performance assessment (e.g., multiple sources representing different perspectives or writing purposes, audio, visual, hands-on experimentation, etc.).

Performance Assessment Quality Rubric (May 2014 version)

6. CURRICULUM CONNECTED

❑ Aligned to the taught curriculum: Performance assessment overview explains how the performance assessment fits within a unit of study.

❑ Aligned to the skills that have been developed over time: Mini-tasks or learning activities, as described by the performance assessment overview, have clear connections to the performance assessment.

7. OPPORTUNITIES FOR SELF-ASSESSMENT, PEER AND TEACHER FEEDBACK

❑ Performance assessment indicates that there will be opportunities for students to gain feedback through self-, peer-, and/or teacher assessment.

❑ Performance assessment indicates that students will have opportunities to revise and resubmit work, and reflect on their learning.

Project Planning Template

Overview: The planning template should be used to develop high quality projects. It is intended to prompt thinking rather than act as a compliance tool. The order of the titles does not suggest that this is the order of planning. This is an organic and evolving process. However, we do suggest starting with outcomes and plan around how students will learn and demonstrate these outcomes. We promote ongoing revision of the planning process and assessing the alignment between intended outcomes, learning activities, and demonstration of learning. As performance assessments are a part of the learning opportunities that comprise the project, use this document to identify the performance assessment(s) within the project and use the separate performance assessment planning template to fully design these.

A **project** is a carefully planned and designed sequence of learning experiences that provide students multiple opportunities to demonstrate learning aligned to pre-determined outcomes.

Project Title:

Grade level(s):		Authors:	
Discipline(s):		Date:	

For additional information as you plan, hover the curser over the __TIP__ to see a screen tip that will help you.

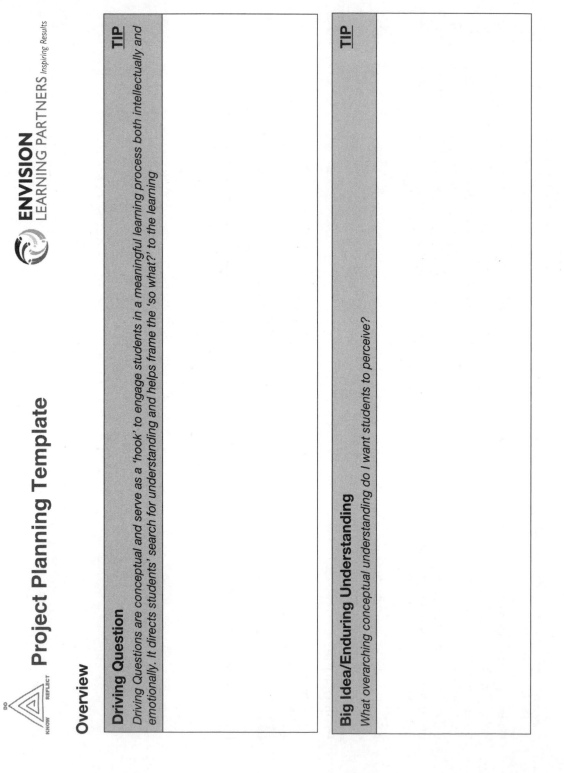

ENVISION
LEARNING PARTNERS *Inspiring Results*

Project Planning Template

Overview

Driving Question   TIP

Driving Questions are conceptual and serve as a 'hook' to engage students in a meaningful learning process both intellectually and emotionally. It directs students' search for understanding and helps frame the 'so what?' to the learning

Big Idea/Enduring Understanding   TIP

What overarching conceptual understanding do I want students to perceive?

ENVISION
LEARNING PARTNERS *Inspiring Results*

Project Planning Template

Narrative/Abstract
TIP

Describe, ideally to the student, what this project is about: the what, the why, and the how of the learning process. Name the skills and concepts to be learned, describe how students will learn these, and explain how students will demonstrate what they learn.

Outcomes

Standards/Skills addressed within this project
TIP

ENVISION
LEARNING PARTNERS *Inspiring Results*

Project Planning Template

Learning Targets

*Learning targets guide learning. They describe, in language that students understand, **the lesson-sized chunk** of information, skills, and reasoning processes that students will come to know deeply.*[1]

Long Term TIP (add rows as needed)	Supporting TIP (add rows as needed)

[1]. Moss and Brookhart. 'Learning Targets Helping Students Aim for Understanding in Today's Lesson'

Project Planning Template

Description of Product or Performance (for summative assessment)
TIP

Performance Assessment(s) within project (use Performance Planning Template)

Title	
Disciplines	
Rubric(s)	

Title	
Disciplines	
Rubric(s)	

Title	
Disciplines	
Rubric(s)	

KNOW   DO   REFLECT

ENVISION
LEARNING PARTNERS *Inspiring Results*

Project Planning Template

Calendar

Sequence of Learning and Assessment
TIP

Date	Long-Term Learning Target	Supporting Learning Targets	Learning Activities/Experiences (That provides knowledge and skills for students to meet the learning target)	Assessment of Learning/Summative Assessments (How students will demonstrate what they know and can do)

Envision Sample Daily Schedule

Monday	Tuesday	Wednesday	Thursday	Friday
Period 0 8:00-8:55	**Period 0** 8:00-8:55	**Period 0** 8:00-8:55	**Period 0** 8:00-8:55	**Period 0** 8:00-8:55
Period 1 9:00 – 9:50	**Period 1** 9:00 – 10:30	**Period 3** 9:00 – 10:30	**Period 1** 9:00 – 10:30	**Period 3** 9:00 – 10:30
	Community Meeting 10:30 – 10:45		**Community Meeting** 10:30 – 10:45	
Period 2 9:55 – 10:45	**Period 2** 10:55 – 12:25	**Period 4** 10:40 – 12:10	**Period 2** 10:55 – 12:25	**Period 4** 10:40 – 12:10
Period 3 10:55 – 11:45				
Lunch 11:45 – 12:15	**Lunch** 12:25 – 1:00	**Lunch** 12:10 – 12:45	**Lunch** 12:25 – 1:00	**Lunch** 12:10 – 12:45
Period 4 12:20 – 1:10	**Advisory Period** 1:05 – 1:50	**Period 5** 12:50 – 2:20	**Advisory Period** 1:05 – 1:35	**Period 5** 12:50 – 2:20
Period 5 1:15 – 2:05				
Period 6 2:10 – 3:00 Elective	**Art Period** 2:00 – 3:30	**Period 6** 2:30 – 3:30 Elective (CAT Staff)	**Art Period** 2:00 – 3:30	**Period 6** 2:30 – 3:30 Elective (CAT Staff)
Staff Meeting 3:15 – 5:00				

PERIOD 1	
Language Arts	A
Social Studies	B
Science	C
Math	D
Digital Media	E

PERIOD 2	
Language Arts	E
Social Studies	A
Science	B
Math	C
Digital Media	D

PERIOD 3	
Language Arts	D
Social Studies	E
Science	A
Math	B
Digital Media	C

PERIOD 4	
Language Arts	C
Social Studies	D
Science	E
Math	A
Digital Media	B

PERIOD 5	
Language Arts	B
Social Studies	C
Science	D
Math	E
Digital Media	A

YOU NEED TO KNOW YOUR LETTER GROUP (A-E) TO KNOW WHICH CLASS YOU ARE TAKING WHICH PERIOD.

EXAMPLE – LETTER GROUP "B" HAS SCIENCE 2ND PERIOD. IT MEETS ON MONDAY(9:55), TUESDAY (10:55), AND THURSDAY(10:55).

9th Grade Envision Schools Advisory Curriculum

Theme	Date	Activity
The purpose of the first block of advisory activities is to prepare for the parent-teacher-student conferences that begin October 25. Students will be expected to prepare a brief presentation that demonstrates their public speaking skills and describes their goals and progress since the beginning of school. *9th grade students will focus on communication, collaboration, and project management Leadership Skills*		*Community and reflection should be considered as underlying themes for all Advisory activities*
Community *Skill: Communication* *Skill: Collaboration*	August 31	Eye Contact exercise Room setup Name Game exercise
Community *Skill: Communication* *Skill: Collaboration*	September 2	Eye Contact exercise Set and post norms Check in Schoolwide expectations
Community *Skill: Communication* *Skill: Collaboration* *Skill: Project management*	September 7	Eye Contact exercise Organization/materials Set up folders
Community *Skill: Communication* *Skill: Collaboration*	September 9	Purpose of Advisory Reflection Journal Play Doh activity

Leadership *Skill: Collaboration*	September 14	Leadership Skills Poster Review rubrics
Leadership *Skill: Collaboration*	September 16	Leadership Skills Poster Eye Contact Exercise
Leadership *Skill: Collaboration*	September 21	Leadership Skills Poster
Community *Skill: Collaboration* *Skill: Communication;* *Skill: Project management*	September 23	Activity: Spaghetti and Gumdrops (45 min)
Community Leadership *Skill: Communication* *Skill: Collaboration*	September 28	Activity: Eye Contact Exercise (mastery) (10 min) *By now or earlier, all students should be able to do this for 3 minutes. Holding them to the mastery level now is important.* Activity: Demonstrate Audience Eye contact exercise (35 min) *Set up the room in audience format. Demonstrate the exercise yourself. Have a volunteer come up. Take the time to have student practice and show mastery, so others can see the criteria for the exercise. This will take about 10 minutes per student. You should be able to do three students.*

Community Leadership *Skill: Communication* *Skill: Collaboration*	September 30	Activity: Audience Eye Contact Exercise (30 min). *3-4 students* Activity: Review the format and dates of the parent conferences (15 min). *Students will prepare a self-assessment of their Leadership Skills, using note cards. Students will answer question "When I graduate from CAT, I expect to..." Bulleted list should include expectations for grades, skills, and college plans. Also, students should reflect on the question, "What does CAT offer me to help me achieve these goals?"*
Community Leadership *Skill: Communication* *Skill: Collaboration*	October 5	Activity: Audience Eye Contact Exercise (25 min) *4-5 students* Activity: Brainstorm presentations (25 min)
Community Leadership *Skill: Communication* *Skill: Collaboration*	October 7	Activity: Audience Eye Contact Exercise (25 min) *4-5 students. Ideally, all students should have completed the exercise by this date* Activity: Students write out note cards and teacher collects for review (25 min)

Community Leadership *Skill: Communication* *Skill: Collaboration*	October 12	Activity: Calendar check – end of quarter discussion (25 min). *Discussion topics: What has been hard this quarter? What has been easy? What was surprising?* Activity: Students record classes and current grade on PLP work in pairs or teams to discuss the content of their presentations (25 min). *Use this time to work individually with students*
Community Leadership *Skill: Communication* *Skill: Collaboration*	October 14	Activity: Demonstrate a two-min speech on goals and accomplishments (15 min) *It is important to model mastery of public speaking skills. Use your own goals and accomplishments during high school as content for your speech.* Activity: Hand back note cards. Students prepare final presentations and final notes (30 min). *Use this time to work individually with students*
Community Leadership *Skill: Communication*	October 19	Activity: Students practice presentation to advisory audience and receive feedback (45 min)

Leadership *Skill: Communication*	October 21	Activity: Students practice presentation to advisory audience and receive feedback (45 min)
	October 25	Parent-student-teacher conferences
In the second block of advisories, students will complete a self-assessment of themselves as learners, develop a personal profile, and create their Personalized Learning Plan. These will be shared in the parent-student- teacher conferences in March.		

Skill: Communication	November 2	Activity: DeBono's Six Thinking Hats
		Three Advisories will be necessary for this activity, which is designed to have students reflect on their thinking styles and multiple intelligences. The thinking styles activity is based on the Six Thinking Hats of Edward DeBono, which denotes thinking styles by color:
		• Blue: cool and controlled, sets the focus, "in charge"
		• Red: emotionas and feelings. Hunch and intuition, opinion. 'This is what I feel.'
		• Black: Devil's advocate. Why it won't work, points out risks and faults. 'This is what could go wrong.'
		• White: facts and figures. Neutral and objective. Imitate a computer. Discipline and direction. 'Just the facts.'
		• Green: Idea person. Looks for alternatives. Creative. What if? 'We can do it this way or this way or...'
		• Yellow: Positive. Happy. Optimistic. 'We can do it, whatever it takes.

		You will need scissors, pens, and poster paper for each of these colors. Staplers will be required to post the hands at the end of the activity.
		Discuss the six thinking styles with students and have them decide which style fits them. Discuss the strengths of each style (refer to handout or Google the Six Thinking Hats).
		Have each student trace their hand on the color of paper that fit their style and cut out the paper hand. On each finger, have students write down one of the strengths of their style.
		Keep hand in class in safe place for next advisory.
Skill: Communication	November 4	Activity: Multiple Intelligences *Have students take and self-score the multiple intelligences survey. Have them write down their top 1-2 intelligence preferences across the <u>palm</u> of their paper hand.*

Skill: Communication	November 9	Activity: De Bono's Six Thinking Hats
		Discussion: How do the six different thinking styles and your intelligence preferences affect creativity and problem solving at school? How do you become tolerant of styles different from your own? How can you use this knowledge of your style and preferences to succeed in school?
		Ask students if they have a favorite quote that inspires them and captures their approach to the world. If they don't have one, suggest finding one in a quote book or on the internet. Have them bring it to the next advisory, or have them write the quote in the <u>center</u> of the hand. The hand is now complete and ready to be put up in the room.
Skill: Collaboration	November 16	Activity: Create Hand
		You will need several staplers for this activity.
		Have students take the completed hands and post them in the room. A circle of hands that runs around the room works best and reinforces the sense of community. Once the hands are posted, have students read all the hands.
		Reflect on the power of the group, the diversity of styles, and inspirational quotes.

Skill: Collaboration	November 18	Activity: Individual reflection and Personal Profile
		Use the hands to focus the beginning of the next unit in advisory, which is designed to encourage self-reflection and goal setting. *Have students begin by discussing and drafting a Personal Profile that will be part of their record at CAT. The profile is part of their Personal Learning Plan (PLP), which will be kept in their digital portfolio over 4 years. The profile should include:* • *Strengths* • *Challenges and stressors* • *Core values/Leadership Skills/personal qualities/learning styles* • *Wellness and fitness reflections* • *Important milestones/life story facts* *Each Advisor will probably approach this differently. The point is to get students thinking about each of these points, and starting on a 1-2 page draft.*

| Skill: Communication | November 23 | Activity: Individual reflection and Personal Profile

Have students complete personal profile. When all students have completed the profile, have students share in large group or small groups. This may take 1-2 advisory periods. |
|---|---|---|
| Skill: Communication | November 30 | Activity: Complete and share Personal Profile/story

Complete the activity. The next step is to enter the profile on the electronic PLP. Advisors may have to schedule computer time. |
| Skill: Creativity | December 2 | Activity: Personal Profile digital entry

Enter profile into PLP. |
| Skill: Project management | December 7 | Activity: Introduce goal setting
Review end of semester goals
Check on grades |
| Skill: Project management | December 9 | Activity: Draft personal goals
End of semester plan |
| Skill: Project management | December 14 | Activity: Draft academic goals |
| | December 16 | Activity: Celebration

End of quarter |
| | January 4 | Activity: Check in discussion; school business |

Skill: Project management	January 6	Activity: Review goals, and grades Add to Personal Profile/story Students begin journaling on study skills
Skill: Project management	January 11	Activity: Set goals for 2nd semester
Skill: Project management	January 13	Activity: Goals for 2nd semester
Skill: Communication Skill: Project management	January 18	Activity: Discuss facilitation and teamwork: what's required
Skill: Communication Skill: Project management	January 20	Activity: Practice project skills
Skill: Communication Skill: Project management	January 25	Activity: Debrief project skills
Skill: Communication	January 27	Activity: SPACE – Ways to listen
Skill: Communication	February 1	Activity: Active listening
Skill: Communication	February 3	Activity: Active listening
Skill: Communication	February 8	Activity: Conflict resolution
Skill: Communication	February 10	Activity: Conflict resolution
Skill: Communication	February 15	Activity: Harassment/bullying
	February 17	Activity: Add to Personal Profile/story
Skill: Communication	March 1	Activity: Share new parts of profile
	March 3	Activity: Upload plan to digital

Skill: Communication	March 8	Activity: Review goals Review Hand Prepare for end of quarter
Skill: Communication	March 10	Activity: Prepare presentations
Skill: Communication	March 15	Activity: Prepare/share presentations in pairs/teams
Skill: Communication	March 17	Activity: Review of public speaking End of quarter
Skill: Communication	March 22	Activity: Practice presentation
Skill: Communication	March 24	Activity: Practice presentations
	March 28	Parent-student-teacher conferences
In the last block of Advisory, 9th grade students will develop their Personalized Learning Plan and ...?		
	April 5	Activity:
	April 7	Activity:
	April 19	Activity:
	April 21	Activity:
	April 26	Activity:
	April 28	Activity:
	May 3	Activity:
	May 5	Activity:
	May 10	Activity:
	May 12	Activity:
	May 17	Activity:
	May 19	Activity:
	May 24	Activity:
	May 31	Activity:
	June 2	Activity:
	June 7	Activity:

	June 9	Activity: Prepare for end of year Update profile/goals for next year
	June 14	Activity: Update Personal Profile
	June 16	Activity: Share goals for next year
	June 21	Activity: Share goals for next year

The Six A's of Designing Projects

(Developed by Adria Steinberg, Jobs for the Future. Used by permission.)

AUTHENTICITY

➤ Does the project emanate from a problem or question that has meaning to the student?

➤ Is it a problem or question that might actually be tackled by an adult at work or in the community?

➤ Do students create or produce something that has personal and/or social value, beyond the school setting?

ACADEMIC RIGOR

➤ Does the project lead students to acquire and apply knowledge central to one or more discipline or content area?

➤ Does it challenge students to use methods of inquiry central to one or more discipline? (e.g., to think like a scientist)

➤ Do students develop higher order thinking skills and habits of mind? (e.g., searching for evidence, taking different perspectives)

APPLIED LEARNING

➤ Does the learning take place in the context of a semi-structured problem, grounded in life and work in the world beyond school?

➤ Does the project lead students to acquire and use competencies expected in high performance work organizations (e.g., teamwork, appropriate use of technology, problem solving, and communications)?

➤ Does the work require students to develop organizational and self-management skills?

ACTIVE EXPLORATION

➤ Do students spend significant amounts of time doing field-based work?

➤ Does the project require students to engage in real investigation, using a variety of methods, media, and sources?

➤ Are students expected to communicate what they are learning through presentation and/or performance?

ADULT RELATIONSHIPS

➤ Do students meet and observe adults with relevant expertise and experience?

➤ Do students have an opportunity to work closely with at least one adult?

➤ Do adults collaborate on the design and assessment of student work?

ASSESSMENT PRACTICES

➤ Do students reflect regularly on their learning using clear project criteria that they have helped to set?

➤ Do adults from outside the classroom help students develop a sense of real world standards for this type of work?

➤ Will there be opportunities for regular assessment of student work through a range of methods, including exhibitions and portfolios?

Six A's Project Examination Tool

Directions: As you investigate a project, use this grid to keep track of evidence you see of each of the Six A's factors.

THE A's	ATTRIBUTES	EVIDENCE
ACADEMIC RIGOR	▪ Students acquire and apply knowledge central to one or more discipline or content area ▪ Students use methods of inquiry central to one or more discipline (e.g., to think like a scientist) ▪ Students develop higher order thinking skills and habits of mind (e.g., searching for evidence, taking different perspectives)	
AUTHENTICITY	▪ Project emanates from a problem or question that has meaning to the student ▪ Problem or question is one that might actually be tackled by an adult at work or in the community ▪ Students create or produce something that has personal and/or social value beyond the school setting	

Six A's project investigation tool continued…

THE A's	ATTRIBUTES	EVIDENCE
APPLIED LEARNING	▪ Students solve a semi-structured problem (e.g., designing a product, improving a system, or organizing an event) that is grounded in a context of life and work beyond the school walls ▪ Students acquire and use competencies expected in high performance work organizations (e.g., teamwork, problem solving) ▪ Work requires students to develop organizational and self-management skills	
ACTIVE EXPLORATION	▪ Students spend significant amounts of time doing field-based work ▪ Students engage in real investigations using a variety of methods, media, and sources ▪ Students communicate what they learn through presentations	
ADULT RELATIONSHIPS	▪ Students meet and observe adults with relevant expertise and experience ▪ Students work closely with at least one adult ▪ Adults collaborate on the design and assessment of student work	

Six A's project investigation tool continued…

THE A's	ATTRIBUTES	EVIDENCE
ASSESSMENT	<ul><li>Students reflect regularly on their learning, using clear project criteria that they have helped to set</li><li>Adults from outside the classroom help students develop a sense of the real world standards for this type of work</li><li>There are opportunities for regular assessment of student work through a range of methods, including exhibitions and portfolios</li></ul>	

Project Sharing Protocol

This sharing protocol is intended to assist you as you describe a project. Please feel free to add any information you feel is salient to the project's design or implementation in order to help the listener understand your thinking and reflection of the project.

1. Begin by telling the listener what you are "working on," or what you might like them to pay special attention to. This will help focus the listener on what you most want feedback on.

2. Describe the project with a brief overview. Please include grade level, context for the project, the theme, topic, or essential question, and significant student products as a result of the project. Have you done this project before? If so, how long have you been doing this project?

3. Describe the student learning from doing this project. What are the key academic concepts learned and applied, and the processes and dispositions (habits of mind) required to complete the project?

4. How does the project relate to your school's academic standards? Please describe the academic standards required to complete the project and their origin, i.e., National, State, or Local.

5. Describe any adjustments made in the project and the rationale behind making the adjustments.

6. How do you give your students ongoing feedback to assess their work? Describe any strategies and techniques used to assess student learning which are unique to this project. How are the work products evaluated? What evidence is collected for assessment and what is used for evaluation?

7. Describe how you develop a project's scaffolding. What elements in the project supported and ensured high quality student work? Are there adjustments that need to be made here? What are they and what do you hope to see as a result of your re-structuring?

8. How are you dealing with the pressures to "teach to the test"? How do you prepare students? How does your project work prepare students?

STUDENT: _____ ADVISOR: _____ COURSE: _____ BLOCK: _____

CITY ARTS AND TECH HIGH SCHOOL
Holistic Grading Rubric

CITY ARTS & TECH HIGH SCHOOL	**NC (No Credit):** *Work does not meet standard*	**C:** *Work minimally meets standard*	**B:** *Work is of sufficient quality*	**A:** *Work is of an excellent quality*
MASTERY OF KNOWLEDGE • **Reports of Information** (including essays, labs, presentations), **Tests & Quizzes** **GRADE:**	☐ Test and Quiz scores are mostly below Basic ☐ Assessments are mostly **1** for content mastery	☐ Test and Quiz scores are mostly basic or higher ☐ Assessments are mostly **2** for content mastery	☐ Test and Quiz scores are mostly proficient or higher ☐ Assessments are mostly **3** for content mastery	☐ Test and Quiz scores are mostly advanced or higher ☐ Assessments are mostly **4** for content mastery
APPLICATION OF KNOWLEDGE • **Work Product & Exhibition Assessments** • **Application of Information** (*essays, labs, presentations*) **GRADE:**	☐ Demonstrates little or no understanding ☐ Assessments are mostly below **1** for understanding	☐ Demonstrates understanding in certain assessments to meet minimum requirements ☐ Assessments are mostly **2** for understanding	☐ Demonstrates understanding of content in large, small, or one to one discussions, essays, portfolios, and/or projects ☐ Assessments are mostly **3** for understanding	☐ Demonstrates a complex and thorough understanding of content in large, small or one to one discussions, essays, portfolios, and/or projects ☐ Assessments are mostly **4** for understanding

CITY
ARTS & TECH HIGH SCHOOL

	NC (No Credit): Work does not meet standard	C: Work minimally meets standard	B: Work is of sufficient quality	A: Work is of an excellent quality
METACOGNITION • **Growth over time** • **Reflections (in class, journals, projects)** • **Self-editing** **GRADE:**	☐ Does not attempt to improve in mastery of content, demonstration of understanding and/or metacognition ☐ Rarely completes reflections in journals, in class, and after projects	☐ Does not demonstrate improvement and growth in mastery of content, demonstration of understanding and/or metacognition ☐ Completes reflections in journals, in class, and after projects	☐ Demonstrates improvement and growth in mastery of content, demonstration of understanding and/or metacognition ☐ Thorough reflections in journals, in class and after projects	☐ Demonstrates tremendous improvement and growth in mastery of content, demonstration of understanding and/or metacognition ☐ Thorough and often insightful reflections in journals, in class and after projects
LEADERSHIP SKILLS Each semester focuses on select Leadership Skills **GRADE:**	Leadership Skills Assessments are mostly 1 _____	Leadership Skills Assessments are mostly 2 _____	Leadership Skills Assessments are mostly 3 _____	Leadership Skills Assessments are mostly 4 _____

CITY
ARTS & TECH HIGH SCHOOL

	NC (No Credit): Work does not meet standard	**C:** Work minimally meets standard	**B:** Work is of sufficient quality	**A:** Work is of an excellent quality
COLLEGE WORK HABITS Engagement Participation Preparedness & Homework	☐ Rarely participates in large and/or small groups ☐ Rarely engaged in the work (lectures, groups, research, writing, projects, etc.) ☐ Rarely completes homework and class work. It is often not acceptable.	☐ Sometimes actively participates in large and/or small groups ☐ Sometimes engaged in the work (lectures, groups, research, writing, projects, etc.) ☐ Sometimes completes homework and class work thoroughly, thoughtfully, and on time	☐ Usually actively participates in large and/or small group by contributing to discussions, doing research, recording, encouraging, and/or reporting ☐ Usually engaged in the work (lectures, groups, research, writing, projects, etc.) ☐ Usually completes homework and class work thoroughly, thoughtfully and on time	☐ Always actively participates in large and/or small group by contributing to discussions, doing research, recording, encouraging, and/or reporting ☐ Always engaged in the work (lectures, groups, research, writing, projects, etc.) ☐ Always completes homework and class work thoroughly, thoughtfully and on time
GRADE:				

OVERALL HOLISTIC GRADE:

TEACHER SIGNATURE: _____   **DATE:** _____

COMMENTS:

Envision Core Values

Our Mission

Envision Schools transforms the lives of students – especially those who will be first in their families to attend college – by preparing them for success in college and in life.

Our Beliefs

We believe that...

by creating authentic and public projects, forming deep relationships, and expecting student to demonstrate mastery of challenging academic work and 21st Century Leadership Skills by performance we engage students in a transformational learning experience.

by entering, succeeding in, and graduating from college our students transform the trajectories of their lives and eventually their communities.

Our Core Values

We are passionate about meeting our mission. In service of our mission, we use these core values to guide our actions and decisions every day with our colleagues, our students, their parents, and our partner organizations.

We are...

Accountable

We set high goals. We hold high expectations. We work relentlessly to achieve our goals and check our progress regularly. We honor our commitments. We don't make excuses.

Respectful

We treat everyone with dignity. We are honest and direct. We assume good intentions. We go to the source.

Collaborative

We believe collegiality creates synergy and a richer solution. We seek the expertise of others to ensure our work is most effective. We work in teams as needed, and consider the consequences of our decisions for others.

Persistent learners

We are determined, deliberate, and learn from our success and failures. Our learning makes us consistently smarter and stronger. We innovate. We never give up.

Decision Making @ Envision Schools

Our commitments:

- ❏ Consider unintended consequences
- ❏ Use the smallest group possible to make the best decision possible
- ❏ Be disciplined in discussions and decision making
- ❏ Use the core values

Envision Core Values

We are…

- ❏ Accountable
- ❏ Respectful
- ❏ Collaborative
- ❏ Persistent Learners

This Team	Makes Decisions About:
CEO	❏ Hiring/firing Management Team ❏ Items that lack time for MT input
Management Team	❏ Future goals and direction of the organization ❏ Significant budget impacts ❏ Additions or subtractions of positions ❏ Policies that impact organizational culture ❏ Large legal issues ❏ Items with significant impact on multiple teams ❏ Major changes to the educational model ❏ PR risk issues
Team Leaders	❏ Budgets within the team budget ❏ Hiring/firing staff ❏ Daily operations of the team ❏ Team professional development ❏ Salary and other personnel decisions within EE guidelines ❏ Discipline up to expulsion (principal specific)
Team	❏ Policy, within the team's domain, where there is appropriate expertise, that creates standardization across the network ❏ Implementation of team work plan ❏ Modifications to the education model (principal team specific)
Team Players	❏ Items within established individual scope of work
Board	❏ Strategic direction ❏ Hiring/firing CEO ❏ Board membership ❏ Fiduciary matters, for example: oversight/governance: budget, investment, policy, auditors ❏ Items required by law ❏ Expulsions ❏ Mission stewardship

ENVISION EDUCATION *Transforming Learning, Transforming Lives*

Ground Rules for Meetings

1. Stay open to influence – be willing to move your stake.

2. Don't just advocate. Inquire into what others think.

3. Put your reasoning on the table, not just your conclusion.

4. Define what important words mean.

5. Test assumptions and mental models.

6. Listen in order to understand, not in order to debate. Listening does not mean waiting.

7. Use data to inform decisions.

8. Have the discussions and disagreements in the meeting, not outside the meeting.

9. Be brief. No war stories. Don't repeat.

10. Focus on interests, not positions.

11. S-L-O-W down the discussion.

Meeting Agenda Template

Management Team Agenda
Thursday, Date 2013
9:30 AM — Noon, Bob's Office

Driving Question(s):

-

Today's Targets:

- I can
-

Core Values:

We are...

Accountable: We set high goals. We hold high expectations. We work relentlessly to achieve our goals and check our progress regularly. We honor our commitments. We don't make excuses.

Respectful: We treat everyone with dignity. We are honest and direct. We assume good intentions. We go to the source.

Collaborative: We believe collegiality creates synergy and a richer solution. We seek the expertise of others to ensure our work is most effective. We work in teams as needed, and consider the consequences of our decisions for others.

Persistent Learners: We are determined, deliberate, and learn from our success and failures. Our learning makes us consistently smarter and stronger. We innovate. We never give up.

Time	Item	Activity, Process, Reading
7:30-7:45 am	Check-in	•
7:45-8:45 am		•
8:45-9:00 am	Close of meeting	• Props • Process Checks

National School Reform Faculty
Harmony Education Center

Tuning Protocol Guidelines

This protocol was developed in the field by educators affiliated with NSRF.

Participation in a structured process of professional collaboration like this can be intimidating and anxiety producing, especially for the teacher presenting student work. Having a shared set of guidelines or norms helps everybody participate in a manner that is respectful as well as conducive to helpful feedback.

Below is one set of guidelines; teachers may want to create their own. In any case, the group should go over the guidelines and the schedule before starting the protocol. The facilitator must feel free to remind participants of the guidelines and schedule at any time in the process.

1. **Be respectful of presenters.** By making their work more public, teachers are exposing themselves to kinds of critiques they may not be used to receiving. If inappropriate comments or questions are posed, the facilitator should make sure they are blocked or withdrawn.

2. **Contribute to substantive discourse.** Resist offering only blanket praise or silence. Without thoughtful, probing questions and comments, the presenter will not benefit from the tuning protocol.

3. **Be appreciative of the facilitator's role**, particularly in regard to following the norms and keeping time. A tuning protocol that doesn't allow for all components (presentation, feedback, response, debrief) to be enacted properly will do a disservice to the teacher-presenters and to the participants.

4. **Facilitators need to keep the conversation constructive.** There is a delicate balance between feedback that only strokes and feedback that does damage. It is the facilitator's job to make sure that balance is maintained. At the end of the session, the presenter should be able to revise the work productively on the basis of what was said.

Protocols are most powerful and effective when used within an ongoing professional learning community such as a Critical Friends Group® and facilitated by a skilled coach. To learn more about professional learning communities and seminars for new or experienced coaches, please visit the National School Reform Faculty website at www.nsrfharmony.org.

National School Reform Faculty

Harmony Education Center

5. **Don't skip the debrief.** It is tempting to move to the next item of business once the feedback section is over. If you do that, the quality of responses will not improve and the presenters will not get increasingly useful kinds of feedback.

Protocols are most powerful and effective when used within an ongoing professional learning community such as a Critical Friends Group® and facilitated by a skilled coach. To learn more about professional learning communities and seminars for new or experienced coaches, please visit the National School Reform Faculty website at www.nsrfharmony.org.

National School Reform Faculty
Harmony Education Center

The Tuning Protocol: Narrative

Developed by Gene Thompson-Grove and David Allen

The Tuning Protocol is best suited to look at particular teacher- or school-created projects and assessments in order to improve them. So, for example, it is often used to look at writing prompts, open-ended problems and other kinds of assignments, research project designs, and rubrics for all kinds of activities and projects. It is less effective for learning in depth about a particular student's understanding, interests, or skills; for these purposes, the structure of the Collaborative Assessment Conference would serve better.

The focus of a Tuning Protocol is on a piece of curriculum, instruction, or assessment selected by the presenting teacher. Typically, the teacher chooses something because some of the students weren't successful. The goal is to help the presenting teacher to improve, or "fine tune," that piece of his or her curriculum or assessment (hence the name Tuning Protocol), so that all students meet the expectations. *If a presenter wants to revise something he or she has done, the structure of the Tuning Protocol will likely provide useful feedback.*

- The scope of the group's work is determined, at least in part, by a "focusing question" framed in advance by the presenting teacher. For example, "How does this project support students' application and development of critical thinking skills in math?"

- A range of student work (typically from several students at different levels of accomplishment) is presented to inform the group's understanding and help the group "tune" the piece of curriculum/ assessment identified by the presenting teacher. The presenter should bring enough copies of the student work, the assignment or prompt, the assessment tool or rubric, and the student learning goals, standards, or expectations.

Protocols are most powerful and effective when used within an ongoing professional learning community such as a Critical Friends Group® and facilitated by a skilled coach. To learn more about professional learning communities and seminars for new or experienced coaches, please visit the National School Reform Faculty website at www.nsrfharmony.org.

- A crucial part of the tuning comes through "warm" and "cool" feedback offered to the presenting teacher by the participants (after they've heard about the instructional context and looked at the student work). The feedback tries to respond to the presenting teacher's focusing question but is not limited by it.

- "Warm" feedback asks participants to identify strengths, both in the teacher-created piece of instruction or assessment and in the student work; "cool" feedback asks participants to identify possible gaps between the teacher's goals for the work and the students' accomplishment—and ways these gaps might be closed.

- The presenting teacher listens to the full range of feedback without responding immediately. Instead, in the next step, s/he is asked to reflect on what s/he heard. In this step, the other participants listen and don't interrupt.

- A final step calls for all the participants to "debrief" the conversation, considering how the structure helped them achieve the goals for the protocol.

Protocols are most powerful and effective when used within an ongoing professional learning community such as a Critical Friends Group® and facilitated by a skilled coach. To learn more about professional learning communities and seminars for new or experienced coaches, please visit the National School Reform Faculty website at www.nsrfharmony.org.

The Tuning Protocol: Tuning a Plan

Developed in the field by educators affiliated with NSRF

When you tune a plan you have two basic components: a set of goals and a set of activities sequenced in a way that you believe will help the people you work with to meet those goals. The general objective is to get feedback from your colleagues about the degree to which the activities you structure seem likely to get your group to these goals. The plan is "in tune" when the goals and activities are most in alignment.

Time: Approximately 1 hour
Roles: Presenter, Participants (seated in small groups of 4-5), Small Group Facilitator (who also participates), and Large Group Facilitator

1. **Presentation to the Large Group** (10 minutes)
   - Context for plan
   - Goals that drive the plan
   - Focusing question for feedback

NOTE: This question should be a more specific version of the general objective above. Participants are silent.

2. **Clarifying Questions from the Large Group** (5 minutes)
   - Clarifying questions are matters of fact. Save substantive issues for later.
   - The facilitator is responsible for making sure that clarifying questions are really clarifying.

3. **Examination of the Plan** (7 minutes)
   - Participants read the plan, taking notes on where the plan seems "in tune" with the stated goals and where there might be problems.

4. **Pause to Reflect on Feedback** (2-3 minutes)

5. Feedback in Small Groups (15-20 minutes)

- Participants talk to each other about the presenter's plan (as if the presenter is not in the room), beginning with the ways the plan seems likely to meet the goals, continuing with possible disconnects and problems, and perhaps ending with one or two probing questions for further reflection on the part of the presenter. These don't need to be in tight sequence, but participants should always begin with some positive feedback.
- The Presenter may walk around the room and listen in on groups, but remains silent and doesn't answer questions or engage in back and forth conversation.
- Facilitator may need to remind participants of presenter's focusing question.
- Recorder takes notes on the warm and cool feedback.

The group chooses one item of warm feedback and one item of cool feedback to share in the large group.

6. Sharing Feedback in the Large Group (5-10 minutes)

- Each group shares one item of warm feedback (in a round). When the first round has been completed, each group shares one item of cool feedback (again, in a round, and going in the opposite direction).

7. Reflection (10 minutes)

- Presenter talks about what s/he has learned from the participants' feedback. This is NOT a time to defend oneself (this is for the presenter and defending isn't necessary), but a time to explore further interesting ideas that came out of the feedback section.

  At any point the presenter may open the conversation to the entire group (or not).

8. Debrief (5 minutes)

- Facilitator-led open discussion of this tuning experience, either in small groups or in the large group.

Index

Culture. *See* School culture

Curriculum: bubble testing and, 5; Campaign Ad Project, 76–77; Envision Schools Advisory Curriculum, 128; integrated classrooms, 135–140; *Understanding by Design*, 21–22

D

Dakarai's story, 105–107

Darling-Hammond, Linda, 2

de Bono, Edward, 158, 159

Debates, 117, 164

Decision making, RAPID, 155–156

Deeper learning, 1–17; for all students, 14–15; *College Knowledge*, 2, 94; Common Core and, 168; competencies of, 7; creativity and, 124–125; defined, 7; depth over breadth, 8–9; design principles (educational philosophy) of, 7–14; essential message of, 6–8; *The Global Achievement Gap*, 2; *Horace's Compromise*, 2, 162; *The Power of Their Ideas*, 2; reasons for, 1–2; reflection and, 12; *The Right to Learn*, 2; transform, not reform, 15–16; Workplace Learning Experiences, 25, 27, 28, 29, 31, 138–140. *See also* Leadership; Project-based learning

Deeper Learning Network, 7, 162, 168

Deeper learning outcomes. *See* Outcomes

Deeper Learning Student Assessment System, 41–63; assessments, distillation of standards, 47–48; assessments, not discipline specific, 48–49; assessments, short list, 47; critical elements in, 27; defined, 20; described, 45–56; key features, 46; nuts and bolts, 26–33; portfolio defenses and, 45–46; purpose of, 48; reflection in, 27; rubrics in, 49; sneak preview of implementation, 34–35. *See also* Performance assessments

Defense of learning, 33–34. *See also* Portfolio defenses

Demographics: demographic fallacy, PBL, 93, 94–95, 148; Envision Schools (2013–2014), 3, 94–95

Depth over breadth (design principle for deeper learning), 8–9

Design principles. *See* Deeper learning

Designing for Deeper Learning: How to Develop Performance Assessments or the Common Core (online course), 56

Determination, "Persistence and Determination are Omnipotent," 147

Dewey, John, 11, 108, 162

Digital presentation, 32

Disaster in the Gulf performance assessment, 50–53

Discipline/management/persistence, 72

Distillation of standards, performance assessments, 47–48

Do. *See* Know-Do-Reflect Triangle

Doing, learning and, 41–42

Drake High School. *See* Sir Francis Drake High School

Driver's test example, 41–42

Driving questions, 80–82

Dweck, Carol, 104–105, 107, 140

E

EdLeader21, 168

edTPA, 168

Education: Buck Institute for Education, 68, 72, 76, 80, 168; changes, books on, 2; Dewey on, 11; Merrow on, 167; No Child Left Behind, 2, 5, 6, 105, 168; Piaget on, 9; scaffolding, 32, 80, 83, 115, 137, 158. *See also* Deeper learning; Envision Schools; Project-based learning

Educational Achievement Authority, 4

Edutopia, 116

EE Times, 118

Eisenhower, Dwight D., 66

ELA (English Language Arts), 30, 53–54, 55, 61, 133–134

Eliza Doolittle (fictional character), 44

ELP. *See* Envision Learning Partners

Emotion: *Social and Emotional Learning* blog, 116; social-emotional interventions, 129

End in itself, 69

English Language Arts. *See* ELA

English Language Learners, 3

Envision Idol, 119

Envision Learning Partners (ELP), 4

structures and, 124–125; scoring difficulties, 58–60; short list, 47; Smarter Balanced, 6, 61; subject disciplines and, 48–49; textual analysis, *Inferno* Mosaic Retelling Project, 53–55; trending, 5. *See also* Deeper Learning Student Assessment System; Fallacies

Performance tasks, 27, 32, 34, 46, 48, 76, 112

Persistence: college persistence rates, 3–4, 105; defined, 105; development of, 26; discipline/management/persistence: metaskill, 72; failure and, 108; "Persistence and Determination are Omnipotent," 147; self-esteem and, 110

Persistent learning, 153

Piaget, Jean, 9

"Picture Me Black," 105–107

Planning: common planning time, 133–134; meetings, as well-designed lessons, 156–157; project planning, 77–80

Portfolio defenses: Dakarai's defense, 106; Deeper Learning Student Assessment System and, 45–46; defined, 33; Kaleb's story, 19–20, 35–38; oral defense, 36–37, 38; PBLs and, 73–74; power of, 33–34

Portfolios: artifacts and, 27–28; components of, 28; cover letter, 28, 32; Deeper Learning Student Assessment System, 26–27

The Power of Their Ideas (Meier), 2

Powerschool, 142

Present moment, focus on (design principle for deeper learning), 11

Productive collaboration, 149–151

Professional development (PD) sessions, 130–133

Profiles. *See* Graduate profiles; Project Profiles

Project Profiles: Campaign Ad Project, 78; *Inferno* Mosaic Retelling Project, 92; Moving Voices Project, 89

Project-based learning (PBL), 65–99; all or nothing, 70; Angel Island project, 130–133; audience and, 68; challenges first, then instruction, 90–91; "Changing the Subject: Making the Case for PBL," 94; in classrooms, 88–96; Common Core and, 71–72, 74;

coverage fallacy, 93–94; creative next step, 90; defined, 68–69; demographic fallacy, 93, 94–95, 148; end in itself, 69; goals and, 69; how it works, at Envision Schools, 74–76; inquiry and, 68, 91; interviews and, 91; medieval apprenticeship and, 69; newness of, 69–70; outcomes and, 15, 74; *PBL in the Elementary Grades*, 168; qualities not found in PBL, 69–70; reasons for, 66–69, 95; reflections and, 87–88; revision and, 85–86; rigor fallacy, 93, 94; school structures and, 124–125; structuredness of, 114–115; as transformational practice, 74; video series, YouTube, 98. *See also* Deeper learning; Projects

Project-based scheduling, 127

Projects: Angel Island project, 130–132; Archaeological Dig Project, 96, 98; assignments *versus*, 65; Campaign Ad Project and, 67; completion of, 25, 88; definitions, 67–68, 88; Disaster in the Gulf project, 50–53; driving questions in, 80–82; Envision Project Planning Template, 77; large-scale, 75, 88; length of, 70; Moving Voices Project, 89; multidisciplinary, 74–77; PBL *versus*, 68; planning, 77–80; proposals in, 83–84; Six A's of Designing Projects, 76, 91, 133; well-designed, 73–74; "Who Am I?" project, 113. *See also* Campaign Ad Project; *Inferno* Mosaic Retelling Project

Proposals, 83–84

Psychometricians, 58, 59

Public speaking, 36, 113

R

Race to the Top, 4

Radford, A. W., 3

Ramos, Carlos, 19

RAPID decision making, 155–156

Real Learning, Real Work (Steinberg), 76

Reflection: on artifacts, 31; in Deeper Learning Student Assessment System, 27; defined, 12; failure and, 110; Know-Do-Reflect Triangle, 24–26, 73–74; PBLs and, 87–88

About the DVD-ROM

INTRODUCTION

This appendix provides you with information on the contents of the DVD that accompanies this book. For the latest information, please refer to the AbouttheDVD.html located at the root of the DVD.

SYSTEM REQUIREMENTS

- A computer with a web browser
- A DVD-ROM drive

USING THE DVD

To access the content from the DVD, follow these steps:

1. Insert the DVD into your computer's DVD-ROM drive.

2. Select Home.html from the list of files.

3. Read through the license agreement by clicking the License link near the top-right of the interface.

4. The interface appears. Simply select the material you want to view.

WHAT'S ON THE DVD

The following sections provide a summary of the software and other materials you'll find on the DVD.

Videos

Video 1. Envision Philosophy, Practices, and Design

Video 2. Envision Defense Montage

Video 3. The Four C's

Video 4. Tiana: Profile of a Deeper Learning Student

Video 5. Student Profile, Portfolio Defense

Video 6. The *Inferno* Mosaic Retelling Project

Video 7. The Envision Assessment Process

Video 8. The Campaign Ad Project

Video 9. Creating a Driving Question for the Watershed Project

Video 16. Envision Idol

Video 17. Advisory: Check in and Support

Video 18. TheWorkplace Learning Experience at Envision

Video 19. Teacher Collaboration

Video 20. Calibration: Assessing Portfolio Defenses

Video 21. Sha'nice — Nasty Attitude to Bright Future

Documents

1. Envision Schools Course Syllabus Template

2. Envision Schools College Success Portfolio Performance Task Requirements: Scientific Inquiry

3. Envision Schools College Success Portfolio Performance Task: English Language Arts Textual Analysis

4. What Is the Most Effective Method for Cleaning Oil, Dispersants or Absorbents?

5. Envision Schools College Success Portfolio Performance Assessment: Creative Expression

6. Performance Assessment Planning Template

7. SCALE Performance Assessment Quality Rubric

8. Envision Project Planning Template

9. Envision Sample Daily Schedule

10. 9th Grade Envision Schools Advisory Curriculum

11. The Six A's of Designing Projects

12. Project Sharing Protocol

13. City Arts and Tech High School Holistic Grading Rubric

14. Envision Core Values

15. Decision Making at Envision Schools

16. Ground Rules for Meetings

17. Meeting Agenda Template

18. NSRF Tuning Protocol Guidelines

TROUBLESHOOTING

If you have difficulty using any of the materials on the companion DVD, try the following solutions:

- Turn off any anti-virus software that you may have running. HTML files sometime mimic virus activity and can make your computer incorrectly believe that it is being infected by a virus. (Be sure to turn the anti-virus software back on later.)

- Close all running programs. The more programs you're running, the less memory is available to other programs.

- Reboot if necessary. If all else fails, rebooting your machine can often clear any conflicts in the system.

CUSTOMER CARE

If you have trouble with the DVD-ROM, please call the Wiley Product Technical Support phone number at (800) 762-2974. Outside the United States, call 1(317) 572-3994. You can also contact Wiley Product Technical Support at http://support.wiley.com. John Wiley & Sons will provide technical support only for installation and other general quality control items. For technical support of the applications themselves, consult the program's vendor or author.

To place additional orders or to request information about other Wiley products, please call (877) 762-2974.